Thomas Jefferson and American Democracy

PROBLEMS IN
AMERICAN CIVILIZATION

Under the editorial direction of
Edwin C. Rozwenc

Thomas Jefferson and American Democracy

Edited and with an Introduction by

Henry C. Dethloff
Texas A & M University

D. C. HEATH AND COMPANY
Lexington, Massachusetts   Toronto   London

CONTENTS

INTRODUCTION

Two centuries ago Thomas Jefferson composed the Declaration of Independence. By this and many other acts and services Jefferson became one of the most important shapers of the historical development of the American people. It has been said that while Washington fought and Patrick Henry talked Jefferson *thought* for the American Revolution. As author of the Declaration of Independence, war-time governor of Virginia, post-war minister to France, first Secretary of State under the new Constitution, Vice-President, and finally President of the United States from 1800 until 1808, Jefferson's impact upon his own time was great. "Thomas Jefferson still survives," John Adams said as he breathed his last words, and indeed, Jefferson's image and his influence seemed to grow greater rather than less with the passage of time. As the image grew, so too did distortions of that image, and so too came an increasing suspicion that the world of Thomas Jefferson was no more. Do the words, the ideas, the ideals of Thomas Jefferson still have relevance for changing, modern America? On the second centennial of American independence does Thomas Jefferson still survive?

The answer to that question depends in part to which Thomas Jefferson you refer. Is it Jefferson the member of the "loyal opposition" who constantly bearded and berated the Federalists; the Jefferson who became the progenitor of the American liberal tradition, a tradition which stresses individualism, equality, democracy, and self-determination? Or is it Jefferson the agrarian democrat? Jefferson, to borrow the terminology of John D. Hicks, was among the first to fight in defense of rural-agricultural America against the devouring jaws of urban-industrial America. "I think," Jefferson said, "our governments will remain virtuous for many centuries as long as they are chiefly agricultural." Jefferson emerges too as a founder of the states rights doctrines. Strongly supporting the Kentucky and Virginia Resolutions and the "compact" theory of government, Jefferson wrote that "the several states composing the United States of America, are not united on the principles of unlimited submission to their general government." Thus Jefferson became the preceptor of states rights, nullification, and agrarianism, none of which appear to be consistent with modern values.

Jefferson's advocacy of agrarianism, states rights, and decentralized government appears archaic in the light of America's development as an urban, collectivist society. Although Jefferson praised the virtues of the simple yeoman farmer, America has intrinsically been a nation of entrepreneurs. Jefferson's image of a politically and commercially isolated nation is paradoxical in view of the nation's developing internationalism. Jefferson's laissez-faire became the byword of the commercial, not of the agricultural interests. States rights became the banner of secession and, later, of racial segregation. Indeed, many of the ideals advocated by Jefferson appear to have been incompatible even with conditions prevailing in his own administration.

As President did Thomas Jefferson fight a holding action against the forces of change and defend principles which were at best utopian and at worst anachronistic? Or did he abandon some of his values and principles when he faced the realities of power? Was the professed "Revolution of 1800" really a revolution or was "Jeffersonian democracy" only another version of the gentry politics already established by the Federalists? Was commercial America sacrificed upon the altar of agricultural supremacy while the Jeffersonians were in power? Did Jefferson revoke or change the commercial and fiscal structure of the Federalists as established by Alexander Hamilton? Did the authority of the national government and the powers of the chief executive suffer in Jefferson's hands? Or through such vehicles as the Louisiana Purchase, the trial of Aaron Burr, and the Embargo Act of 1807, did the authority of the central government and of the executive actually expand? How should we measure the relationship between the philosophical

Jefferson and Jefferson the practicing politician? Herein lies the Jeffersonian paradox.

Thomas Jefferson and Alexander Hamilton have been widely accepted as symbols of fairly distinct and virtually incompatible social values. Historians have tended to choose their champion and then proceed from there in the reconstruction of American history. Few historians have been able to embrace both men or symbols with equal charity, forbearance, or compassion. Alexander Hamilton is traditionally conceived of as the aristocratic, authoritarian, business and urban-oriented skeptic of democracy. Hamilton believed that the rich, well-born, and able should govern; Jefferson believed that the people could be trusted to choose men of virtue and wisdom to lead them. It has nonetheless been somewhat unnerving to draw these two diverse buckets from the same historical well. Is the Hamilton-Jeffersonian dialogue more accurately one of conflict or of consensus?

Alexander Hamilton wrote of Thomas Jefferson: "I admit that his politics are tinctured with fanaticism; that he is too much in earnest in his democracy; . . . that he is crafty and persevering in his objects; that he is not scrupulous about the means of success, nor very mindful of truth, and that he is a contemptible hypocrite. But it is not true, *as alleged,* that he is an enemy to the power of the Executive, or that he is for confounding all the powers in the House of Representatives. . . . He is as likely as any man I know to temporize." He would, Hamilton concluded, be far more acceptable as President than Aaron Burr, and would be unlikely to make any changes in the established order.

The historiographical distinctions between the Hamiltonian and Jeffersonian systems may be more analytic than real. There is a noticeable trend among historians to close the gap. Increasingly, phrases such as gentry politician, pragmatist, and mercantilist, are being applied to Thomas Jefferson. Such evaluations suggest that Jefferson the idealist was confounded by Jefferson the realist. As President, did Jefferson do what he said he was going to do, or what we are led to think he would do? The problem is complex and provocative.

A resolution of the Jefferson problem is far from complete, but effective and intriguing answers have been offered by many outstanding historians.

This volume begins by presenting Jeffersonian principles as defined by their author, Thomas Jefferson, before he assumed the Presidency. It then proceeds to an evaluation of those principles and finally to an effort to comprehend the meaning of Jeffersonianism in today's world. For example, A. Whitney Griswold ably presents the classic view of Jefferson as the agrarian democrat. Jefferson believed that America's political and economic future depended upon her development as a nation of small, independent, yeoman farmers. Stuart Bruchey argues, however, that although Jefferson often praised agriculture he was not hostile to a broad-based economy, neither did he refrain from using the power of the national government to promote economic expansion. William A. Williams concludes that Jefferson's label as an agrarian democrat is a misnomer. Rather, Jefferson conceived of continuing economic expansion, not a static agricultural society, as America's social ideal. The expanding frontier and economic progress are the key elements in Jefferson's social philosophy, he argues. The interpretations of Williams and Bruchey make Jefferson's values more accommodating to urban twentieth-century America. There remains, however, the lurking suspicion that Jefferson really was a genuine agrarian.

Similarly, modern uneasiness over the Jefferson image has been produced by his association with states rights, nullification, decentralization, and laissez-faire, issues that now seem virtually incompatible with contemporary life. Historians have tended to suggest that these conceptions were not in themselves Jeffersonian objectives, but rather vehicles for achieving greater purposes which *are* consistent with modern values. Bernard Mayo suggests that Jefferson valued individual freedom above all things. Agrarianism, states rights, and at times nationalism, he asserts, were invoked by Jefferson to achieve the greater objective of maintaining and safeguarding personal liberties. Thus Jefferson's ideals, says Mayo, are the universal values of the American democratic society. Charles M. Wiltse, on the other hand, describes the development of a Jeffersonian commonwealth that was broad enough to tolerate manufacturing and agriculture, states rights and nationalism, aristocracy and democracy. But this delicately-balanced Jeffersonian state crumbled and poured into two distinct channels of American thought concerning the relationship between the states and the nation.

The political role of Thomas Jefferson has recently aroused as much interest as his philosophy. James MacGregor Burns suggests that the political Jefferson is far more "real" and relevant than the philosophical Jefferson. William Nisbet Chambers credits Jefferson with being the architect of the modern party system; Richard P. McCormick, however, finds that the American party system has undergone a transformation to the extent that the modern party structure is no longer that of the Jeffersonians or Federalists. In the first American party system, McCormick argues, policies and decisions came from the "top down" rather than from the "bottom up."

Other historians have been preoccupied with the essential nature of Jefferson's democracy. Progressive historians, such as Charles Beard and Vernon L. Parrington, interpreted that democracy in terms of a broad-based, popular rule of the masses, and of a continuing struggle against entrenched aristocracy, privilege, and minority rule. Thus Jefferson, according to Parrington and others, is one of the philosophical founders of the American liberal tradition which has wended its way up to the present via Jackson, Lincoln, Theodore Roosevelt, Wilson, Franklin Roosevelt, and John F. Kennedy. This view of American history as a continuing struggle between liberal and conservative, good and evil, has produced some problems and paradoxes. How can one reconcile the Jeffersonian system stressing laissez-faire with the New Deal which stressed positive governmental action? Some historians conclude that it simply cannot be done.

On the other hand, Richard Hofstadter argues effectively that the line between the Jeffersonian and Hamiltonian systems was not so great as is often depicted. The point at issue between them, Hofstadter said, was not philosophy, but property. In reality Jefferson was a pragmatist rather than a resolute agrarian who yielded a good part of his agrarianism in defense of democracy.

But Thomas Jefferson is more than a historical personage who belongs to a particular time and place. He is a culture hero whose image has evoked changing responses from succeeding generations. In *The Jefferson Image in the American Mind*, Merrill D. Peterson concerns himself primarily with the question of "what history made of Thomas Jefferson." Peterson's study reveals that Jefferson has been many things to many people at many different times.

Whatever one makes of him, Thomas Jefferson is profoundly significant to students of American history. He is either the favorite son of an America that once was, or the godfather of an America that came to be. To understand the relevance of Thomas Jefferson to our own time requires an enriched understanding of American historical development. By knowing Thomas Jefferson we can better know ourselves. He can be accepted or rejected, criticized, defended or amended, but he cannot be ignored. The image of Jefferson is woven into the fabric of American culture.

Conflict of Opinion

Jefferson's principles as expressed in his Inaugural Address of 1801:

> It is proper that you should understand what I deem the essential principles of our government. . . . Equal and exact justice to all men . . . ; peace, commerce, and honest friendship with all nations . . . ; the support of the state governments in all their rights . . . ; a jealous care of the right of election by the people . . . ; absolute acquiescence in the decisions of the majority . . . ; encouragement of agriculture, and of commerce as its handmaid.
>
> THOMAS JEFFERSON

Is the best characterization of Jefferson that of an agrarian democrat?

> There is no name in American history so intimately associated with the twofold theme of agrarianism and democracy as that of Thomas Jefferson.
>
> A. WHITNEY GRISWOLD

> In fine, I do not argue that Jefferson advocated industrialization to the extent Hamilton had. But he did advocate it, and the development of other sections of the economy as well.
>
> STUART BRUCHEY

> It seems doubtful that Jefferson ever became a mercantilist in the full philosophical sense. . . . Yet under the tutoring of Madison and the pressure of the changes that were taking place in America, Jefferson accepted and employed mercantilist programs and policies between 1791 and 1820.
>
> WILLIAM A. WILLIAMS

As President, did Thomas Jefferson remain true to his professed principles of states rights, agrarianism, and decentralization?

> Nothing does greater injustice to him and to the "sanctity of history" than to confuse the changing methods he used in his generation with his unchangeable democratic goals.
>
> BERNARD MAYO

> If the Jeffersonian philosophy developed on its aristocratic side through Calhoun and Stephens into a theory of class sovereignty which precipitated the Civil War, it developed also on its egalitarian side through Andrew Jackson.
>
> CHARLES M. WILTSE

Is the American political system derived from Jeffersonian antecedents?

> The Jefferson that feared national power and presidential tenure in the new Constitution is the Jefferson that has emerged most vividly in our national heritage. . . . There is another, quite different Jefferson that needs to be brought much more sharply into our national vision. . . . This second Jefferson, the politician and pragmatist, is, I think, as "real" as the first, and far more relevant to the America of the 1960's.
>
> JAMES MacGREGOR BURNS

> The party of Jefferson in the 1790's was a new political engine, the first of its kind in modern history. It exhibited little continuity with antecedent formations, and it developed political relationships which carried it well beyond the Federalists as an archetype of a modern, "popular" party.
>
> WILLIAM NISBET CHAMBERS

> In many other respects, the political environment had altered between the age of Jefferson and the age of Jackson. As long as politics could be managed informally, without the agency of elaborate party apparatus, those who were recognized at the time as "the gentry" wielded decisive influence.
>
> RICHARD P. McCORMICK

Has the Jeffersonian democracy survived in America and if so in what form?

> Far more completely than any other American of his generation he embodied the idealisms of the great revolution—its faith in human nature, its economic individualism, its conviction that here in America, through the instrumentality of political democracy, the lot of the common man should somehow be made better.
>
> VERNON L. PARRINGTON

> The relentless advance of modern capitalism . . . has gradually emptied the practical content out of Jefferson's agrarian version of democracy. This process had its earliest beginnings during Jefferson's lifetime, and, as we shall see, he yielded a good part of his agrarian prejudices (like the pragmatic, undoctrinaire soul that he was) without sacrificing his democratic preferences.
>
> RICHARD HOFSTADTER

I JEFFERSONIAN PRINCIPLES

Thomas Jefferson, 1776

THE DECLARATION OF INDEPENDENCE

As author of the Declaration of Independence, Thomas Jefferson set forth the revolutionary proposition that authority in government derived solely from the people governed. Not only did the Declaration of Independence announce the right of revolution and proclaim the Lockean principles of representative government, but it embraced the concept that government should be based on popular consent and should secure the "inalienable" rights of man. The second paragraph of the Declaration, which follows, is Jefferson's most significant and succinct statement of political philosophy.

We hold these truths to be self-evident, that all men are created equal, that they are endowed by their Creator with certain unalienable Rights, that among these, are Life, Liberty, and the pursuit of Happiness. That, to secure these rights, Governments are instituted among Men, deriving their just Powers from the consent of the governed. That, whenever any form of Government becomes destructive of these ends, it is the Right of the People to alter or to abolish it, and to institute new Government, laying its foundation on such Principles, and organizing its Powers in such form, as to them shall seem most likely to effect their Safety and Happiness. Prudence, indeed, will dictate that Governments long established should not be changed for light and transient causes; and, accordingly, all experience hath shewn, that mankind are more disposed to suffer, while evils are sufferable, than to right themselves by abolishing the forms to which they are accustomed. But, when a long train of abuses and usurpations, pursuing invariably the same Object, evinces a design to reduce them under absolute Despotism, it is their right, it is their duty, to throw off such Government, and to provide new Guards for their future Security. Such has been the patient sufferance of these Colonies; and such is now the necessity which constrains them to alter their former Systems of Government. The history of the present King of Great Britain is a history of repeated injuries and usurpations, all having in direct object the

establishment of an absolute Tyranny over these States. To prove
this, let Facts be submitted to a candid world.

Thomas Jefferson, 1781

NOTES ON THE STATE OF VIRGINIA

*Written in 1780 and 1781 as a response to French queries about their new
ally, the United States, Jefferson's* Notes on the State of Virginia *is an
American classic containing a wide range of information and many insights
into Jefferson's ideals. In the following selection on "Manufactures" Jefferson
states some of his social and economic values. He proposes to "let our
work-shops remain in Europe"; America should remain chiefly agricultural,
for "Those who labour in the earth are the chosen people of God, if ever
he had a chosen people."*

MANUFACTURES

We never had an interior trade of any importance. Our exterior commerce
has suffered very much from the beginning of the present
contest. During this time we have manufactured within our families
the most necessary articles of cloathing. Those of cotton will bear
some comparison with the same kinds of manufacture in Europe;
but those of wool, flax and hemp are very coarse, unsightly, and
unpleasant: and such is our attachment to agriculture, and such our
preference for foreign manufactures, that be it wise or unwise, our
people will certainly return as soon as they can, to the raising raw
materials, and exchanging them for finer manufactures than they
are able to execute themselves.

The political economists of Europe have established it as a
principle that every state should endeavour to manufacture for
itself: and this principle, like many others, we transfer to America,
without calculating the difference of circumstance which should

From *Notes on the State of Virginia* by Thomas Jefferson, edited and with an introduction
and notes by William Peden (University of North Carolina Press, 1955),
pp. 164–165, 137–138, 146–149, 223–225. Reprinted by permission of the publisher
and the Institute of Early American History and Culture. Notes to the original have
been omitted.

often produce a difference of result. In Europe the lands are either cultivated, or locked up against the cultivator. Manufacture must therefore be resorted to of necessity not of choice, to support the surplus of their people. But we have an immensity of land courting the industry of the husbandman. Is it best then that all our citizens should be employed in its improvement, or that one half should be called off from that to exercise manufactures and handicraft arts for the other? Those who labour in the earth are the chosen people of God, if ever he had a chosen people, whose breasts he has made his peculiar deposit for substantial and genuine virtue. It is the focus in which he keeps alive that sacred fire, which otherwise might escape from the face of the earth. Corruption of morals in the mass of cultivators is a phaenomenon of which no age nor nation has furnished an example. It is the mark set on those, who not looking up to heaven, to their own soil and industry, as does the husbandman, for their subsistance, depend for it on the casualties and caprice of customers. Dependance begets subservience and venality, suffocates the germ of virtue, and prepares fit tools for the designs of ambition. This, the natural progress and consequence of the arts, has sometimes perhaps been retarded by accidental circumstances: but, generally speaking, the proportion which the aggregate of the other classes of citizens bears in any state to that of its husbandmen, is the proportion of its unsound to its healthy parts, and is a good-enough barometer whereby to measure its degree of corruption. While we have land to labour then, let us never wish to see our citizens occupied at a work-bench, or twirling a distaff. Carpenters, masons, smiths, are wanting in husbandry: but, for the general operations of manufacture, let our work-shops remain in Europe. It is better to carry provisions and materials to workmen there, than bring them to the provisions and materials, and with them their manners and principles. The loss by the transportation of commodities across the Atlantic will be made up in happiness and permanence of government. The mobs of great cities add just so much to the support of pure government, as sores do to the strength of the human body. It is the manners and spirit of a people which preserve a republic in vigour. A degeneracy in these is a canker which soon eats to the heart of its laws and constitution.

SLAVERY

In his Notes on the State of Virginia *Jefferson engages in a comprehensive commentary on the "Laws." He explains that a plan for the revision and clarification of the laws of Virginia had been proposed and would likely be approved when hostilities ceased. Included in these "revisals" as he termed them was a bill to emancipate all slaves born after the passage of the act and to provide for the colonization of those slaves to another place. Jefferson actually drafted legislation which would have ended slavery in Virginia and a bill forbidding slavery in the western territory of the United States; but the legislation was not adopted in either case. Although a slave owner himself, he was one of the foremost opponents of the slave system in his time. Nevertheless, most of his discussion of Negro slavery in the* Notes *contains arguments as to why, after emancipation, the races should be separated.*

[The plan of the revisal was this] . . . to emancipate all slaves born after passing the act. The bill reported by the revisors does not itself contain this proposition; but an amendment containing it was prepared, to be offered to the legislature whenever the bill should be taken up, and further directing, that they should continue with their parents to a certain age, then be brought up, at the public expence, to tillage, arts or sciences, according to their geniusses, till the females should be eighteen, and the males twenty-one years of age, when they should be colonized to such place as the circumstances of the time should render most proper, sending them out with arms, implements of houshold and of the handicraft arts, seeds, pairs of the useful domestic animals, &c. to declare them a free and indepandant people, and extend to them our alliance and protection, till they shall have acquired strength; and to send vessels at the same time to other parts of the world for an equal number of white inhabitants; to induce whom to migrate hither, proper encouragements were to be proposed. It will probably be asked, Why not retain and incorporate the blacks into the state, and thus save the expence of supplying, by importation of white settlers, the vacancies they will leave? Deep rooted prejudices entertained by the whites; ten thousand recollections, by the blacks, of the injuries they have sustained; new provocations; the real distinctions which nature has made; and many other circumstances, will divide us into parties, and produce convulsions which will probably never end but in the extermination of the one or the other race.—To these objections, which are political, may be added others, which are physical and moral.

EDUCATION

Among the revisals of the "Laws" mentioned by Jefferson was included a bill to establish a system of public education in Virginia. Here Jefferson blazed new paths in social philosophy. Significantly, public education was to him an integral part of a responsible democratic society. "Every government degenerates when trusted to the rulers of the people alone. The people themselves therefore are its only safe depositories. And to render even them safe their minds must be improved to a certain degree."

Another object of the revisal is, to diffuse knowledge more generally through the mass of the people. This bill proposes to lay off every county into small districts of five or six miles square, called hundreds, and in each of them to establish a school for teaching reading, writing, and arithmetic. The tutor to be supported by the hundred, and every person in it entitled to send their children three years gratis, and as much longer as they please, paying for it. These schools to be under a visitor, who is annually to chuse the boy, of best genius in the school, of those whose parents are too poor to give them further education, and to send him forward to one of the grammar schools, of which twenty are proposed to be erected in different parts of the country, for teaching Greek, Latin, geography, and the higher branches of numerical arithmetic. Of the boys thus sent in any one year, trial is to be made at the grammar schools one or two years, and the best genius of the whole selected, and continued six years, and the residue dismissed. By this means twenty of the best geniusses will be raked from the rubbish annually, and be instructed, at the public expence, so far as the grammar schools go. At the end of six years instruction, one half are to be discontinued (from among whom the grammar schools will probably be supplied with future masters); and the other half, who are to be chosen for the superiority of their parts and disposition, are to be sent and continued three years in the study of such sciences as they shall chuse, at William and Mary college, the plan of which is proposed to be enlarged, as will be hereafter explained, and extended to all the useful sciences. The ultimate result of the whole scheme of education would be the teaching all children of the state reading, writing, and common arithmetic: turning out ten annually of superior genius, well taught in Greek, Latin, geography, and the higher branches of arithmetic: turning out ten others annually, of still superior parts, who, to those branches of learning, shall have added such of the sciences as their genius shall have led them to: the furnishing to the wealthier part of the people convenient schools, at which their children may be educated, at their own expence.—The general objects of this law are to provide an education adapted to the years, to the capacity, and the condition of every one, and directed to their freedom and happiness. Specific details were not proper for the law. These must be the business of the visitors entrusted with its execution. The first stage of this education being the schools of the hundreds, wherein the great mass of the people will receive their instruction, the principal foundations of future order will be laid here. Instead therefore of putting the Bible and Testament into the hands of the children, at an age when their judgments are not sufficiently matured for religious enquiries, their memories may here be stored with the most useful facts from Grecian, Roman, European and American history. The first elements of morality too may be instilled into their minds; such as, when further developed as their judgments advance in strength, may teach them how to work out their own greatest happiness, by shewing them that it does not depend on the condition of life in which chance has placed them, but is always the result of a good conscience, good health, occupation, and freedom in all just pursuits.— Those whom either the wealth of their parents or the adoption of the state shall destine to higher degrees of learning, will go on to the grammar schools, which constitute the next stage, there to be instructed in the languages. The learning Greek and Latin, I am told, is going into disuse in Europe. I know not what their manners and occupations may call for: but it would be very ill-judged in us to follow their example in this instance. There is a certain period of life, say from eight to fifteen or sixteen years of age, when the mind, like the body, is not yet firm enough for laborious and close operations. If applied to such, it falls an early victim to premature exertion; exhibiting indeed at first, in these young and tender subjects, the flattering appearance of their being men while they are yet children, but ending in reducing them to be children when they should be men. The memory is then most susceptible and tenacious of impressions; and the learning of languages being chiefly a work of memory, it seems precisely fitted to the powers of this period, which is long enough too for acquiring the most useful languages antient and modern. I do not pretend that language is science. It is only an instrument for the attainment of science. But that time is not lost which is employed in providing tools for future operation: more especially as in this case the books put into the hands of the youth for this purpose may be such as will at the same time impress their minds with useful facts and good principles. If this period be suffered to pass in idleness, the mind becomes lethargic and impotent, as would the body it inhabits if unexercised during the same time. The sympathy between body and mind during their rise, progress and decline, is too strict and obvious to endanger our being misled while we reason from the one to the other.—As soon as they are of sufficient age, it is supposed they will be sent on from the grammar schools to the university, which constitutes our third and last stage, there to study those sciences which may be adapted to their views. —By that part of our plan which prescribes the selection of the youths of genius from among the classes of the poor, we hope to avail the state of those talents which nature has sown as liberally among the poor as the rich, but which perish without use, if not sought for and cultivated.—But of all the views of this law none is more important, none more legitimate, than that of rendering the people the safe, as they are the ultimate, guardians of their own liberty. For this purpose the reading in the first stage, where *they* will receive their whole education, is proposed, as has been said, to be chiefly historical. History by apprising them of the past will enable them to judge of the future; it will avail them of the experience of other times and other nations; it will qualify them as judges of the actions and designs of men; it will enable them to know ambition under every disguise it may assume; and knowing it, to defeat its views. In every government on earth is some trace of human weakness, some germ of corruption and degeneracy, which cunning will discover, and wickedness insensibly open, cultivate, and improve. Every government degenerates when trusted to the rulers of the people alone. The people themselves therefore are its only safe depositories. And to render even them safe their minds must be improved to a certain degree. This indeed is not all that is necessary, though it be essentially necessary. An amendment of our constitution must here come in aid of the public education. The influence over government must be shared among all the people. If every individual which composes their mass participates of the ultimate authority, the government will be safe; because the corrupting the whole mass will exceed any private resources of wealth: and public ones cannot be provided but by levies on the people. In this case every man would have to pay his own price. The government of Great-Britain has been corrupted, because but one man in ten has a right to vote for members of parliament. The sellers of the government therefore get nine-tenths of their price clear. It has been thought that corruption is restrained by confining the right of suffrage to a few of the wealthier of the people: but it would be more effectually restrained by an extension of that right to such numbers as would bid defiance to the means of corruption.

Lastly, it is proposed, by a bill in this revisal, to begin a public library and gallery, by laying out a certain sum annually in books, paintings, and statues.

RELIGIOUS FREEDOM

Jefferson authored Virginia's "Act for Establishing Religious Freedom" and included it in the appendix to the English edition (1787) of the Notes on Virginia. *Announced as one of the great "natural rights of man" the concept of religious freedom was undoubtedly inherent in the developing American social fabric from the earliest colonization. It was an integral part of the revolutionary movement, and its appearance as an act of the Virginia Assembly and in the Bill of Rights is the result of a logical historical progression. Jefferson believed in the complete separation of civil and religious affairs.*

Well aware that Almighty God hath created the mind free; that all attempts to influence it by temporal punishments or burthens, or by civil incapacitations, tend only to beget habits of hypocrisy and meanness, and are a departure from the plan of the Holy Author of our religion, who, being Lord both of body and mind, yet chose not to propagate it by coercions on either, as was in his Almighty power to do; that the impious presumption of legislators and rulers, civil as well as ecclesiastical, who, being themselves but fallible and uninspired men have assumed dominion over the faith of others, setting up their own opinions and modes of thinking as the only true and infallible, and as such endeavouring to impose them on others, hath established and maintained false religions over the greatest part of the world, and through all time; That to compel a man to furnish contributions of money for the propagation of opinions which he disbelieves, is sinful and tyrannical; that even the forcing him to support this or that teacher of his own religious persuasion, is depriving him of the comfortable liberty of giving his contributions to the particular pastor whose morals he would make his pattern, and whose powers he feels most persuasive to righteousness, and is withdrawing from the ministry those temporal rewards which, proceeding from an approbation of their personal conduct, are an additional incitement to earnest and unremitting labours for the instruction of mankind; that our civil rights have no dependence on our religious opinions, more than on our opinions in physics or geometry; that therefore the proscribing any citizen as unworthy the public confidence by laying upon him an incapacity of being called to offices of trust and emolument, unless he profess or renounce this or that religious opinion, is depriving him injuriously of those privileges and advantages to which in common with his fellow citizens he has a natural right; that it tends also to corrupt the principles of that very religion it is meant to encourage, by bribing, with a monopoly of worldly honors and emoluments, those who will externally profess and conform to it; that though indeed these are criminal who do not withstand such temptation, yet neither are those innocent who lay the bait in their way; that to suffer the civil magistrate to intrude his powers into the field of opinion, and to restrain the profession or propagation of principles, on supposition of their ill tendency, is a dangerous fallacy, which at once destroys all religious liberty, because he being of course judge of that tendency, will make his opinions the rule of judgment, and approve or condemn the sentiments of others only as they shall square with or differ from his own; that it is time enough for the rightful purposes of civil government for its officers to interfere when principles break out into overt acts against peace and good order; and finally, that truth is great and will prevail if left to herself, that she is the proper and sufficient antagonist to error, and has nothing to fear from the conflict, unless by human interposition disarmed of her natural weapons, free argument and debate, errors ceasing to be dangerous when it is permitted freely to contradict them.

Be it therefore enacted by the General Assembly, That no man shall be compelled to frequent or support any religious worship, place or ministry whatsoever, nor shall be enforced, restrained, molested, or burthened in his body or goods, nor shall otherwise suffer on account of his religious opinions or belief; but that all men shall be free to profess, and by argument to maintain, their opinions in matters of religion, and that the same shall in no wise diminish, enlarge, or affect their civil capacities.

And though we well know that this Assembly, elected by the people for the ordinary purposes of legislation only, have no power to restrain the acts of succeeding Assemblies, constituted with powers equal to our own, and that therefore to declare this act irrevocable, would be of no effect in law, yet we are free to declare, and do declare, that the rights hereby asserted are of the natural rights of mankind, and that if any act shall be hereafter passed to repeal the present, or to narrow its operation, such act will be an infringement of natural right.

Thomas Jefferson to James Madison
Paris, December 20, 1787
VIEWS ON THE CONSTITUTION

Jefferson served as minister to France from 1785 to 1789 and so missed much of the activity surrounding the drafting and adoption of the Constitution. Through correspondence with James Madison and others he main-

From *The Writings of Thomas Jefferson* edited by Andrew A. Lipscomb (Washington, D.C.: Thomas Jefferson Memorial Association, 1903), Vol. VI, pp. 385–393.

tained close surveillance over the Constitutional question. The following letter finds two primary faults with the proposed Constitution: (1) the lack of a Bill of Rights, and (2) the failure to limit the term of the President. Jefferson feared too much power lodged in the hands of the executive. He reaffirms his faith in majority rule, an educated electorate, and in an agricultural society.

The season admitting only of operations in the cabinet, and these being in a great measure secret, I have little to fill a letter. I will, therefore, make up the deficiency, by adding a few words on the Constitution proposed by our convention.

I like much the general idea of framing a government, which should go on of itself, peaceably, without needing continual recurrence to the State legislatures. I like the organization of the government into legislative, judiciary and executive. I like the power given the legislature to levy taxes, and for that reason solely, I approve of the greater House being chosen by the people directly. For though I think a House so chosen, will be very far inferior to the present Congress, will be very illy qualified to legislate for the Union, for foreign nations, etc., yet this evil does not weigh against the good, of preserving inviolate the fundamental principle, that the people are not to be taxed but by representatives chosen immediately by themselves. I am captivated by the compromise of the opposite claims of the great and little States, of the latter to equal, and the former to proportional influence. I am much pleased, too, with the substitution of the method of voting by person, instead of that of voting by States; and I like the negative given to the Executive, conjointly with a third of either House; though I should have liked it better, had the judiciary been associated for that purpose, or invested separately with a similar power. There are other good things of less moment. I will now tell you what I do not like. First, the omission of a bill of rights, providing clearly, and without the aid of sophism, for freedom of religion, freedom of the press, protection against standing armies, restriction of monopolies, the eternal and unremitting force of the habeas corpus laws, and trials by jury in all matters of fact triable by the laws of the land, and not by the laws of nations. To say, as Mr. Wilson does, that a bill of rights was not necessary, because all is reserved in the case of the general government which is not given, while in the particular ones, all is given which is not reserved, might do for the audience to which it was addressed; but it is surely a *gratis dictum,* the reverse of which might just as well be said; and it is opposed by strong inferences from the body of the instrument, as well as from the omission of the cause of our present Confederation, which had made the reservation in express terms. It was hard to conclude, because there has been a want of uniformity among the States as to the cases triable by jury, because some have been so incautious as to dispense with this mode of trial in certain cases, therefore, the more prudent States shall be reduced to the same level of calamity. It would have been much more just and wise to have concluded the other way, that as most of the States had preserved with jealousy this sacred palladium of liberty, those who had wandered, should be brought back to it; and to have established general right rather than general wrong. For I consider all the ill as established, which may be established. I have a right to nothing, which another has a right to take away; and Congress will have a right to take away trials by jury in all civil cases. Let me add, that a bill of rights is what the people are entitled to against every government on earth, general or particular; and what no just government should refuse, or rest on inference.

The second feature I dislike, and strongly dislike, is the abandonment, in every instance, of the principle of rotation in office, and most particularly in the case of the President. Reason and experience tell us, that the first magistrate will always be re-elected if he may be re-elected. He is then an officer for life. This once observed, it becomes of so much consequence to certain nations, to have a friend or a foe at the head of our affairs, that they will interfere with money and with arms. A Galloman, or an Angloman, will be supported by the nation he befriends. If once elected, and at a second or third election outvoted by one or two votes, he will pretend false votes, foul play, hold possession of the reins of government, be supported by the States voting for him, especially if they be the central ones, lying in a compact body themselves, and separating their opponents; and they will be aided by one nation in Europe, while the majority are aided by another. The election of a President of America, some years hence, will be much more interesting to certain nations of Europe, than ever the election of a King of Poland was. Reflect on all the instances in history, ancient and modern, of elective monarchies, and say if they do not give foundation for my fears; the Roman Emperors, the Popes while they were of any importance, the German Emperors till they became hereditary in practice, the Kings of Poland, the Deys of the Ottoman dependencies. It may be said, that if elections are to be attended with these disorders, the less frequently they are repeated the better. But experience says, that to free them from disorder, they must be rendered less interesting by a necessity of change. No foreign power, nor domestic party, will waste their blood and money to elect a person, who must go out at the end of a short period. The power of removing every fourth year by the vote of the people, is a power which they will not exercise, and if they were disposed to exercise it, they would not be permitted. The King of Poland is removable every day by the diet. But they never remove him. Nor would Russia, the Emperor, etc., permit them to do it. Smaller objections are, the appeals on matters of fact as well as laws; and the binding all persons, legislative, executive, and judiciary by oath, to maintain that constitution. I do not pretend to decide, what would be the best method of procuring the establishment of the manifold good things in this constitution, and of getting rid of the bad. Whether by adopting it, in hopes of future amendment; or after It shall have been duly weighed and canvassed by the people, after seeing the parts they generally dislike, and those they generally approve, to say to them, "We see now what you wish. You are willing to give to your federal government such and such powers; but you wish, at the same time, to have such and such fundamental rights secured to you, and certain sources of convulsion taken away. Be it so. Send together deputies again. Let them establish your fundamental rights by a sacrosanct declaration, and let them pass the parts of the Constitution you have approved. These will give powers to your federal government sufficient for your happiness."

This is what might be said, and would probably produce a speedy, more perfect and more permanent form of government. At all events, I hope you will not be discouraged from making other trials, if the present one should fail. We are never permitted to despair of the commonwealth. I have thus told you freely what I like, and what I dislike, merely as a matter of curiosity; for I know it is not in my power to offer matter of information to your judgment, which has been formed after hearing and weighing everything which the wisdom of man could offer on these subjects. I own, I am not a friend to a very energetic government. It is always oppressive. It places the governors indeed more at their ease, at the expense of the people. The late rebellion in Massachusetts has given more alarm, than I think it should have done. Calculate that one rebellion in thirteen States in the course of eleven years, is but one for each State in a century and a half. No country should be so long without one. Nor will any degree of power in the hands of government, prevent insurrections. In England, where the hand of power is heavier than with us, there are seldom half a dozen years without an insurrection. In France, where it is still heavier, but less despotic, as Montesquieu supposes, than in some other countries, and where there are always two or three hundred thousand men ready to crush insurrections, there have been three in the course of the three years I have been here, in every one of which greater numbers were engaged than in Massachusetts, and a great deal more blood was spilt. In Turkey, where the sole nod of the despot is death, insurrections are the events of every day. Compare again the ferocious depredations of their insurgents, with the order, the moderation and the almost self-extinguishment of ours. And say, finally, whether peace is best preserved by giving energy to the government, or information to the people. This last is the most certain, and the most legitimate engine of government. Educate and inform the whole mass of the people. Enable them to see that it is their interest to preserve peace and order, and they will preserve them. And it requires no very high degree of education to convince them of this. They are the only sure reliance for the preservation of our liberty. After all, it is my principle that the will of the majority should prevail. If they approve the proposed constitution in all its parts, I shall concur in it cheerfully, in hopes they will amend it, whenever they shall find it works wrong. This reliance cannot deceive us, as long as we remain virtuous; and I think we shall be so, as long as agriculture is our principal object, which will be the case, while there remains vacant lands in any part of America. When we get piled upon one another in large cities, as in Europe, we shall become corrupt as in Europe, and go to eating one another as they do there. I have tired you by this time with disquisitions which you have already heard repeated by others a thousand and a thousand times; and therefore, shall only add assurances of the esteem and attachment with which I have the honor to be, dear Sir, your affectionate friend and servant.

P.S. The instability of our laws is really an immense evil. I think it would be well to provide in our constitutions, that there shall always be a twelvemonth between the engrossing a bill and passing it; that it should then be offered to its passage without changing a word; and that if circumstances should be thought to require a speedier passage, it should take two-thirds of both Houses, instead of a bare majority.

Thomas Jefferson, February 15, 1791

OPINION AGAINST THE CONSTITUTIONALITY OF A NATIONAL BANK

Appointed Secretary of State by President Washington in 1790, Jefferson rendered an opinion against the constitutionality of the proposed First Bank of the United States, supported by Alexander Hamilton. He feared that loose construction of the Constitution would lead to the unbridled power of the federal government. He viewed strict construction as a check on the tyranny of a national majority. His support of majority rule was tempered by the very nature of the agrarian society he envisioned, by the systems of checks and balances among the branches of the national government, by the retention of "sovereign" powers within the separate states, and by strict interpretation of the Constitution.

The bill for establishing a National Bank undertakes among other things:—

1. To form the subscribers into a corporation.

From *The Writings of Thomas Jefferson*, Lipscomb, ed., Vol. III, pp. 145–153.

2. To enable them in their corporate capacities to receive grants of land; and so far is against the laws of *Mortmain.**

3. To make alien subscribers capable of holding lands; and so far is against the laws of *alienage.*

4. To transmit these lands, on the death of a proprietor, to a certain line of successors; and so far changes the course of *Descents.*

5. To put the lands out of the reach of forfeiture or escheat; and so far is against the laws of *Forfeiture and Escheat.*

6. To transmit personal chattels to successors in a certain line; and so far is against the laws of *Distribution.*

7. To give them the sole and exclusive right of banking under the national authority; and so far is against the laws of Monopoly.

8. To communicate to them a power to make laws paramount to the laws of the States; for so they must be construed, to protect the institution from the control of the State legislatures; and so, probably, they will be construed.

I consider the foundation of the Constitution as laid on this ground: That "all powers not delegated to the United States, by the Constitution, nor prohibited by it to the States, are reserved to the States or to the people." [XIIth amendment.] To take a single step beyond the boundaries thus specially drawn around the powers of Congress, is to take possession of a boundless field of power, no longer susceptible of any definition.

The incorporation of a bank, and the powers assumed by this bill, have not, in my opinion, been delegated to the United States, by the Constitution.

1. They are not among the powers specially enumerated: for these are: 1st. A power to lay taxes for the purpose of paying the debts of the United States; but no debt is paid by this bill, nor any tax laid. Were it a bill to raise money, its origination in the Senate would condemn it by the Constitution.

2d. "To borrow money." But this bill neither borrows money nor ensures the borrowing it. The proprietors of the bank will be just as free as any other money holders, to lend or not to lend their money to the public. The operation proposed in the bill, first, to lend them

---

* Though the Constitution controls the laws of Mortmain so far as to permit Congress itself to hold land for certain purposes, yet not so far as to permit them to communicate a similar right to other corporate bodies.

two millions, and then to borrow them back again, cannot change the nature of the latter act, which will still be a payment, and not a loan, call it by what name you please.

3d. To "regulate commerce with foreign nations, and among the States, and with the Indian tribes." To erect a bank, and to regulate commerce, are very different acts. He who erects a bank, creates a subject of commerce in its bills; so does he who makes a bushel of wheat, or digs a dollar out of the mines; yet neither of these persons regulates commerce thereby. To make a thing which may be bought and sold, is not to prescribe regulations for buying and selling. Besides, if this was an exercise of the power of regulating commerce, it would be void, as extending as much to the internal commerce of every State, as to its external. For the power given to Congress by the Constitution does not extend to the internal regulation of the commerce of a State, (that is to say of the commerce between citizen and citizen,) which remain exclusively with its own legislature; but to its external commerce only, that is to say, its commerce with another State, or with foreign nations, or with the Indian tribes. Accordingly the bill does not propose the measure as a regulation of trade, but as "productive of considerable advantages to trade." Still less are these powers covered by any other of the special enumerations.

II. Nor are they within either of the general phrases, which are the two following:—

1. To lay taxes to provide for the general welfare of the United States, that is to say, "to lay taxes for *the purpose* of providing for the general welfare." For the laying of taxes is the *power*, and the general welfare the *purpose* for which the power is to be exercised. They are not to lay taxes *ad libitum for any purpose they please;* but only *to pay the debts or provide for the welfare of the Union.* In like manner, they are not *to do anything they please* to provide for the general welfare, but only to *lay taxes* for that purpose. To consider the latter phrase, not as describing the purpose of the first, but as giving a distinct and independent power to do any act they please, which might be for the good of the Union, would render all the preceding and subsequent enumerations of power completely useless.

It would reduce the whole Instrument to a single phrase, that of instituting a Congress with power to do whatever would be for the good of the United States; and, as they would be the sole judges of the good or evil, it would be also a power to do whatever evil they please.

It is an established rule of construction where a phrase will bear either of two meanings, to give it that which will allow some meaning to the other parts of the instrument, and not that which would render all the others useless. Certainly no such universal power was meant to be given them. It was intended to lace them up straitly within the enumerated powers, and those without which, as means, these powers could not be carried into effect. It is known that the very power now proposed *as a means* was rejected as *an end* by the Convention which formed the Constitution. A proposition was made to them to authorize Congress to open canals, and an amendatory one to empower them to incorporate. But the whole was rejected, and one of the reasons for rejection urged in debate was, that then they would have a power to erect a bank, which would render the great cities, where there were prejudices and jealousies on the subject, adverse to the reception of the Constitution.

2. The second general phrase is, "to make all laws *necessary* and proper for carrying into execution the enumerated powers." But they can all be carried into execution without a bank. A bank therefore is not *necessary,* and consequently not authorized by this phrase.

It has been urged that a bank will give great facility or convenience in the collection of taxes. Suppose this were true: yet the Constitution allows only the means which are *"necessary,"* not those which are merely "convenient" for effecting the enumerated powers. If such a latitude of construction be allowed to this phrase as to give any non-enumerated power, it will go to every one, for there is not one which ingenuity may not torture into a *convenience* in some instance *or other,* to *some one* of so long a list of enumerated powers. It would swallow up all the delegated powers, and reduce the whole to one power, as before observed. Therefore it was that the Constitution restrained them to the *necessary* means, that is to say, to those means without which the grant of power would be nugatory.

But let us examine this convenience and see what it is. The report on this subject . . . states the only *general* convenience to be, the

preventing the transportation and re-transportation of money between the States and the treasury (for I pass over the increase of
circulating medium, ascribed to it as a want, and which, according
to my ideas of paper money, is clearly a demerit). Every State will
have to pay a sum of tax money into the treasury; and the treasury
will have to pay, in every State, a part of the interest on the public
debt, and salaries to the officers of government resident in that
State. In most of the States there will still be a surplus of tax money
to come up to the seat of government for the officers residing there.
The payments of interest and salary in each State may be made by
treasury orders on the State collector. This will take up the great
export of the money he has collected in his State, and consequently
prevent the great mass of it from being drawn out of the State. If
there be a balance of commerce in favor of that State against the
one in which the government resides, the surplus of taxes will be
remitted by the bills of exchange drawn for that commercial balance.
And so it must be if there was a bank. But if there be no balance of
commerce, either direct or circuitous, all the banks in the world
could not bring up the surplus of taxes, but in the form of money.
Treasury orders then, and bills of exchange may prevent the displacement of the main mass of the money collected, without the aid
of any bank; and where these fail, it cannot be prevented even with
that aid.

Perhaps, indeed, bank bills may be a more *convenient* vehicle
than treasury orders. But a little *difference* in the degree of *convenience,* cannot constitute the necessity which the Constitution makes
the ground for assuming any non-enumerated power.

Besides; the existing banks will, without a doubt, enter into ar-
rangements for lending their agency, and the more favorable, as
there will be a competition among them for it; whereas the bill
delivers us up bound to the national bank, who are free to refuse
all arrangement, but on their own terms, and the public not free, on
such refusal, to employ any other bank. That of Philadelphia, I believe, now does this business, by their post-notes, which, by an
arrangement with the treasury, are paid by any State collector to
whom they are presented. This expedient alone suffices to prevent
the existence of that *necessity* which may justify the assumption of
a non-enumerated power as a means for carrying into effect an

enumerated one. The thing may be done, and has been done, and well done, without this assumption; therefore, it does not stand on that degree of *necessity* which can honestly justify it.

It may be said that a bank whose bills would have a currency all over the States, would be more convenient than one whose currency is limited to a single State. So it would be still more convenient that there should be a bank, whose bills should have a currency all over the world. But it does not follow from this superior conveniency, that there exists anywhere a power to establish such a bank; or that the world may not go on very well without it.

Can it be thought that the Constitution intended that for a shade or two of *convenience,* more or less, Congress should be authorized to break down the most ancient and fundamental laws of the several States; such as those against Mortmain, the laws of Alienage, the rules of descent, the acts of distribution, the laws of escheat and forfeiture, the laws of monopoly? Nothing but a necessity invincible by any other means, can justify such a prostitution of laws, which constitute the pillars of our whole system of jurisprudence. Will Congress be too straitlaced to carry the Constitution into honest effect, unless they may pass over the foundation-laws of the State government for the slightest convenience of theirs?

The negative of the President is the shield provided by the Constitution to protect against the invasions of the legislature: 1. The right of the Executive. 2. Of the Judiciary. 3. Of the States and State legislatures. The present is the case of a right remaining exclusively with the States, and consequently one of those intended by the Constitution to be placed under its protection.

It must be added, however, that unless the President's mind on a view of everything which is urged for and against this bill, is tolerably clear that it is unauthorized by the Constitution; if the pro and the con hang so even as to balance his judgment, a just respect for the wisdom of the legislature would naturally decide the balance in favor of their opinion. It is chiefly for cases where they are clearly misled by error, ambition, or interest, that the Constitution has placed a check in the negative of the President.

Thomas Jefferson, 1798

RESOLUTIONS RELATIVE TO THE ALIEN AND SEDITION LAWS

Jefferson viewed the Alien and Sedition Laws passed under Federalist auspices in 1798 during controversies with France as a threat to the political life of the new Democratic-Republican Party. Moreover, the laws created an arbitrary power over individuals in the federal government, trampled upon state authority, and set aside individual rights and liberties guaranteed by the Constitution. The acts, he argued, in a handwritten draft which became the text of the famous Kentucky Resolutions, could be ignored or nullified by the states. Writing to Madison, who authored the Virginia Resolutions on the same topic, from Monticello on November 17, 1798, Jefferson said, "I enclose you a draught of the Kentucky resolutions. I think we should distinctly affirm all the important principles they contain. . . ."

1. *Resolved,* That the several States composing the United States of America, are not united on the principle of unlimited submission to their General Government; but that, by a compact under the style and title of a Constitution for the United States, and of amendments thereto, they constituted a General Government for special purposes,—delegated to that government certain definite powers, reserving, each State to itself, the residuary mass of right to their own self-government; and that whensoever the General Government assumes undelegated powers, Its acts are unauthoritative, void, and of no force: that to this compact each State acceded as a State, and is an integral party, its co-States forming, as to itself, the other party: that the government created by this compact was not made the exclusive or final judge of the extent of the powers delegated to itself; since that would have made its discretion, and not the Constitution, the measure of its powers; but that, as in all other cases of compact among powers having no common judge, each party has an equal right to judge for itself, as well of infractions as of the mode and measure of redress.

2. *Resolved,* That the Constitution of the United States, having delegated to Congress a power to punish treason, counterfeiting the

From *The Writings of Thomas Jefferson*, Lipscomb, ed., Vol. XVII, pp. 379–391; for the letter to Madison see Vol. X, pp. 62–63.

securities and current coin of the United States, piracies, and felonies committed on the high seas, and offences against the law of nations, and no other crimes whatsoever; and it being true as a general principle, and one of the amendments to the Constitution having also declared, that "the powers not delegated to the United States by the Constitution, nor prohibited by it to the States, are reserved to the States respectively, or to the people," therefore the act of Congress, passed on the 14th day of July, 1798, and intituled "An Act in addition to the act intituled An Act for the punishment of certain crimes against the United States," as also the act passed by them on the — day of June, 1798, intituled "An Act to punish frauds committed on the bank of the United States," (and all their other acts which assume to create, define, or punish crimes, other than those so enumerated in the Constitution,) are altogether void, and of no force; and that the power to create, define, and punish such other crimes is reserved, and, of right, appertains solely and exclusively to the respective States, each within its own territory.

3. *Resolved,* That it is true as a general principle, and is also expressly declared by one of the amendments to the Constitution, that "the powers not delegated to the United States by the Constitution, nor prohibited by it to the States, are reserved to the States respectively, or to the people;" and that no power over the freedom of religion, freedom of speech, or freedom of the press being delegated to the United States by the Constitution, nor prohibited by it to the States, all lawful powers respecting the same did of right remain, and were reserved to the States or the people: that thus was manifested their determination to retain to themselves the right of judging how far the licentiousness of speech and of the press may be abridged without lessening their useful freedom, and how far those abuses which cannot be separated from their use should be tolerated, rather than the use be destroyed. And thus also they guarded against all abridgment by the United States of the freedom of religious opinions and exercises, and retained to themselves the right of protecting the same, as this State, by a law passed on the general demand of its citizens, had already protected them from all human restraint or interference. And that in addition to this general principle and express declaration, another and more special provision has been made by one of the amendments to the Constitution,

which expressly declares, that "Congress shall make no law respecting an establishment of religion, or prohibiting the free exercise thereof, or abridging the freedom of speech or of the press:" thereby guarding in the same sentence, and under the same words, the freedom of religion, of speech, and of the press: insomuch, that whatever violated either, throws down the sanctuary which covers the others, and that libels, falsehood, and defamation, equally with heresy and false religion, are withheld from the cognizance of federal tribunals. That, therefore, the act of Congress of the United States, passed on the 14th day of July, 1798, intituled "An Act in addition to the act intituled An Act for the punishment of certain crimes against the United States," which does abridge the freedom of the press, is not law, but is altogether void, and of no force.

4. *Resolved,* That alien friends are under the jurisdiction and protection of the laws of the State wherein they are: that no power over them has been delegated to the United States, nor prohibited to the individual States, distinct from their power over citizens. And it being true as a general principle, and one of the amendments to the Constitution having also declared, that "the powers not delegated to the United States by the Constitution, nor prohibited by it to the States, are reserved to the States respectively, or to the people," the act of the Congress of the United States, passed on the — day of July, 1798, intituled "An Act concerning aliens," which assumes powers over alien friends, not delegated by the Constitution, is not law, but is altogether void, and of no force.

5. *Resolved,* That in addition to the general principle, as well as the express declaration, that powers not delegated are reserved, another and more special provision, inserted in the Constitution from abundant caution, has declared that "the migration or importation of such persons as any of the States now existing shall think proper to admit, shall not be prohibited by the Congress prior to the year 1808;" that this commonwealth does admit the migration of alien friends, described as the subject of the said act concerning aliens: that a provision against prohibiting their migration, is a provision against all acts equivalent thereto, or it would be nugatory: that to remove them when migrated, is equivalent to a prohibition of their migration, and is, therefore, contrary to the said provision of the Constitution, and void.

6. *Resolved,* That the imprisonment of a person under the protection of the laws of this commonwealth, on his failure to obey the simple *order* of the President to depart out of the United States, as is undertaken by said act intituled "An Act concerning aliens," is contrary to the Constitution, one amendment to which has provided that "no person shall be deprived of liberty without due process of law;" and that another having provided that "in all criminal prosecutions the accused shall enjoy the right to public trial by an impartial jury, to be informed of the nature and cause of the accusation, to be confronted with the witnesses against him, to have compulsory process for obtaining witnesses in his favor, and to have the assistance of counsel for his defence," the same act, undertaking to authorize the President to remove a person out of the United States, who is under the protection of the law, on his own suspicion, without accusation, without jury, without public trial, without confrontation of the witnesses against him, without hearing witnesses in his favor, without defence, without counsel, is contrary to the provision also of the Constitution, is therefore not law, but utterly void, and of no force: that transferring the power of judging any person, who is under the protection of the laws, from the courts to the President of the United States, as is undertaken by the same act concerning aliens, is against the article of the Constitution which provides that "the judicial power of the United States shall be vested in courts, the judges of which shall hold their offices during good behavior;" and that the said act is void for that reason also. And it is further to be noted, that this transfer of judiciary power is to that magistrate of the General Government who already possesses all the Executive, and a negative on all legislative powers.

7. *Resolved,* That the construction applied by the General Government (as is evidenced by sundry of their proceedings) to those parts of the Constitution of the United States which delegate to Congress a power "to lay and collect taxes, duties, imports, and excises, to pay the debts, and provide for the common defence and general welfare of the United States," and "to make all laws which shall be necessary and proper for carrying into execution the powers vested by the Constitution in the government of the United States, or in any department or officer thereof," goes to the destruction of all limits prescribed to their power by the Constitution: that words

meant by the instrument to be subsidiary only to the execution of limited powers, ought not to be so construed as themselves to give unlimited powers, nor a part to be so taken as to destroy the whole residue of that instrument: that the proceedings of the General Government under color of these articles, will be a fit and necessary subject of revisal and correction, at a time of greater tranquillity, while those specified in the preceding resolutions call for immediate redress.

8th. *Resolved,* That a committee of conference and correspondence be appointed, who shall have in charge to communicate the preceding resolutions to the legislatures of the several States; to assure them that this commonwealth continues in the same esteem of their friendship and union which it has manifested from that moment at which a common danger first suggested a common union: that it considers union, for specified national purposes, and particularly to those specified in their late federal compact, to be friendly to the peace, happiness and prosperity of all the States: that faithful to that compact, according to the plain intent and meaning in which it was understood and acceded to by the several parties, it is sincerely anxious for its preservation: that it does also believe, that to take from the States all the powers of self-government and transfer them to a general and consolidated government, without regard to the special delegations and reservations solemnly agreed to in that compact, is not for the peace, happiness or prosperity of these States; and that therefore this commonwealth is determined, as it doubts not its co-States are, to submit to undelegated, and consequently unlimited powers in no man, or body of men on earth: that in cases of an abuse of the delegated powers, the members of the General Government, being chosen by the people, a change by the people would be the constitutional remedy; but, where powers are assumed which have not been delegated, a nullification of the act is the rightful remedy: that every State has a natural right in cases not within the compact, (casus non foederis,) to nullify of their own authority all assumptions of power by others within their limits: that without this right, they would be under the dominion, absolute and unlimited, of whosoever might exercise this right of judgment for them: that nevertheless, this commonwealth, from motives of regard and respect for its co-States, has wished to communicate

with them on the subject: that with them alone it is proper to communicate, they alone being parties to the compact, and solely authorized to judge in the last resort of the powers exercised under it,
Congress being not a party, but merely the creature of the compact,
and subject as to its assumptions of power to the final judgment of
those by whom, and for whose use itself and its powers were all
created and modified: that if the acts before specified should stand,
these conclusions would flow from them; that the General Government may place any act they think proper on the list of crimes, and
punish it themselves whether enumerated or not enumerated by the
Constitution as cognizable by them: that they may transfer its cognizance to the President, or any other person, who may himself be the
accuser, counsel, judge and jury, whose *suspicions* may be the
evidence, his *order* the sentence, his *officer* the executioner, and his
breast the sole record of the transaction: that a very numerous and
valuable description of the inhabitants of these States being, by this
precedent, reduced, as outlaws, to the absolute dominion of one
man, and the barrier of the Constitution thus swept away from us all,
no rampart now remains against the passions and the powers of a
majority in Congress to protect from a like exportation, or other
more grievous punishment, the minority of the same body, the legislatures, judges, governors, and counsellors of the States, nor their
other peaceable inhabitants, who may venture to reclaim the constitutional rights and liberties of the States and people, or who for
other causes, good or bad, may be obnoxious to the views, or
marked by the suspicions of the President, or be thought dangerous
to his or their election, or other interests, public or personal: that
the friendless alien has indeed been selected as the safest subject
of a first experiment; but the citizen will soon follow, or rather, has
already followed, for already has a sedition act marked him as its
prey: that these and successive acts of the same character, unless
arrested at the threshold, necessarily drive these States into revolution and blood, and will furnish new calumnies against republican
government, and new pretexts for those who wish it to be believed
that man cannot be governed but by a rod of iron: that it would be a
dangerous delusion were a confidence in the men of our choice to
silence our fears for the safety of our rights: that confidence is
everywhere the parent of despotism—free government is founded in

jealousy, and not in confidence; it is jealousy and not confidence which prescribes limited constitutions, to bind down those whom we are obliged to trust with power: that our Constitution has accordingly fixed the limits to which, and no further, our confidence may go; and let the honest advocate of confidence read the alien and sedition acts, and say if the Constitution has not been wise in fixing limits to the government it created, and whether we should be wise in destroying those limits. Let him say what the government is, if it be not a tyranny, which the men of our choice have conferred on our President, and the President of our choice has assented to, and accepted over the friendly strangers to whom the mild spirit of our country and its laws have pledged hospitality and protection: that the men of our choice have more respected the bare *suspicions* of the President, than the solid right of innocence, the claims of justification, the sacred force of truth, and the forms and substance of law and justice. In questions of power, then, let no more be heard of confidence in man, but bind him down from mischief by the chains of the Constitution. That this commonwealth does therefore call on its co-States for an expression of their sentiments on the acts concerning aliens, and for the punishment of certain crimes herein before specified, plainly declaring whether these acts are or are not authorized by the federal compact. And it doubts not that their sense will be so announced as to prove their attachment unaltered to limited government, whether general or particular. And that the rights and liberties of their co-States will be exposed to no dangers by remaining embarked in a common bottom with their own. That they will concur with this commonwealth in considering the said acts as so palpably against the Constitution as to amount to an undisguised declaration that that compact is not meant to be the measure of the powers of the General Government, but that it will proceed in the exercise over these States, of all powers whatsoever: that they will view this as seizing the rights of the States, and consolidating them in the hands of the General Government, with a power assumed to bind the States, (not merely as the cases made federal, casus foederis) but in all cases whatsoever, by laws made, not with their consent, but by others against their consent: that this would be to surrender the form of government we have chosen, and live under one deriving its powers from its own will, and not from our authority; and that the co-States, recurring to their natural right in cases not made federal, will concur in declaring these acts void, and of no force, and will each take measures of its own for providing that neither these acts, nor any others of the General Government not plainly and intentionally authorized by the Constitution, shall be exercised within their respective territories.

9th. *Resolved,* That the said committee be authorized to communicate by writing or personal conferences, at any times or places whatever, with any person or persons who may be appointed by any one or more co-States to correspond or confer with them; and that they lay their proceedings before the next session of Assembly.

Thomas Jefferson to Gideon Granger
Monticello, August 13, 1800

FEDERALIST VERSUS REPUBLICAN PRINCIPLES OF GOVERNMENT

On the eve of the elections of 1800 which brought Jefferson into the Presidency, Jefferson views the Federalists as attempting to consolidate all state governments under the authority of a single general government and to set aside individual rights and liberties in pursuit of their own self-interests. He counseled dependence upon state authority in domestic affairs, isolation, peace, simple and economical government, and advised Americans to "rally round the Constitution."

Dear Sir, I received with great pleasure your favor of June the 4th, and am much comforted by the appearance of a change of opinion in your State; for though we may obtain, and I believe shall obtain, a majority in the Legislature of the United States, attached to the preservation of the federal Constitution according to its obvious principles, and those on which it was known to be received; attached equally to the preservation to the States of those rights unquestionably remaining with them; friends to the freedom of religion,

From *The Writings of Thomas Jefferson,* Lipscomb, ed., Vol. X, pp. 166–169.

freedom of the press, trial by jury and to economical government; opposed to standing armies, paper systems, war, and all connection, other than commerce, with any foreign nation; in short, a majority firm in all those principles which we have espoused and the federalists have opposed uniformly; still, should the whole body of New England continue in opposition to these principles of government, either knowingly or through delusion, our government will be a very uneasy one. It can never be harmonious and solid, while so respectable a portion of its citizens support principles which go directly to change of the federal Constitution, to sink the State governments, consolidate them into one, and to monarchize that. Our country is too large to have all its affairs directed by a single government. Public servants at such a distance, and from under the eye of their constituents, must, from the circumstance of distance, be unable to administer and overlook all the details necessary for the good government of the citizens, and the same circumstance, by rendering detection impossible to their constituents, will invite the public agents to corruption, plunder and waste. And I do verily believe, that if the principle were to prevail, of a common law being in force in the United States, (which principle possesses the General Government at once of all the powers of the State governments, and reduces us to a single consolidated government,) it would become the most corrupt government on the earth. You have seen the practises by which the public servants have been able to cover their conduct, or, where that could not be done, delusions by which they have varnished it for the eye of their constituents. What an augmentation of the field for jobbing, speculating, plundering, office-building and office-hunting would be produced by an assumption of all the State powers into the hands of the General Government! The true theory of our Constitution is surely the wisest and best, that the States are independent as to everything within themselves, and united as to everything respecting foreign nations. Let the General Government be reduced to foreign concerns only, and let our affairs be disentangled from those of all other nations, except as to commerce, which the merchants will manage the better, the more they are left free to manage for themselves, and our General Government may be reduced to a very simple organization, and a very inexpensive one; a few plain duties to be performed by a few servants. But I repeat, that this simple and economical mode of government can never be secured, if the New England States continue to support the contrary system. I rejoice, therefore, in every appearance of their returning to those principles which I had always imagined to be almost innate in them. In this State, a few persons were deluded by the X. Y. Z. duperies. You saw the effect of it in our last Congressional representatives, chosen under their influence. This experiment on their credulity is now seen into, and our next representation will be as republican as it has heretofore been. On the whole, we hope, that by a part of the Union having held on to the principles of the Constitution, time has been given to the States to recover from the temporary frenzy into which they had been decoyed, to rally round the Constitution, and to rescue it from the destruction with which it had been threatened even at their own hands. I see copied from the American Magazine two numbers of a paper signed Don Quixote, most excellently adapted to introduce the real truth to the minds even of the most prejudiced. . . .

Thomas Jefferson, March 4, 1801
INAUGURATION ADDRESS

Although Jefferson referred earlier to the elections of 1800 as a "revolution," his inaugural address was remarkably restrained. He reaffirmed his faith in republican government, the inviolability of personal liberties, a wise and frugal government, and in majority rule. "We are all republicans—we are all federalists," he said. Now that he was President would or could Thomas Jefferson fully implement the ideal government which he had so long envisioned and espoused? Would the philosophical Jefferson and Jefferson the practicing politician be one and the same?

Friends and Fellow Citizens: Called upon to undertake the duties of the first executive office of our country, I avail myself of the presence of that portion of my fellow citizens which is here assembled,

From *The Writings of Thomas Jefferson,* Lipscomb, ed., Vol. III, pp. 317–323.

to express my grateful thanks for the favor with which they have been pleased to look toward me, to declare a sincere consciousness that the task is above my talents, and that I approach it with those anxious and awful presentiments which the greatness of the charge and the weakness of my powers so justly inspire. A rising nation, spread over a wide and fruitful land, traversing all the seas with the rich productions of their industry, engaged in commerce with nations who feel power and forget right, advancing rapidly to destinies beyond the reach of mortal eye—when I contemplate these transcendent objects, and see the honor, the happiness, and the hopes of this beloved country committed to the issue and the auspices of this day, I shrink from the contemplation, and humble myself before the magnitude of the undertaking. Utterly indeed, should I despair, did not the presence of many whom I here see remind me, that in the other high authorities provided by our constitution, I shall find resources of wisdom, of virtue, and of zeal, on which to rely under all difficulties. To you, then, gentlemen, who are charged with the sovereign functions of legislation, and to those associated with you, I look with encouragement for that guidance and support which may enable us to steer with safety the vessel in which we are all embarked amid the conflicting elements of a troubled world.

During the contest of opinion through which we have passed, the animation of discussion and of exertions has sometimes worn an aspect which might impose on strangers unused to think freely and to speak and to write what they think; but this being now decided by the voice of the nation, announced according to the rules of the constitution, all will, of course, arrange themselves under the will of the law, and unite in common efforts for the common good. All, too, will bear in mind this sacred principle, that though the will of the majority is in all cases to prevail, that will, to be rightful, must be reasonable; that the minority possess their equal rights, which equal laws must protect, and to violate which would be oppression. Let us, then, fellow citizens, unite with one heart and one mind. Let us restore to social intercourse that harmony and affection without which liberty and even life itself are but dreary things. And let us reflect that having banished from our land that religious intolerance under which mankind so long bled and suffered, we have yet gained little if we countenance a political intolerance as despotic, as wicked, and capable of as bitter and bloody persecutions. During the throes and convulsions of the ancient world, during the agonizing spasms of infuriated man, seeking through blood and slaughter his long-lost liberty, it was not wonderful that the agitation of the billows should reach even this distant and peaceful shore; that this should be more felt and feared by some and less by others; that this should divide opinions as to measures of safety. But every difference of opinion is not a difference of principle. We have called by different names brethren of the same principle. We are all republicans —we are all federalists. If there be any among us who would wish to dissolve this Union or to change its republican form, let them stand undisturbed as monuments of the safety with which error of opinion may be tolerated where reason is left free to combat it. I know, indeed, that some honest men fear that a republican government cannot be strong; that this government is not strong enough. But would the honest patriot, in the full tide of successful experiment, abandon a government which has so far kept us free and firm, on the theoretic and visionary fear that this government, the world's best hope, may by possibility want energy to preserve itself? I trust not. I believe this, on the contrary, the strongest government on earth. I believe it is the only one where every man, at the call of the laws, would fly to the standard of the law, and would meet invasions of the public order as his own personal concern. Sometimes it is said that man cannot be trusted with the government of himself. Can he, then, be trusted with the government of others? Or have we found angels in the forms of kings to govern him? Let history answer this question.

Let us, then, with courage and confidence pursue our own federal and republican principles, our attachment to our union and representative government. Kindly separated by nature and a wide ocean from the exterminating havoc of one quarter of the globe; too high-minded to endure the degradations of the others; possessing a chosen country, with room enough for our descendants to the hundredth and thousandth generation; entertaining a due sense of our equal right to the use of our own faculties, to the acquisitions of our industry, to honor and confidence from our fellow citizens, resulting not from birth but from our actions and their sense of them; enlightened by a benign religion, professed, indeed, and practiced in various forms, yet all of them including honesty, truth, temperance, gratitude, and the love of man; acknowledging and adoring an overruling Providence, which by all its dispensations proves that it delights in the happiness of man here and his greater happiness hereafter; with all these blessings, what more is necessary to make us a happy and prosperous people? Still one thing more, fellow citizens—a wise and frugal government, which shall restrain men from injuring one another, which shall leave them otherwise free to regulate their own pursuits of industry and improvement, and shall not take from the mouth of labor the bread it has earned. This is the sum of good government, and this is necessary to close the circle of our felicities.

About to enter, fellow citizens, on the exercise of duties which comprehend everything dear and valuable to you, it is proper that you should understand what I deem the essential principles of our government, and consequently those which ought to shape its administration. I will compress them within the narrowest compass they will bear, stating the general principle, but not all its limitations. Equal and exact justice to all men, of whatever state or persuasion, religious or political; peace, commerce, and honest friendship, with all nations—entangling alliances with none; the support of the state governments in all their rights, as the most competent administrations for our domestic concerns and the surest bulwarks against anti-republican tendencies; the preservation of the general government in its whole constitutional vigor, as the sheet anchor of our peace at home and safety abroad; a jealous care of the right of election by the people—a mild and safe corrective of abuses which are lopped by the sword of the revolution where peaceable remedies are unprovided; absolute acquiescence in the decisions of the majority—the vital principle of republics, from which there is no appeal but to force, the vital principle and immediate parent of despotism; a well-disciplined militia—our best reliance in peace and for the first moments of war, till regulars may relieve them; the supremacy of the civil over the military authority; economy in the public expense, that labor may be lightly burdened; the honest payment of our debts and sacred preservation of the public faith; encouragement of agriculture, and of commerce as its handmaid; the diffusion of information and the arraignment of all abuses at the bar of public reason; freedom of religion; freedom of the press; freedom of person under the protection of the *habeas corpus;* and trial by juries impartially selected—these principles form the bright constellation which has gone before us, and guided our steps through an age of revolution and reformation. The wisdom of our sages and the blood of our heroes have been devoted to their attainment. They should be the creed of our political faith—the text of civil instruction—the touch-stone by which to try the services of those we trust; and should we wander from them in moments of error or alarm, let us hasten to retrace our steps and to regain the road which alone leads to peace, liberty, and safety.

I repair, then, fellow citizens, to the post you have assigned me. With experience enough in subordinate offices to have seen the diffi-culties of this, the greatest of all, I have learned to expect that it will rarely fall to the lot of imperfect man to retire from this station with the reputation and the favor which bring him into it. Without pretensions to that high confidence reposed in our first and great revolutionary character, whose preeminent services had entitled him to the first place in his country's love, and destined for him the fairest page in the volume of faithful history, I ask so much con-fidence only as may give firmness and effect to the legal adminis-tration of your affairs. I shall often go wrong through defect of judgment. When right, I shall often be thought wrong by those whose positions will not command a view of the whole ground. I ask your indulgence for my own errors, which will never be intentional; and your support against the errors of others, who may condemn what they would not if seen in all its parts. The approbation implied by your suffrage is a consolation to me for the past; and my future solicitude will be to retain the good opinion of those who have bestowed it in advance, to conciliate that of others by doing them all the good in my power, and to be instrumental to the happiness and freedom of all.

Relying, then, on the patronage of your good will, I advance with obedience to the work, ready to retire from it whenever you become sensible how much better choice it is in your power to make. And may that Infinite Power which rules the destinies of the universe, lead our councils to what is best, and give them a favorable issue for your peace and prosperity.

II JEFFERSON'S AGRARIANISM

A. Whitney Griswold

JEFFERSON'S AGRARIAN DEMOCRACY

Griswold's Farming and Democracy *contains one of the finest studies of Jefferson's personal philosophy. Griswold believes that Jefferson was an agrarian democrat, and that he remained true to his ideals throughout his life. Jefferson's values did not change, but those of America did. Jefferson refused to impose his will upon that of the majority. In his capacity as the author of the Declaration of Independence or of the* Notes on Virginia, *and as President of the United States, he reflected the mind of the people which may not always have been his own. Jefferson, then, may have been both the consistent idealist as well as the practical politician.*

There is no name in American history so intimately associated with the twofold theme of agrarianism and democracy as that of Thomas Jefferson. On the two hundredth anniversary of his birth, in 1943, the entire American agricultural community paid tribute to him "as a man of abiding passion for the sacred rights of the common people, and as one who, throughout his entire career, remained pre-eminently and above all a farmer"—this from the preamble to a joint resolution of Congress establishing the National Agricultural Jefferson Bicentenary Committee, representing the Department of Agriculture, the land-grant colleges, the national farm organizations, the agricultural press, scientific and learned agricultural societies, and the federal Office of Education. Not as a digression, but as an integral part of the war effort in which American democracy was then engaged, the Bicentenary Committee spread the agrarian and the democratic fame of Jefferson throughout the nation; and at Monticello, on the two hundred and first anniversary of his birthday, Secretary of Agriculture Claude Wickard acclaimed Jefferson as "father of the idea of the family-sized farm."

Historians might question the merits of this accolade, but they cannot deny the fact of it. To living Americans, Jefferson is the foremost exemplar of agrarian democracy. No one believed so implicitly as he in a causal connection between the occupation of farming and the political system of democracy, and no one, before

From *Farming and Democracy* by A. Whitney Griswold (Harcourt, Brace & Co., 1948), pp. 18–46. Reprinted by permission of Mary B. Griswold. The title of the selection is that of the editor. Notes to the original have been omitted.

or since his time, has given that belief a greater impetus among his countrymen. His writings take us as near to the origin of the agrarian tradition as any American's; and this fact, together with his labors for the republican government of his day that became the democratic government of ours, commends them to us as the most representative American expression of the tradition.

Jefferson did not originate the tradition. He appropriated it. It was centuries old when he first took notice of it. From time immemorial, agriculture had been exalted above all other human occupations. The writings of Aristotle, Xenophon, and Hesiod reflect its prestige among the ancient Greeks, as do those of Cicero, Virgil, Horace, Pliny, Cato, Varro, and Columella, among the Romans. It was Socrates who, in the pages of Xenophon, contributed to the French Physiocrats of the eighteenth century the motto, "Husbandry is the mother and nurse of the other arts. For when husbandry flourishes, all the other arts are in good fettle, but whenever the land is compelled to lie waste, the other arts . . . well-nigh perish." Medieval and Renaissance writers venerated agriculture, and with the poets and essayists of the eighteenth century the veneration developed into a cult. Cicero spoke for them all, and for the host of writers since their day that has carried on their tradition, when he declared that "of all the occupations by which gain is secured, none is better than agriculture, none more profitable, none more delightful, none more becoming to a freeman."

Much of this writing, all of it, perhaps, was an idealization of the circumstances in which men had lived and labored throughout most of their history. For thousands of years agriculture had been their principal means of livelihood. Even today it employs two-thirds of the human race. Only for a brief moment in history and in a few places on earth have men known anything but an agrarian environment. Since agriculture was the basic economic enterprise, the traditional calling of mankind, it is not surprising to find it sanctioned by religion, by secular idealism, by whatever forms in which the human propensity for rationalization found expression. Almost all men were farmers, therefore to think well of man was to think well of farming. As Cato says of his ancestors, "when they were trying to praise a good man they called him a good farmer and a good tiller of the soil, and the one who received this compliment was considered to have received the highest praise." Man's universal respect for the producers of food, his first necessity, and his love of nature, which has grown as his distance from it has increased, have added mystic and romantic elements to the agrarian theme. Cicero was an indifferent farmer, an intellectual who enjoyed his country estates but whose chief contributions to agriculture were literary and forensic. He has had a numerous following: farmers have never lacked friends among writers and politicians. A farm is still the best place for a politician to be born. The annual list of best sellers invariably contains a votive offering to the country.

The moral ascendancy of agriculture reached its peak during the second half of the eighteenth century in England and France. In those years, which saw the beginning of the Industrial revolution in England and culminated in political revolutions in America and France, farming and rural life, the practical fulfillment of the increasingly popular philosophy of nature, became a craze among the British and French. British royalty and aristocracy vied with one another in enclosing and exploiting great agricultural estates. The enclosure movement, whose social consequences Goldsmith deplored in *The Deserted Village,* had its enthusiastic spokesman in the agricultural writer Arthur Young. The farming gentry eagerly read Young, founded agricultural societies, introduced technical improvements on their estates, and turned husbandry into big business. The extent of the fashion may be measured by the fact that King George III himself operated a model farm at Windsor, contributed to Young's *Annals of Agriculture,* carried Young's books about with him when he traveled, and did not conceal his pleasure in the nickname "Farmer George." "Perhaps," Arthur Young wrote, "we might, without any great impropriety, call farming the reigning taste of the present times."

In France, meanwhile, François Quesnay and his disciples, Mirabeau, Mercier de la Rivière, Le Trosne, and Du Pont de Nemours, were propounding an economic system known as Physiocracy, from the law of nature upon which it was based. The Physiocrats taught that all human affairs were governed by a divinely ordained natural order, *l'ordre naturel,* in which agriculture was the only productive occupation, the only true source of wealth. It was therefore the duty of the government to remove all taxes upon the land and its cultivators except a single tax on its net product, that is, after the deduction of costs. Apart from this, the state should keep its hands off economic enterprise: *laissez faire, laissez passer.* Whatever favored agriculture favored the public welfare; whatever harmed it was by definition unnatural and immoral. There were mixed motives in this as in all doctrines. The Physiocrats were applying John Locke's philosophy of natural rights to economic life, partly in conscientious protest against the tax-ridden mercantilist economy of Colbert, partly in the interests of a rising class of well-to-do bourgeois landowners (of whom Quesnay himself was one), who bought large estates, affected the manners of the nobility, and wanted to make money out of farming. Whatever their motives, by claiming divine sanction for agriculture as the sole source of wealth and the touchstone of human welfare, they carried its economic and moral prestige to its historic peak.

It was against this background that Jefferson and his colleagues composed their thoughts on agriculture and the agrarian way of life. George Washington ran a model farm like George III, corresponded with Arthur Young about its management, and avowed that agriculture was "amongst the most favourite amusements" of his life. Jefferson's political disciple and heir, James Madison, was one of the founders and early presidents of the Albermarle Agricultural Society of Virginia. John Taylor, a fellow-planter from Caroline County, Virginia, has been called "the philosopher and statesman of agrarianism." Jefferson was born to farming, as were most of his countrymen. He loved the land, trying again and again to escape to it from "the hated occupations of politics." His years at Monticello were unquestionably his happiest. "I return to farming with an ardor which I scarcely knew in my youth," he wrote Adams in 1794, and in later years:

> I have often thought that if heaven had given me choice of my position and calling, it should have been on a rich spot of earth, well watered, and near a good market for the productions of the garden. No occupation is so delightful to me as the culture of the earth. . . .

These were no idle sentiments. As his correspondence and notebooks show, his interest in farming was sincere and consistent throughout his life. They also reveal him as an experimental agriculturist of distinction. His observations and adaptations of European crops, livestock, and methods of farming put him in the vanguard of his contemporaries. He introduced the threshing machine in America and was one of the first importers of Merino sheep from Spain. His improved mold-board plow won him international awards. The agricultural societies he founded and encouraged and his recommended inclusion of scientific agriculture in the curriculum of the University of Virginia foreshadowed our whole national system of agricultural education. Instead of patenting his innovations and improvements, moreover, he gave them freely to the public, and instead of profiting from them he ended his years in virtual bankruptcy. This he attributed to the "disgusting dish of politics" which had lured him from his chosen vocation and cost him proficiency in it.

His political concern for agriculture was equally obvious. He had espoused the cause of the common man. At that time in our history, the common man was a farmer. Ninety per cent of all Americans, common or uncommon, were farmers. To champion the people, therefore, was to champion agriculture, a political theorem no politician could deny, however lofty or disinterested his purposes. The character of these people and their geographical surroundings might have determined their economic life without benefit of political theory. Lack of capital and a wilderness that yielded only to hard, slow manual labor made small-scale family farming the rule long before Jefferson became its advocate. The tobacco, rice, and cotton plantations of his southern compatriots were exceptions to the rule. It would be possible to ascribe his solicitude for small landholders to an astute rationalization of things as they were among his largest and most sympathetic political constituency.

But Jefferson was more than a farmer and a politician. He was a serious student of philosophy. The diligence with which he applied himself to his philosophical studies, to a search for moral guidance and for counsels of law and government, is collateral for the sincerity of his political and economic ideas. We know from his letters and commonplace books the time and thought he devoted to the Greek and Latin classics, to Locke, Bolingbroke, Hume, Montesquieu, Adam Smith, Destutt de Tracy, and many another English and French writer represented on the shelves of his library. We know from the

Declaration of Independence, his principal state paper, the degree to which he had steeped himself in the natural rights philosophy of John Locke. During his residence in Paris (1784–1789), he made the acquaintance of the Physiocrat, Du Pont de Nemours, and the economist, Destutt de Tracy.

Du Pont, who took up residence in America, and whose son founded the "gunpowder manufactory" that was eventually to gain un-Physiocratic fame as the eighth largest industrial corporation in the United States, became one of Jefferson's closest intellectual friends. Their correspondence over a period of seventeen years (1800–1817) weighed and appraised not only the principles of Physiocracy but most of the leading ideas of government and political economy current at the time. Jefferson's admiration for Destutt de Tracy was extravagant. He translated and edited De Tracy's *Commentary and Review of Montesquieu's Spirit of Laws* and his *Treatise on Political Economy,* which he considered the leading works in "civil government" and political economy. He persuaded the president of his alma mater, William and Mary, to adopt the *Commentary* as a text and spoke so enthusiastically about it to his friends that Du Pont, for one, accused him of having written it.

What is of interest to us in all this intellectual trafficking is not the genealogy of Jefferson's ideas, at best a speculative theme, but their substance, the elements of which they were composed, the process of composition. His general views on agriculture may require no more complicated explanation than, as already suggested, that they were perfectly logical deductions from his own tastes and environment. Undoubtedly he found moral support for them in his reading, especially in the classics. But the character of the views, their obviousness, generality, and fundamental simplicity, discourages a search for more specific doctrinal influences. The Physiocratic influence that is sometimes inferred in this connection has been discounted not only by historical scholars but by Jefferson himself. The inference derived largely from their common emphasis of agriculture, the similarity of the moral philosophy which both drew independently of each other from Locke, and from Jefferson's friendship with Du Pont. But Jefferson's homespun agrarianism stopped far short of the elaborate "arithmetical formularies," as Adam Smith called them, by which Quesnay proved agriculture the sole source of wealth and a single tax upon its net product the best source of public revenue. As Chinard has pointed out, Jefferson was never an economist in the formal sense of the word. There is no trace of Physiocratic or any other systematic economic analysis in any of his writings. He did not make Du Pont's acquaintance until some time during his tour of duty in Paris (1784–1789), nearly a decade after he had formulated and published his political philosophy, and at least two years after he had done the same with his views on agriculture. The latter he had set forth in his *Notes on Virginia,* which he had written in 1781 and revised in the winter of 1782–83. His exposure to the revolutionary intellectual ferment of Paris, far from revising his political opinions, strengthened them.

When he did enter into a specific discussion of Physiocratic economic policies in his correspondence with Du Pont, he exhibited a sturdy pragmatism and a practical sense of proportions which included commerce and industry, and to which, in the end, he partially converted Du Pont. Finally, in the "prospectus" to his edition of De Tracy's *Political Economy,* he stated his preference for Adam Smith, J. B. Say, and De Tracy, and disposed of Physiocracy thus:

> *Political Economy, in modern times, assumed the form of a regular science, first in the hands of the political sect in France, called the Economists. They made it a branch only of a comprehensive system, on the natural order of Societies. Quesnia [sic] first, Gournay, Le Trosne, Turgot, & Du Pont de Nemours, the enlightened, philanthropic, and venerable citizen now of the United States, led the way in these developments, and gave to our enquiries the direction they have since observed. Many sound and valuable principles, established by them, have received the sanction of general approbation. Some, as in the infancy of a science, might be expected, have been brought into question, and have furnished occasion for much discussion; their opinions on production, and on the proper subjects of taxation, have been particularly controverted and whatever may be the merit of their principles of taxation, it is not wonderful that they have not prevailed, not on the questioned score of correctness, but because not acceptable to the people, whose will must be the supreme law. Taxation is, in fact, the most difficult function of government, and that against which, their citizens are most apt to be refractory. The general aim is, therefore, to adopt the mode most consonant with the circumstances and sentiments of the country.*

One fundamental difference between Jefferson and the Physiocrats brings out his own views on agriculture in sharp relief. The Physiocrats stood for large-scale farming and great estates, in conscious emulation of Arthur Young and the British aristocracy. They represented a group of prosperous magistrates and bureaucrats then rising in French society, seeking (and gaining) titles, and determined, like the British, to make their newly acquired estates pay. Quesnay, Mercier de la Rivière, and Du Pont himself were all men of this type. They believed in scientific estate farming, which they called *la grande culture*; and their single tax, which ensured the owner a comfortable margin of profit, was conceived in its interest. The welfare of the peasants to them was of minor consideration, save in so far as all would gain from a simplification of the prevailing tax system. They favored, in other words, the interests of new and prosperous recruits to the landed aristocracy and proposed detailed methods of furthering those interests.

Jefferson from the outset directed his thoughts to small frontier farmers and never, even in their interest, conceived of economic measures so complex in detail or specific in purpose as those of the Physiocrats. Agriculture, to him, was not primarily a source of wealth but of human virtues and traits most congenial to popular self-government. It had a sociological rather than an economic value. This is the dominant note in all his writings on the subject. In Europe, he says in his *Notes on Virginia,* manufacturing was being promoted to support the surplus population that could not gain access to the land.

> But we have an immensity of land courting the industry of the husbandman. Is it best then that all our citizens should be employed in its improvement, or that one half should be called off from that to exercise manufactures and handicraft arts for the others? Those who labour in the earth are the chosen people of God, if ever He had a chosen people, whose breasts He has made His peculiar deposit for substantial and genuine virtue. It is the focus in which He keeps alive that sacred fire, which otherwise might escape from the face of the earth. Corruption of morals in the mass of cultivators is a phenomenon of which no age, nor nation has furnished an example. It is the mark set on those, who, not looking up to heaven, to their own soil and industry, as does the husbandman, for their subsistence, depend for it on casualties and caprice of customers. Dependence begets subservience and venality, suffocates the germ of virtue, and prepares fit tools for the designs of

ambition. *This, the natural progress and consequence of the arts, has sometimes perhaps been retarded by accidental circumstances; but, generally speaking the proportion which the aggregate of the other classes of citizens bears in any state to that of its husbandmen, is the proportion of its unsound to its healthy parts, and is a good enough barometer whereby to measure its degree of corruption. While we have land to labour then, let us never wish to see our citizens occupied at a workbench, or twirling a distaff. Carpenters, masons, smiths, are wanting in husbandry; but, for the general operations of manufacture, let our workshops remain in Europe. It is better to carry provisions and materials to workmen there, than bring them to the provisions and materials, and with them their manners and principles. The loss by the transportation of commodities across the Atlantic will be made up in happiness and permanence of government. The mobs of great cities add just so much to the support of pure government, as sores do to the strength of the human body. It is the manners and spirit of a people which preserve a republic in vigor. A degeneracy in these is a canker which soon eats to the heart of its laws and constitution.*

This is a recurrent theme: "Cultivators of the earth are the most valuable citizens. They are the most vigorous, the most independent, the most virtuous, and they are tied to their country, and wedded to its liberty and interests by the most lasting bonds. . . . I consider the class of artificers as the panders of vice, and the instruments by which the liberties of a country are generally overturned." Again: "I think our governments will remain virtuous for many centuries; as long as they are chiefly agricultural; and this will be as long as there shall be vacant lands in any part of America. When they get piled up upon one another in large cities, as in Europe, they will become corrupt as in Europe." Jefferson came almost as near to claiming a monopoly of good morals for farmers as the Physiocrats did of the sources of material wealth.

He never changed these views, though he never permitted them or any other theoretical consideration to obscure his sense of the practical. He had bitterly opposed Hamilton in the creation of a national bank (1790), having gone so far as to call the funding of the public debt an iniquitous and unconstitutional levy on farmers for the benefit of "stock-jobbers." Yet, when he became President, he maintained Hamilton's policies. He had inherited the "half lettered ideas of Hamilton," he explained to Du Pont, but they were law and he was bound to defend them. "We can pay off his debt in 15 years but we can never get rid of his financial system. It mortifies me to be strengthened by principles which I deem radically vicious, but this vice is entailed on us by a just error." Then follows a sentence that provides the key to his whole character: "What is practicable must often countrol what is pure theory, and the habits of the governed determine in a great degree what is practicable." He displays here that pragmatic empiricism which has governed Anglo-American political thought and action through history, confounding European critics in our time as it perplexed Du Pont in his. The logical Frenchman wanted things planned, ordered, consistent, directed from the top down, having no more faith than Hamilton in the capacity of the common people to know their own best interests. Jefferson's faith in the people was complete. He considered it "a duty in those entrusted with the administration of their affairs, to conform themselves to the decided choice of their constituents." Toward the end of their long correspondence he admonished Du Pont: "We both consider the people as our children, and love them with parental affection. But you love them as infants whom you are afraid to trust without nurses, and I as adults, whom I freely leave to self government."

True to this basic philosophy, which not infrequently drew charges of hypocrisy from his enemies, when the people began to manifest an interest in commerce and industry, Jefferson went along with them. This is how he answered a direct query on the point in 1785:

> *You ask what I think on the expediency of encouraging our States to be commercial? Were I to indulge my own theory, I should wish them to practice neither commerce nor navigation, but to stand, with respect to Europe, precisely on the footing of China. We should thus avoid wars, and all our citizens would be husbandmen. Whenever, indeed, our numbers should so increase as that our produce would overstock the markets of those nations who should come to seek it, the farmers must either employ the surplus of their time in manufactures, or the surplus of our hands must be employed in manufactures or in navigation. But that day would, I think, be distant, and we should long keep our workmen in Europe, while Europe should be drawing rough materials, and even subsistence from America. But this is theory only, and a theory which the servants of America are not at liberty to follow.*

Again the practical qualifications, the acceptance of what was in place of what ought to be. A quarter century later, he had moved so far with the times as to prescribe an "equilibrium of agriculture, manufactures, and commerce":

> Manufactures, sufficient for our own consumption, of what we raise the raw material (and no more). Commerce sufficient to carry the surplus produce of agriculture, beyond our own consumption, to a market for exchanging it for articles we cannot raise (and no more). These are the true limits of manufactures and commerce. . . . These three important branches of human industry will then grow together, and be really handmaids to each other.

Finally, in 1816, this thoroughgoing discussion of the matter:

> You tell me I am quoted by those who wish to continue our dependence on England for manufactures. There was a time when I might have been so quoted with more candor, but within the thirty years which have since elapsed, how are circumstances changed! We were then in peace. Our independent place among the nations was acknowledged. A commerce which offered the raw material in exchange for the same material after receiving the last touch of industry, was worthy of welcome to all nations. It was expected that those especially to whom manufacturing industry was important, would cherish the friendship of such customers by every favor, by every inducement, and particularly cultivate their peace by every act of justice and friendship. Under this prospect the question seemed legitimate, whether, with such an immensity of unimproved land, courting the hand of husbandry, the industry of agriculture, or that of manufactures, would add most to the national wealth? And the doubt was entertained on this consideration chiefly, that to the labor of the husbandman a vast addition is made by the spontaneous energies of the earth on which it is employed: for one grain of wheat committed to the earth, she renders twenty, thirty, and even fifty fold, whereas to the labor of the manufacturer nothing is added. Pounds of flax, in his hands, yield, on the contrary, but pennyweights of lace. This exchange, too, laborious as it might seem, what a field did it promise for the occupations of the ocean; what a nursery for that class of citizens who were to exercise and maintain our equal rights on that element? This was the state of things in 1785, when the "Notes on Virginia" were first printed; when, the ocean being open to all nations, and their common right in it acknowledged and exercised under regulations sanctioned by the assent and usage of all, it was thought that the doubt might claim some consideration. But who in 1785 could foresee the rapid depravity which was to render the close of that century the disgrace of the history of man? Who could have imagined that the two most distinguished in the rank of nations, for science and civilization, would have suddenly descended from that honorable eminence, and setting at defiance all those moral

laws established by the Author of nature between nation and nation, as between man and man, would cover earth and sea with robberies and piracies, merely because strong enough to do it with temporal impunity; and that under this disbandment of nations from social order, we should have been despoiled of a thousand ships, and have thousands of our citizens reduced to Algerine slavery. Yet all this has taken place. . . . Compare this state of things with that of '85, and say whether an opinion founded in the circumstances of that day can be fairly applied to those of the present. We have experienced what we did not then believe, that there exists both profligacy and power enough to exclude us from the field of interchange with other nations: that to be independent for the comforts of life we must fabricate them ourselves. We must now place the manufacturer by the side of the agriculturist. The former question is suppressed, or rather assumes a new form. Shall we make our own comforts, or go without them, at the will of a foreign nation? He, therefore, who is now against domestic manufacture, must be for reducing us either to dependence on that foreign nation, or to be clothed in skins, and to live like wild beasts in dens and caverns. I am not one of these; experience has taught me that manufactures are now as necessary to our independence as to our comfort. . . .

Several features of Jefferson's conversion are of interest. In the first place, it was incomplete. The farthest he would go was to approve a balanced, self-sufficient economy in which he expected agriculture to occupy the most important position. Secondly, it was reluctant: he attributed it to the "depravity" of the times. Thirdly, it was decided not on the merits of the question but by international politics and war. The Napoleonic Wars were not the first in which American domestic issues had been confused by the whims and ambitions of foreign powers, nor would they be the last. The dominant role they played in the conversion of Jefferson, if we may call it such, shows the extent to which the conversion was one of expediency rather than of principle. The world war in which we became a belligerent in 1812 forced him to forego as statesman and patriot views which, as farmer and philosopher, he never formally renounced. To the end of his days, agriculture remained the occupation nearest his heart, his ideal of a good society: a society of farmers.

We should say, as he did, a society of small farmers, for as we shall see, he considered these "the most precious part of a state." The political freedom of the individual was his *summum bonum,* and the political value that Jefferson expected agriculture to yield was exactly that, a value best produced on a small farm. For it was pre-eminently on a small farm that those qualities of independence and self-reliance, of "looking up to heaven, to their own soil and industry," that were most readily convertible into enlightened self-government were most thoroughly developed in farmers. Political independence rested upon social equality and economic security, of which a small farm was the surest foundation. The tiller of another man's fields could never feel the sense of economic security nor the pride of possession of the independent farmer, still less could those dependent upon "casualties and caprice of customers . . . or twirling a distaff." Democracy meant self-government. Who would govern himself must own his soul. To own his soul he must own property, the means of economic security. Everyone in America could own land. Thus everyone, "by his property, or by his satisfactory situation, is interested in the support of law and order. And such men may safely and advantageously reserve to themselves a wholesome control over their public affairs. . . ." The typical form of private property was land, and the typical use for land was farming. Thus we find in Jefferson's conception of the property right another link between his agrarianism and his democracy.

A search for the intellectual basis of this conception again leads back to Locke. "The earth is given as a common stock for man to labour and live on," Jefferson wrote from Paris in 1785. The "right to labour the earth" was "fundamental." And in 1816, in a detailed summary of his political creed, he stated the belief "that a right of property is founded in our natural wants, in the means with which we were endowed to satisfy these wants, and the right to what we acquire by those means without violating the similar rights of other sensible beings." A century and a quarter earlier, Locke had written:

> God, who hath given the world to men in common, hath also given them reason to make use of it to the best advantage of life and convenience. The earth and all that is therein is given to men for the support and comfort of their being. And though all the fruits it naturally produces, and beasts it feeds, belong to mankind in common, as they are produced by the spontaneous hand of Nature, and nobody has originally a private dominion exclusive of the rest of mankind in any of them, as they are thus in their natural state, yet being given for the use of men, there

*must of necessity be a means to appropriate them some way or other
before they can be of any use, or at all beneficial, to any particular men.*

Even the phrasing sounds like Jefferson's, and both echo the psalm
Locke quotes as his authority: "The heaven, even the heavens, are
the Lord's: but the earth hath he given to the children of men."

Whether consciously or indirectly and unconsciously borrowed
from Locke, Jefferson's theory of property was essentially Locke's.
What was Locke's in essence had evolved out of pre-Christian custom, Roman law, and medieval doctrine to find philosophical definition at Locke's hands and to be transmitted by him to most political
philosophers of the eighteenth, and many of the nineteenth, century.
By the time Locke's ideas on property had reached Jefferson, many
tributaries had flowed into the stream, broad as it was even in
Locke's day. The texts Jefferson studied at William and Mary, the
authorities he consulted as a law student, the more specific writings,
such as Kames' *Historical Law Tracts,* that he extracted in his commonplace book, all reflected the general sanction civilized society
had long since placed upon the institution of private property.

The colonists had brought this sanction with them to America.
The Protestant churches, to which most of them belonged, had improved upon it with the doctrine of the calling, according to which
material possessions were a proof of virtue and a sign of heavenly
grace. Taxation without representation, the *cause célèbre* of the
Revolution, had made every American acutely conscious of the
property right and its relation to government. The first resolution of
the Declaration and Resolves of the First Continental Congress, Oc-
tober 14, 1774, proclaimed the right "to life, liberty and property."
Jefferson's own draft of the Declaration on Taking up Arms, July 6,
1775, declared: "The political institutions of America, its various
soils and climates opened a certain resource to the unfortunate and
to the enterprising of every country and ensured to them the acquisition and free possession of property." The first resolution of the
famous Virginia Bill of Rights, written by George Mason, adopted
June 12, 1776, and honored by imitation in both America and France
read:

*That all men are by nature equally free and independent, and have
certain inherent rights, of which, when they enter into a state of*

*society, they cannot by any compact deprive or divest their posterity;
namely, the enjoyment of life and liberty, with the means of acquiring
and possessing property, and pursuing and obtaining happiness and
safety.*

Property, in this context, was the means of freedom, not the end—as
it later became. The right to private property was taken for granted,
and the duty of the government to protect it assumed, by Jefferson
when he sat down to compose the Declaration of Independence,
and that document is anything if not representative of the times.
When some of his contemporaries criticized it as "a commonplace
compilation, its sentiments hacknied in Congress for two years
before" and "as copied from Locke's treatise on Government,"
Jefferson explained that he was not trying to invent new principles
or ideas "but to place before mankind the common sense of the
subject, in terms so plain and firm as to command their respect";
that the Declaration was intended as "an expression of the American mind" based on "the harmonizing sentiments of the day."

In England, Locke's ideas on property were construed in the
interests of the rich as well as the poor, whereas to Jefferson they
provided the moral basis for a pattern of small landowners. The substance of these ideas was that the right to private property existed
in the state of nature that preceded formal government. Although
the earth and its fruits were given to mankind in common, a man's
person and his labor were his and his alone. "Whatsoever, then, he
removes out of the state that Nature hath provided and left it in, he
hath mixed his labour with it, and joined to it something that is his
own, and thereby makes it his property." By picking up fruit or
tilling a field or filling his pitcher at a fountain, a man appropriated
exclusively to himself what was given by nature to all men equally
and in common, with two important qualifications: there must be
"enough, and as good left in common for others," and no one must
take more than he can use. Upon this second qualification Locke
placed special emphasis:

*It will, perhaps, be objected to this, that if gathering the acorns or
other fruits of the earth, etc., makes a right to them, then any one may
engross as much as he will. To which answer, Not so. The same law of
Nature that does by this means give us property, does also bound that*

property too. "God has given us all things richly." Is the voice of reason confirmed by inspiration? But how far has He given it us—"to enjoy"? As much as any one can make use of to any advantage of life before it spoils, so much he may by his labour fix a property in. Whatever is beyond this is more than his share, and belongs to others.

Applied to land, which Locke called "the chief matter of property," this meant "as much land as a man tills, plants, improves, cultivates, and can use the product of." Thus defined and qualified, the natural right to private property must be recognized and protected by government as a basic condition of the social order.

The qualifications are important. Both Locke and Jefferson believed they would be automatically enforced by the great "immensity of land" behind the American frontier. Where they failed, according to Locke, was in those parts of the world where the increase of population "with the use of money" made land scarce and caused its distribution to be regulated "by compact and agreement." Where there was plenty of land and a minimum of commerce, "there men will not be apt to enlarge their possessions of land, were it never so rich, never so free for them to take."

> *For I ask, what would a man value ten thousand or an hundred thousand acres of excellent land, ready cultivated and well stocked, too, with cattle, in the middle of the inland parts of America, where he had no hopes of commerce with other parts of the world, to draw money to him by the sale of the product? It would not be worth the enclosing, and we should see him give up again to the wild common of Nature whatever was more than would supply the conveniences of life, to be had there for him and his family.*
> *Thus, in the beginning, all the world was America. . . .*

Was this not a suggestion to Jefferson by the foremost political philosopher of the age, of a fall from grace and a hope of redemption in a rural democracy across the seas?

Here, surely, was confirmation, if not inspiration, for his ideal community of small landholders. If Locke was more interested in defending the right to private property than in promoting its equal division, to Jefferson both were important. Like Locke, he wished to make the strongest possible political case for the principle, as Locke put it, that "the supreme power cannot take from any man

any part of his property without his own consent." But the benefi-
ciaries of the principle as Jefferson conceived it were small frontier
farmers, not landed Parliamentarians as was the case with Locke.
Locke's limitations on landowning came to the fore in Jefferson's
thinking. There was a hint of them in the constitution he drew up
for the state of Virginia in June, 1776, one title of which provided
that every person of full age who neither owned nor had owned fifty
acres of land should be entitled to an appropriation of fifty acres
"in full and absolute dominion. And no other person shall be capable
of taking an appropriation."

There was more than a hint of them in the laws he drew up to
abolish primogeniture and entail. So vital did he consider these that
he obtained leave from Congress soon after the adoption of the
Declaration of Independence to return to the Virginia legislature
and see that they were carried out in his own state. He first brought
in a bill doing away with entail, the means by which "a distinct set
of families who, being privileged by law in the perpetuation of their
wealth were thus formed into a Patrician order."

> To annul this privilege, and instead of an aristocracy of wealth, of
> more harm and danger, than benefit, to society, to make an opening
> for the aristocracy of virtue and talent, which nature has wisely provided
> for the direction of the interests of society, and scattered with equal
> hand through all its conditions, was deemed essential to a well ordered
> republic. To effect it no violence was necessary, no deprivation of
> natural right, but rather an enlargement of it by a repeal of the law.
> For this would authorize the present holder to divide the property among
> his children equally, as his affections were divided; and would place
> them by natural generation on the level of their fellow citizens.

Next he turned his attention to primogeniture:

> As the Law of Descents, & the criminal law fell of course within my
> portion, I wished the commee [sic.] to settle the leading principles of
> these, as a guide for me in framing them. And with respect to the first,
> I proposed to abolish the law of primogeniture, and to make real estate
> descendible in parcenary to the next of kin, as personal property is by
> the statute of distribution. Mr. Pendleton wished to preserve the right
> of primogeniture, but seeing at once that that could not prevail, he pro-
> posed we should adopt the Hebrew principle, and give a double portion
> to the elder son. I observed that if the eldest son could eat twice as

much, or do double work, it might be a natural evidence of his right to a double portion; but being on a par in his powers & wants, with his brothers and sisters, he should be on a par also in the partition of the patrimony, and such was the decision of the other members.

These bills he considered "as forming a system by which every fibre would be eradicated of ancient or future aristocracy; and a foundation laid for a government truly republican."

The repeal of the laws of entail would prevent the accumulation and perpetuation of wealth in select families, and preserve the soil of the country from being daily more and more absorbed in Mortmain. The abolition of primogeniture, and equal partition of inheritances removed the feudal and unnatural distinctions which made one member of every family rich, and all the rest poor, substituting equal partition, the best of all Agrarian laws.

Jefferson was too shrewd a politician to believe that a perfectly equal division of the land was possible. It was another of those ideals that he tried to realize pragmatically, as practical politics and human nature would permit. Yet it was an ideal. In a letter he wrote from Fontainebleau to the president of William and Mary College in 1785, he reduced the whole subject to its simplest terms. He was inspired to write by a chance encounter with an old peasant woman who had guided him on a walk through the countryside and answered his questions about "the condition of the labouring poor." When he had rewarded her for this service with twenty-four sous, she had burst into tears of gratitude.

This little attendrissement, with the solitude of my walk, led me into a train of reflections on that unequal division of property which occasions the numberless instances of wretchedness which I had observed in this country & is to be observed all over Europe. The property of this country is absolutely concentrated in a very few hands, having revenues of from half a million of guineas a year downwards. These employ the flower of the country as servants, some of them having as many as 200 domestics, not labouring. They employ also a great number of manufacturers, & tradesmen, & lastly the class of labouring husbandmen. But after all there comes the most numerous of all the classes, that is, the poor who cannot find work. I asked myself what could be the reason that so many should be permitted to beg who are willing to work, in a country where there is a very considerable proportion of uncultivated lands? These lands are undisturbed only for the sake of game. It should seem then that it must be because of the enormous wealth of the proprietors which places them above attention to the encrease of their revenues by permitting these lands to be laboured. I am conscious that an equal division of property is impracticable. But the consequences of this enormous inequality producing so much misery to the bulk of mankind, legislators cannot invent too many devices for subdividing property, only taking care to let their subdivisions go hand in hand with the natural affections of the human mind.

The descent of property of every kind therefore to all the children, or to all the brothers & sisters, or other relations in equal degree is a politic measure and a practicable one. Another means of silently lessening the inequality of property is to exempt all from taxation below a certain point, & to tax the higher portions of property in geometrical progression as they rise. Whenever there is in any country, uncultivated lands and unemployed poor, it is clear that the laws of property have been so far extended as to violate natural right. The earth is given as a common stock for man to labour & live on. If for the encouragement of industry we allow it to be appropriated, we must take care that other employment be provided to those excluded from the appropriation. If we do not the fundamental right to labour the earth returns to the unemployed. It is too soon yet in our country to say that every man who cannot find employment but who can find uncultivated land shall be at liberty to cultivate it, paying a moderate rent. But it is not too soon to provide by every possible means that as few as possible shall be without a little portion of land. The small land holders are the most precious part of a state.

The ancient agrarian tradition; the personal love of the soil; the theory of natural rights bequeathed by Locke to all liberal politicians of the age; the cause of American independence which became the cause of popular government versus the government of kings; the existing circumstances of the American frontier; the horror of the industrial revolution, fed by imagination as much as by a fleeting impression of England; the conception of the earth as a common stock; the immensity of land with which America might redeem Europe's loss; the belief in individual freedom and in private property as its means; the fact that farm land was the most typical and useful form of private property—the philosophical insight and the political sagacity—what does it matter which came first? All were present in the conclusion that small landholders, i.e., family farmers, were "the most precious part of a state," the classic American statement of the political theory of the family farm.

Are they still the most precious part of the state? Were they ever? Jefferson's dream of a rural republic, isolated from European commercialism and industrialism and composed entirely of self-governing farmers, had begun to fade before it was full-blown. As the intransigent John Taylor lamented to Monroe in 1810, "There were a number of people who soon thought, and said to one another, that Mr. Jefferson did many good things, but neglected some better things; and who now view his policy as very like a compromise with Mr. Hamilton's." Although Taylor continued to prompt him with such sentiments as "the divine intelligence which selected an agricultural state as a paradise for its first favourites, has . . . prescribed the agricultural virtues as the means for the admission of their posterity into heaven," and to sandbag the dikes with ponderous arguments, both he and Jefferson saw that the rising tide of commerce and industry could not be held in check. The unpent genie of industrialism was moving about the world and had visited America. By 1791, Hamilton could say with confidence, in his *Report on Manufactures,* "The expediency of encouraging manufactures in the United States, which was not long since deemed very questionable, appears at this time to be pretty generally admitted." So it came to be, even by Thomas Jefferson. But his ideal of democracy as a community of family farms has lived on to inspire the modern lawmakers and color the thoughts of their constituents when they turn their minds to rural life.

Stuart Bruchey

JEFFERSON, THE LATENT INDUSTRIALIST

Traditionally Thomas Jefferson is viewed as the philosophical and political antagonist of Alexander Hamilton who favored strong centralized government, manufacturing, trade and urban development. Stuart Bruchey takes issue with the "agrarianism" of Thomas Jefferson and with the view that

From "Federal Legislation and Community Will," pp. 114–122 in *The Roots of American Economic Growth, 1607–1861* by Stuart Bruchey. Copyright © 1965 by Stuart Bruchey. Reprinted by permission of Harper & Row, Publishers, and Hutchinson Publishing Group Ltd. The title of the selection is that of the editor.

Jeffersonian and Hamiltonian objectives were indeed hostile. Both, he effectively argues, sought to utilize the national government in the interest of promoting a broad economic development.

A familiar tradition makes Hamilton spokesman for the interests of an elite in commerce, finance, and manufacturing, and associates him with intervention by central government in behalf of these interests. Jefferson is depicted as the champion of a rural America in which the rights of the states are viewed as the bulwarks of republicanism. Occasionally substantive parts of this tradition are challenged, as occurred some three decades ago with the publication of a distinguished study of Jefferson by Gilbert Chinard. The most recent and most vigorous statement of an opposing point of view is that of E. A. J. Johnson, who is convinced that "great national policy decisions concerning economic development must be based on agreement not on discord, variance, or uncompromising truculence," and that "it is only meretricious to contrast Hamiltonian with Jeffersonian policy or solemnly to attribute intervention to one party and libertarianism to another." We may determine which of these views lies closer to the truth by tracing the rise of opposition to the Hamiltonian program and then comparing Jefferson's presidential principles to the measures he proposed for enactment by the federal government.

Unquestionably, much of the early legislation enjoyed widespread support. As Ferguson says, the "remarkable ease" with which the transfer of the substance of political power to the central government was accomplished testifies to the "growth in national feeling." It would be a mistake, he adds, to assume that Hamilton's proposals regarding the public debt "seriously divided either the people or their delegates in Congress." Madison's suggestion that the government discriminate between original and present holders of securities was rejected by the great majority of Congress. Ethically attractive, it appears to have arisen out of Madison's desire to restore his declining political prestige in Virginia, and while it might have been possible to identify "a great many" original holders, discrimination, as Hamilton forcefully argued, would have jeopardized the security of future transfers and damaged public credit. The proposal to assume the debts of the states encountered far more opposition, especially on the part of the South, where "to a relatively greater extent than elsewhere" the costs of the war had already been absorbed by the states. The circumstances in which Jefferson put aside his initial hostility and entered into his famous "bargain" with Hamilton are familiar.

It proved otherwise with Hamilton's proposal in December 1790 that the government charter a national bank. Jefferson feared that the resort by the Secretary of the Treasury to loose constructionism to justify the constitutionality of the bank would prove a foot in the door that would enable him to move increasingly in the direction of the more consolidated government he was known to favor. Jefferson attributed to motives of personal profit the support given Hamilton by a number of Congressmen who owned securities. "Are the people in your quarter as well contented with the proceedings of our government as their representatives say they are?" he asked New York's Robert R. Livingston on February 4, 1791. Affirming the existence of "a vast mass of discontent gathered in the South," Jefferson sought to reverse the trend in government by increasing the weight in the "republican scale" in Congress. His letter of the same date to George Mason of Virginia shows how he hoped to accomplish this: the "only corrective of what is corrupt in our present form of government will be the augmentation of the numbers in the lower house, so as to get a more agricultural representation, which may put that interest above that of stockjobbers."

Parties began to form in Congress in 1792, and such was the success of Jefferson, Madison, and other leaders of the opposition that it is perhaps possible to speak of a Democratic-Republican majority in the House in the Third Congress (1793–95). Certainly by the end of that Congress in 1795 differences in reactions to the Hamiltonian program and to issues growing out of the behavior of revolutionary France had produced two apparently rigidly formed parties. Thereafter the electorate returned Federalist majorities to the Congresses of the 1790's, but with the election of Jefferson in 1800 a Democratic-Republican majority appeared in both House and Senate. And in both chambers the size of that majority increased steadily during Jefferson's two administrations.

Now Jefferson occasionally remarked that political opposition served the useful purpose of criticism, but fundamentally he did not believe in the party system. Both during his presidency and later he was convinced that "the mass of our countrymen, even of those who call themselves Federalists, are republicans." This did not apply to the Federalist leaders, whom he considered irredeemable monarchists, a mere faction he wished to sink into an abyss so deep as to make its resurrection impossible, as he once put it. "I will not say our *party,* the term is false and degrading, but our *nation,*" he wrote in 1811. "For the republicans are the *nation.* Their opponents are but a faction, weak in numbers, but powerful and profuse in the command of money, and backed by England." The bulk of the membership he believed to have been "decoyed into the net of the monarchists by the X. Y. Z. contrivance" and he made it a cardinal point of his presidency to win it back to republicanism. "The greatest good we can do our country is to heal its party divisions & make them one people," he wrote in July 1801. Both during his presidency and afterwards he rejoiced in the electoral evidence of mounting republican ascendancy, and in 1825, the year before his death, it pained him to observe that "the parties exist as heretofore." It is clear Jefferson believed that republicans composed, as he expressed it in the fall of 1801, "a very great majority of the nation."

As spokesman for that majority Jefferson subordinated his own private views to those he believed were held by his fellow citizens. "However, their will, not mine, be done." In November 1801 he spoke of "a sense of obligation imposed on me by the public will." "My idea is that where two measures are equally right, it is a duty to the people to adopt that one which is most agreeable to them," he wrote earlier in that same year. "What is practicable must often controul what is pure theory," he said in 1802, "and the habits of the governed determine in a great degree what is practicable."

The historical tradition which emphasizes Jefferson's "Vergilian vision," his hostility to banks of issue, speculation, and the fluctuant values of a "paper system," to great cities, to manufactures other than those made in households, and to commerce other than that necessary for the carrying off of the agricultural surplus, calls attention to the private, not the public, values of the President. Indeed, despite undoubted change in his opinions, as for example may be seen in his famous letters to John Jay in April 1809 and to Benjamin Austin in January 1816, I am convinced that the weight of his private preference from the writing of *Notes on Virginia* to the last years of his life falls on the side of agrarian simplicity. The nation's experience before and during the War of 1812 does not mark, as it is sometimes implied, his permanent shift to the cause of industrialism. He reacted angrily to the Tariff of 1824, and six months before his death deplored, in a letter to Madison, that "the general prostration of the farming business, under levies for the support of manufacturers, etc. with the calamitous fluctuations of value in our paper medium, have kept agriculture in a state of abject depression."

But Jefferson's agrarian preferences, as Chinard has said, "remained largely theoretical, sentimental, and personal." They do not help us understand why John Randolph, John Taylor of Caroline, Nathaniel Macon, and other "Old Republicans" among his contemporaries and many historians since have believed, as Joseph Dorfman expresses it, that Jefferson, "anti-Hamiltonian out of supreme office, became in good part Hamiltonian as President." His behavior in office becomes clear when we realize that he sought to give expression not to his private values but to the majority will. As Chinard has noted, "one may find a flagrant contradiction between his public utterances and the private letters he wrote to his friends." These contradictions attest neither to hypocrisy nor insincerity but rather to Jefferson's feeling that he had no "right to attempt to shape the destinies of his country according to his own preferences."

In both his public pronouncements and official acts we see a President desirous of furthering the nation's economic development. Believing a large territory necessary for the preservation of a republic, he instructed government agents to "familiarize . . . [the Indians] to the idea that it is for their interest to cede lands at times to the U.S." If the Indians gave up hunting and adopted agriculture and household manufactures, and Jefferson was "disposed to aid and encourage it liberally," they would be enabled "to live on smaller portions of land. . . . While they are learning to do better on less land, our increasing numbers will be calling for more land." By purchasing the Louisiana Territory he more than doubled the land area of the United States. Protection of the western trade via New Orleans prompted the original negotiations, and his desire to expand that trade to the Pacific induced him to dispatch Lewis and Clark on their famed expedition of 1803. "The object of your mission," he informed Captain Meriwether Lewis in April 1803, "is to explore the Missouri river, & such principal streams of it, as, by its course & communication with the water of the Pacific Ocean may offer the most direct & practicable water communication across this continent, for the purposes of commerce." Wishing to encourage population growth as well as trade and increases in the size of the national domain, he recommended to Congress in 1801 a liberalization of the naturalization laws. And in 1802 he suggested to Congress the probable expediency of encouraging western settlement in areas to which Indian titles had been extinguished.

An expanding population, territory, and domestic trade required improved communications with the interior, and in both his sixth and eighth Annual Messages Jefferson invited Congress to consider the application of surplus revenues "to the improvement of roads, canals, rivers, education, and other great foundations of prosperity and union, under the powers which Congress may already possess, or such amendment of the constitution as may be approved by the states." The federal government had already taken steps which would culminate in its construction of the National Road. In April 1802 Congress admitted Ohio to the Union by an enabling act which also provided that five per cent of the net proceeds of sale of public lands within that state should constitute a fund for the building of roads. In this act lay the origins of the National Road, and in 1806 Congress adopted "An Act to Regulate the Laying Out and Making of a Road from Cumberland, in the State of Maryland."

Following the President's Annual Message of that year, the Senate directed Secretary of the Treasury Albert Gallatin to draw up "a plan for the application of such means as are within the power of Congress, to the purposes of opening roads and making canals, together with a statement of the undertakings of that nature, which, as objects of public improvement, may require and deserve the aid of Government." Gallatin's resultant Report on Roads and Canals, which Carter Goodrich characterizes as "a notable ten-year plan of national action," was predicated on "the maintenance of peace, the continuation of substantial revenues from customs, and the absence of great military expenditure." Since none of these conditions obtained, it proved impossible to implement the report. Its existence, as well as the passage of the Ohio Enabling Act, nevertheless reveals the willingness of a Democratic-Republican President and Congress to employ the resources of the national government for purposes of development.

President Jefferson also revealed this willingness on other occasions and in relation to other areas of economic expansion and national development. In 1802 he invited Congress to "protect the manufactures adapted to our circumstances" and to "foster our fisheries and nurseries of navigation." "On my part," his message concluded, "you may count on a cordial concurrence in every measure for the public good." Two years later he called attention to an even broader array of "great interests," all of which he had identified in his First Annual Message:

> Agriculture, manufactures, commerce, and navigation, the four pillars of our prosperity, are the most thriving when left most free to individual enterprise. Protection from casual embarrassments, however, may sometimes be interposed. If in the course of your observations or inquiries they should appear to need any aid within the limits of our constitutional power, your sense of their importance is a sufficient assurance they will occupy your attention.*

As Chinard observes, this last sentence "could only mean one thing, that the President was not ready to depart entirely and radically from Hamilton's policy of giving encouragement to manufactures." "If it is true," Chinard adds, "that during Jefferson's administration industrial and agricultural interests clashed for the first time in America, I fail to see that the President made any effort to favor agriculture at the expense of industry."

If the Hamiltonians stood for a protective tariff, so too did the Jeffersonians. Reporting on various petitions for protection addressed to Congress, the House Committee of Commerce and Manufactures observed in February 1803 that "sound policy" justified "granting governmental aid for the protection of such manufactures as are obviously capable of affording to the United States an adequate supply" of the numerous products specified in the peti-

---

* *The Works of Thomas Jefferson,* ed. Paul L. Ford (New York, 1905), IX, 339. The date is December 8, 1801.

tions. Facing a prospect of government surplus in 1806, Jefferson did not recommend abandoning protective duties: "Shall we suppress the impost and give that advantage to foreign over domestic manufactures?" he asked rhetorically. It would be preferable, he said, to continue the impost and apply its proceeds to "the great purposes of the public." "People generally have more feeling for canals and roads than education," he confessed to Joel Barlow at the end of 1807. "However, I hope we can advance them with equal pace." Noting at the end of 1808 the increasing application "of our industry and capital to internal manufactures and improvements" as a result of the suspension of foreign commerce, Jefferson commented: "little doubt remains that the establishments formed and forming will—under the auspices of cheaper materials and subsistence, the freedom of labor from taxation with us, and of protecting duties and prohibitions—become permanent."

Anyone remembering Jefferson's four-year tenure as Secretary of State could hardly have been surprised by the direction taken by his policies as President. In 1793, as Taussig says, he had "advocated vigorous measures of protection directed against England." In that year, says Jefferson's biographer Dumas Malone, the future president "was more concerned with the total economic life and development of the country" than was Hamilton!

As President, he was only less so. Jefferson's essential economic difference with Hamilton concerned fiscal matters, and his larger difference he believed to be a moral one. He deplored a system he believed contrived for deluging the states with paper money instead of specie, "for withdrawing our citizens from the pursuits of commerce, manufactures, buildings, and other branches of useful industry, to occupy themselves and their capitals in a species of gambling, destructive of morality, and which has introduced its poison in the government itself." He set his face against note-issuing banks, with no more understanding of their economic function than Jackson or Benton were later to display. Yet precisely as the Jackson administration was to do following the Bank War, he favored a policy of depositing public monies in banks that were politically friendly: "I am decidedly in favor of making all the banks Republican, by sharing deposits among them in proportion to the dispositions they show," he informed Gallatin in July 1803. "It is material to the safety

of Republicanism to detach the mercantile interests from its enemies
and incorporate them into the body of its friends. A merchant is
naturally a Republican, and can be otherwise only from a vitiated
state of things."

In fine, I do not argue that Jefferson advocated industrialization
to the extent that Hamilton had. But he did advocate it, and the
development of other sectors of the economy as well. He did so
despite private preferences to the contrary, believing that this was
what "a very great majority of the nation" wanted. If he was right
in his judgment, and his constantly increasing support by the electorate suggests he was, does it not become difficult to maintain that
whereas Jefferson served majority interests, Hamilton served those
of a minority? Both employed the resource of government to promote
development; both wished to employ it even more than either was
allowed to do. And if these things are true, does it not follow that
E. A. J. Johnson is right in maintaining that there is no essential
difference between the economic objectives and political means of
the groups represented respectively by Hamiltonianism and Jeffersonianism? Both bespoke the interests and wishes of a nation
anxious to root its political independence in the soil of economic
development.

William A. Williams
JEFFERSONIAN MERCANTILISM

*Jefferson's social ideal, according to Williams, reflected a "feudal system
of republics" operating in a constant state of expansion. That is, change for
the sake of change, expansion for the sake of expansion, rather than a
literal agrarianism was at the heart of the Jeffersonian ideal. The Jeffersonian mercantile system embraced the frontier and a belief in continuing
economic expansion as the American utopia. This kind of an ideal society
could only thrive where no strong direction, controls, policing or institutional*

Reprinted by permission of The World Publishing Company and Jonathan Cape Ltd.
from *The Contours of American History* by William A. Williams. Copyright © 1961
by William Appleman Williams. Pp. 181–191. The title of the selection is that of
the editor.

inhibitions existed. Yet the paradox of the Jeffersonian "laissez-faire" mercantile system was that it weakened the "sense of community and made it difficult to establish a check on private and group property interests" which might impose a vassalage upon the individual and the government.

I know and see every day the extent of geographical feeling and the necessity of prudence, if we mean to preserve and invigorate the Union.
— *Albert Gallatin, 1816*

The Founding Fathers and the Frontier Thesis

Set alongside De Tocqueville's remark that Americans were "haunted by visions of what will be," Jefferson's persistent concern with his physiocratic dream raises the perplexing question of why no one provided a classic didactic statement or fictional presentation of the American Utopia. Americans were strong on propaganda and vague assertion, but weak on firm conceptions. That loyal nabob and royal Governor of Massachusetts, Thomas Pownall, had said about as much as anyone. He defined America merely as a "New System of Things and Men, which treats all as they actually are, esteeming nothing the true End and perfect Good of Policy, but that effect which produces, as equality of Rights, so equal Liberty, universal Peace, and unobstructed intercommunication of happiness in Human Society."

The same absence of particulars, of some idea of how people were to *live,* strikes the reader of the famous poem "The Rising Glory of America" by Freneau and Brackenridge. They spoke of empire "Stretch'd out from thence far to the burning line," and of "num'rous ships of trade," but not of the society itself. Hector St. John de Crèvecoeur said little more in *Letters from an American Farmer.* He saw empire as the circumstance that "tended to regenerate" the colonist: "new laws, a new mode of living, a new social system." Of the new system, however, he said nothing. He merely talked about the existing order revived by a surplus of property: "to become a free man, invested with lands, to which every municipal blessing is annexed!"

A stronger case might be made for saying that James Fenimore Cooper defined the American utopia in his series of novels. Yet in fact he outlined two American utopias. One was the eastern aristocracy, and that was hardly either unique or idealistic in 1800. The other was the frontier of Natty Bumppo. *But that was not a society.* It was a man and a few comrades establishing a rudimentary ecology. Cooper's women were singularly lacking in substance and almost literally absent in fact. As for the men, D. H. Lawrence described a typical one rather aptly: "hard, isolate, stoic, and a killer." Bumppo killed only when necessary, and with a piety, to be sure, but piety toward nature and animals is not necessarily piety toward men; transferred to humans, the attitude often produces an appalling arrogance.

Only Jefferson's *Notes on Virginia* remains for serious consideration. Here, at any rate, was a society of human beings. But here also was the traditional stress on property, land, and freedom within a hierarchical order. "Those who labor in the earth are the chosen people of God, if ever he had a chosen people, whose breasts he has made his peculiar deposit for substantial and genuine virtue." But that definition of the good society as a stratified, corporate community based on private property in land was far less significant *as a utopia* than the vision which had been advanced by one wing of the English Revolution, that of a corporate Christian commonwealth based on social property. Along with a few others, Sam Adams sustained parts of this ideal, but even he cramped it into a conservative, property-bound form. And for Jefferson as for Adams, expansion was the only way that the benefits of the system could be extended. Indeed, expansion was the only thing that made sense of Jefferson's famous motto about letting each generation make its own decisions. Either the phrase documented his total naïveté, which is of course absurd, or it meant that there had to be room and resources for everyone to start over.

Like Cooper, therefore, Jefferson had to accept the frontier as the only possible definition of an American utopia. All else already existed. But the frontier in this meaning was a process of becoming, not of being, and hence substituted motion for structure as its end. Motion as a substitute for structure is possible only so long as there is unlimited room to move in. When confined without the discipline provided by an ideal, such social motion produces aimlessness or chaos—or perhaps the final ordering of some utopia. And when it actually came to be so confined, Jefferson's south had nothing to guide it but the image of a feudal utopia created for it by Jefferson himself and John Taylor. That trapped the south, for by definition the utopia of Taylor and Jefferson had to expand or stagnate. The first act of that southern expansion was of necessity a move to acquire the freedom of action to extend itself. Secession was that first act of expansion.

But the industrial and agrarian utopias of the north and west also relied on expansion for success. Free farmers were Jefferson's ideological camp followers; merchants and industrialists could choose between the expansion explicit in mercantilism or inherent in laissez faire. Men who had neither the education nor the wealth to live as aristocrats naturally placed a similar emphasis on the frontier. For that matter, the frontier in some ways took the place of formal education; a kind of nonintellectual learning by surviving and succeeding became part of the American attitude at an early date. That Jefferson, who valued the intellect so highly and did so much to establish the University of Virginia, should also have contributed to that side of the educational ledger is an often neglected facet of his physiocracy.

As should be apparent, this conception of the frontier defined it not as a boundary but as an area to enter and occupy. Reinforcing the old antagonism toward England, such aspects of the frontier as a utopia would seem to do a great deal to explain America's steadily growing conviction that it could not live with any other nation occupying any significant part of the North American continent. Viewed through Lewis Carroll's looking-glass, this attitude could be defined as isolationism. But like the very expansionism implicit in mercantilism's static view of the world, this definition of utopia as a frontier produced a policy that was anything but isolationist. It was militantly, even aggressively, expansionist.

Jefferson moved quickly to initiate a western advance. His confidential message to the Congress of January 18, 1803, requested money for an expedition "to provide an extension of territory which the rapid increase of our numbers will call for." Avoiding all euphemisms, this meant that he was preparing expansion not only south, but west *across* the Mississippi *before* he knew that France was willing to sell the Louisiana Territory. His argument was bold even though his procedure was a classic of guile: expansion was necessary for democracy and prosperity. The Indians, for example, would thus be removed, and control of the Mississippi would end the question of egress to world markets. "The interests of commerce," Jefferson concluded in reference to the Pacific trade, "place the principle object within the constitutional powers and care of Congress, and that it should incidentally advance the geographic knowledge of our own continent can not but be an additional gratification." Expansion, not science, was the engine of the Lewis and Clark Expedition.

Had Jefferson and other Americans been forced to choose between a war with France and no further expansion at that time, they might have worked out some clear conception of the kind of society they wanted to build. But the fortuitous ease with which they acquired the 828,000 square miles of the Louisiana Territory served to convince them that expansion was a safe and cheap cure-all for their needs and difficulties. The Senate vote of 24 to 7 was an index of the national sentiment on expansion in its ideological as well as its obvious economic aspects.

Although they may appear a bit surprising in view of his vigorously expansionist messages of 1801 and 1802, Jefferson's qualms about the constitutionality of the purchase may have been completely sincere. He was far too astute to miss the implications of the move for the feudal balance of republics that Madison kept worrying about. But as Madison had done in 1787, and obviously paraphrasing Madison's argument as his own, Jefferson resolved the dilemma in favor of expansion. His second inaugural address, March 4, 1804, was a hymn to Madison's theory. The taxes to pay for the expansion, Jefferson explained, made expansion possible; the expansion would lower taxes. "Who can limit the extent to which the federative principle may operate effectively?" he concluded. "The larger our association, the less it will be shaken by local passions."

Westerners enthusiastically embraced this expansionist theory of democracy and prosperity. A Kentuckian boasted, for example, that his countrymen were "full of enterprise and although not poor, are greedy after plunder as ever the old Romans were, Mexico glitters in our Eyes—the word is all we wait for." It was not so much the word that they awaited as it was the election of enough of their fellow expansionists to control Congress. That came in 1810 and 1811; meanwhile the region developed rapidly as a producer of agricultural surpluses for commercial markets. Continued settlement of the Appalachian and Upper Ohio regions, as well as of Kentucky and Tennessee, tripled the population of the west between 1800 and 1810. Moving along the Mohawk River route, the trail to Pittsburgh, and the Wilderness Road in the Shenandoah Valley, a good many of the increasing number of immigrants simply by-passed the east. These people made the west function as a safety valve for the eastern seaboard in the truest sense. The cities and other settled regions never had to contend with them as economic, political, or social problems.

Westerners were soon enjoying their own religious revivals under the leadership of men like James McGready, whose Cane Ridge Meeting of 1801 rivaled anything George Whitefield had produced in colonial New England. Methodist and Baptist churches grew rapidly, and in Kentucky finally merged with Barton W. Stone's followers to form the Christian Church. Although some western ministers were vigorously anti-education, the revivals not only led to the rise of a large number of religious schools (thus delaying secular state-supported education), but also provided an impetus for the organization in 1810 of the American Board of Commissioners for Foreign Missions. While the Board's activities in the Mediterranean and the Far East ultimately contributed to the character (and the problems) of American foreign policy, the immediate result of such religious enthusiasm was to strengthen the west's self-consciousness. As a partner on the frontier, God provided reassurance in the wilderness and strong sanction for action against opponents who blocked the way to more land and trade.

The Achievements and Dilemmas of Jeffersonian Mercantilism

This rapid economic development in the west produced an export trade from Tennessee and Mississippi as early as 1801. Kentucky, Indiana, Michigan, and Ohio were shipping surpluses down the Mississippi by 1806. And Pittsburgh, which was rapidly becoming known as "the western workshop," had its first iron-rolling mill in operation by 1811. It was not Pittsburgh, however, that undercut Washington's plan for a Virginia iron and industrial complex that would subvert slavery.

That blueprint was torn up by the businessmen who built a textile industry in England and by the American inventors who produced the cotton gin that handled the rough processing of the crop. Although antislavery sentiment continued to grow in line with Jefferson's cry of anguish—"We are truly to be pitied"—southern planters, after the slave uprising known as the Gabriel Plot of 1801 in Virginia, tightened up their controls and turned their gangs of black labor into the fields with renewed confidence. By 1820 they had captured the British market. But they also sold increasing amounts to northern industrialists. By the time that Jefferson retired in 1809, there were over 80 cotton mills in the country. And one of them, the Boston (Waltham) Manufacturing Company, had organized all its operations into one integrated system.

Other manufacturers were producing nails and cards by semi-automatic machines, and Seth Thomas clocks had become an established commodity. Indeed, almost half of the immigrants who came between 1783 and 1812 established themselves in nonagrarian jobs. Usually known as the inventor of the cotton gin (which he probably was not), Eli Whitney actually made a far more important contribution to America's industrial development. Along with Simeon North, he worked out the idea—and the production line—for interchangeable parts in manufactured goods. Starting with guns, the application of the principle became in many respects the key to modern industrial society. Other Americans were beginning to make machines, a particularly important element in economic independence.

Between 1800 and 1816, banking operations expanded from 29 institutions to 246. Society was becoming stable enough for life insurance companies to begin entering the field alongside their maritime predecessors. And the corporation form of organization received a big boost from the New York law of 1811, which permitted general incorporation without special applications and restrictions. Most of the early corporations were in transportation, an indication that the merchant capitalist and the commercial trader played key roles in the early economy. American ships handled over 90 per cent of the nation's trade by 1805, and exports had zoomed to $108,000,000 by 1808. Three years later, John Jacob Astor's American Fur Company had established a base on the Pacific at the mouth of the Columbia River, close co-operation by Jefferson providing a striking indication of the evolving mercantilism of the Republican party leadership.

In the meantime, however, the central issues of politics and government were defined by the problems of building such an American mercantilist system. As a prime source of wealth and welfare, the great western reserve of land presented several of those problems. Indian policy, for example, continued to provoke arguments between those who wanted to be more equitable and those who stressed expansion. Despite the excited, even wild, enthusiasm for land, a surprising number of Americans were uneasy about the policy of unrestrained conquest and tried to halt the aggressive destruction of Indian society. Jefferson often borrowed their rhetoric but his practice was rather different. His economic policy toward the Indians provided a good summary of his attitude. He was "glad to see the good and influential individuals among them in debt; because we observe that when these debts get beyond what the individuals can pay, they become willing to lop them off by a cession of lands."

Land policy was in essence a problem of resolving three competing claims in a workable program. As a source of wealth, the land could be used for the accumulation of private or social riches. And, given a system of politics based on property, land was crucially important in maintaining the political balance of a large nation. Designed to establish settlers on the soil and also provide national revenue, the evolving pattern culminated in the law of 1820. Concluding that the earlier credit system stimulated speculation, the Congress re-established cash payments while lowering the price to $1.25 per acre and permitted sales of 80 acres and more. Speculators still accumulated fortunes, but the law worked well enough to dramatize the central problem of creating a national economic system. Westerners demanded government aid in transportation and commerce.

Both in theory and practice, the principle of government assistance had become widely accepted. South Carolina, for example, passed a typical law in 1808 for "the establishment and encouragement" of manufactures. Pennsylvania helped finance various enterprises, granted cash subsidies to others, and proclaimed "the duty and interest of all governments to prevent fraud, and promote the interests of just and useful commerce." A typical writer in Massachusetts thought it "manifestly erroneous" that people "are the judges of their interests, and consequently should be allowed to regulate them unobstructed." Such laissez faire was "subversive to the end and aim of all governments." As the governor pointed out in 1809, the state had accepted the responsibility of "making and executing just and practicable laws of inspection on manufactured articles." John Adams summarized the situation accurately in his comment that "democrats and aristocrats all unite" on the basic axioms of mercantilism.

National debate centered on four issues: internal improvements, banking and monetary policy, commercial discriminations, and aid to manufacturers. Mechanics and merchants alike petitioned for continued trade discriminations, predicting "a total stagnation in our shipbuilding" and commerce if these were lowered or abandoned. Any relaxation would be "a fatal blow," explained still others, and would be "extremely injurious to the agricultural and the mechanical classes of our citizens." Jefferson responded by maintaining the discriminations that he had recommended in 1793 and by undertaking the naval war against the Mediterranean pirates that he had suggested even earlier. These policies did not completely solve the crisis confronting a weak and backward country caught in the middle of a world war; yet for a time, as the profits of neutral trade brought a flamboyant prosperity, two purely domestic issues gained priority.

Both of these, internal improvements and national finance, became the principal concern of Albert Gallatin. A vigorous defender of civil and religious liberties and a strong advocate of an educational system, Gallatin had favored internal improvements and central banking ever since his service in the Pennsylvania legislature during the 1790s. Other Jeffersonians such as Senator Thomas Worthington of Ohio and Superintendent of Patents William Thornton advocated similar plans and provided important support, but Gallatin was the central figure in both areas. His plan was simple: use the receipts from land sales to promote economic development, and then sustain, control, and balance it through assistance to manufactures and by a national financial system.

Gallatin's masterpiece was his majestic report of April 8, 1808, on a national transportation and communications network designed to strengthen the sense and reality of "community." His proposed ten-year plan made Hamilton appear a fumbling amateur. Having accepted Madison's stress on expansion, Gallatin sought to make the theory work. Concerned with "justice" and a "still more intimate community of interests," he tried to minimize the dangers of separatism "by opening speedy and easy communications" throughout the nation. He proposed four main avenues: coastwise from Maine to Georgia; across the mountains through New York, Pennsylvania, and Virginia into Kentucky and Tennessee; across the four major isthmian blocks (Cape Cod, Delaware, New Jersey, and the Dismal Swamp in Virginia and North Carolina); and into the Great Lakes region.

Two years later, in 1810, he reported on manufactures. Stressing their vital importance to balanced growth and independence, he recommended a program of cash subsidies and other government aid to accelerate their development. But, as he realized, the long-range solution would be provided by an expanding home market stable enough to encourage large investment, *and by the establishment of economic independence vis-à-vis England's superior industrial system.* As did Madison and others, Gallatin understood perfectly the unfavorable consequences of free trade to a relatively backward, underdeveloped economy. This very issue of England's power over the American economy finally subverted his program. As he put it, his ten-year plan became "inexpedient" during a war with the most advanced industrial power in the world.

In the meantime, Gallatin encountered difficulties at home. While he secured an initial grant from land sales in Ohio and with that money began construction of the National Road west to the Ohio River in 1806, he promptly ran into the kind of particularistic opportunism that produced a hodgepodge of pork-barrel legislation instead of a coherent program. Here, of course, was the other side of Madison's expansionist solution to the danger of faction. For it also weakened the sense of community and made it difficult to establish a check on private and group property interests that undercut the general welfare. But supported by such men as John Quincy Adams, who also favored integrated development in preference to a patchwork of local projects, Gallatin initiated and preserved the idea of a truly *national* system.

Jefferson accepted the principle of such internal improvements, emphasizing education as well as canals, but he raised the issue of constitutionality. So did Madison, who feared that such a plan would unbalance his "feudal system of republics." Both men put their case directly: if the Congress undertook a ten-year plan of the magnitude and with the consequences inherent in Gallatin's program without explicit public approval in the form of a constitutional amendment, then a process of interpreting the constitution would have started that could end only in monarchy or some other form of tyranny.

Both men had similar reservations about continuing the national bank. But understanding and accepting Gallatin's argument that it would balance and stabilize the monetary system, and agreeing that destroying it would cause "much individual and probably . . . no inconsiderable public injury," Madison concluded that the bank should be maintained. Jefferson, on the other hand, never overcame two fundamental reservations, and his skepticism helped block a recharter in 1811. Like Madison, but with more insistence, he worried lest the bank in time become an institution that cut across all regional and political lines. Doing so, he reasoned, it would subvert the authority of the states and hence replace or override them as an institution in the political economy. It would do so, moreover, outside the constitutional framework. This would not only recast the entire balance of power that the constitution established, but the bank would effect the change as an institution which was not in any way directly responsible to the people. He feared the end result would be a kind of "vassalage" imposed on both the individual and the government.

Jefferson's analysis was extremely perceptive, and basically his criticism was valid. Any economic institution organized on a national basis but essentially controlled by a group of private citizens would make economic decisions that affected all aspects of society without its powers being defined in the Constitution or checked by public participation and direct responsibility. This was anything but an irrational or irrelevant argument by an agrarian who did not understand economics. It was an astute analysis of the relationship between economic power and its social and political consequences, and our modern industrial corporations, together with the Federal Reserve Board itself, have verified it.

In his own physiocratic way, Jefferson had raised once again the crucial issue for mercantilists: How does one use private property to accomplish social ends without giving way to the narrower view? But to raise the question was not enough, and Jefferson's position had a fundamental weakness. He answered his own intelligent analysis of danger with an anti-intellectual conclusion that there was no way to have the benefits of the bank while controlling its potential harm. Without any doubt, Jefferson's position strengthened the coalition of businessmen such as Henry Clay of Kentucky and Isaac McKim of Maryland and agrarians such as John Taylor of Virginia and his western followers who fought the bank for the greater glory of their interests and principles. Symbolizing such opposition, Vice-President Clinton of New York in 1811 cast the deciding vote against rechartering the bank.

Despite their victory, Taylor and his physiocrat compatriots were by that time caught in a difficult contradiction between their theory and the mercantilist reality of their world. Given the general attack by Britain and France on American shipping, Taylor and Randolph had two choices: they could go to war, or they could simply acquiesce in British domination of the seas and its comparable industrial power vis-à-vis the American economy. As the philosophers of a faction, their logic took them, by quite a different route, to an agreement with the pro-British merchant group: no war with England. Put simply, the opposition to the War of 1812 was a coalition of the groups that had never wholly accepted an American mercantilism.

Neither Jefferson nor Madison wanted a war with Great Britain. They were not fanatic Anglophiles. But both men did fear the long-run consequences of the economic imbalance between the two systems and sought by economic power to break out of the relationship by persuading England to acknowledge America's right to trade throughout the British Empire and with other nations. When they first came to power, Madison and Jefferson kept Rufus King in London, hoping that his long associations and sympathies would facilitate some kind of equitable settlement. England continued its economic warfare. So next they sent Monroe on a special mission, just as Washington had sent Jay, but backed him up with economic measures to indicate the seriousness of their policy.

Jefferson and Madison refused to consider the draft treaty that Monroe negotiated as anything more than a basis for further discussions. With considerable justification, Monroe insisted that he had secured everything that could be obtained without recourse to war. But Madison favored using the economic measures that, at the request of the British, had been postponed during the negotiations. Madison admitted that they would cut into the wartime prosperity but emphasized that manufactures would be "efficiently fostered. . . . No event can be more desirable." His feelings hurt and his confidence undercut, Monroe came home. Taylor and Randolph welcomed him as a potential ally in their campaign against the mercantilism of Madison and Jefferson. Arguing that nothing more than the parasitic carrying trade was at issue, Randolph turned his full fury on the administration. "What!" he demanded. "Shall this great mammoth of the American forest leave his native element and plunge into the water in a mad contest with the shark? . . . I, for one, will not mortgage my property and my liberty. . . . You will come out without your constitution."

III THE FORKED ROAD OF STATES RIGHTS

Bernard Mayo

THE STRANGE CASE OF
THOMAS JEFFERSON

Not only did Jefferson advocate agrarianism, but support for decentralization and states rights permeates his writings. Did Jefferson then weaken the authority and power of the national government when he became President? Mayo suggests that states rights, laissez-faire, agrarianism, and on occasion nationalism were merely vehicles for achieving Jefferson's basic objective of individual freedom. Thus, although agrarianism, states rights, and laissez-faire may no longer be applicable to American life, Jefferson's fundamental beliefs are "universal, timeless, and very much alive."

Champions of the Old South used [Jefferson's] states rights views as a defensive weapon. But they rejected as "glittering generalities" his basic principles of the Declaration of Independence that "all men are created equal" and have inalienable rights. Abolitionists abused him as a slaveholder. But they made effective use of his inalienable rights and his many denunciations of slavery. The Democratic party long used him as its father-image. But it was challenged by the new major party formed in 1854 which appropriated the very name of his old Republican party. Its chieftain, Abraham Lincoln, a democratic nationalist in the Clay tradition, held high the banner of a Jefferson whose principles, he declared, "are the definitions and axioms of free society . . . applicable to all men and all times." But against Lincoln, Southerners who in the 1860s fought for their independence cited as precedent Jefferson's Declaration of 1776, which had justified secession from Britain.

As a result of this confusion of symbols and myths, this welter of half-truths and distortions, the frankly-spoken, complex, and many-sided Jefferson was made to appear the most inconsistent of men. Of his many symbols which partisans used, and misused, most firmly established was that of states rights, with its various connotations. When states rights with its connotations of nullification and disunion

From *Myths and Men: Patrick Henry, George Washington, Thomas Jefferson,* by Bernard Mayo. Harper & Row, 1963, pp. 72–82. Copyright by University of Georgia Press, 1959. Reprinted by permission of the University of Georgia Press.

met defeat at Appomattox his popularity declined. It was low in the Age of Big Business and of Robber Barons, which made Hamilton its hero. In the conservative Age of William McKinley his reputation was such that William E. Curtis, in his rather oddly entitled *The True Thomas Jefferson* of 1901, gave serious attention to those who compared him unfavorably as a statesman even to a General Grant.

Most surprising in this Strange Case of Thomas Jefferson is to find his dark image predominating in the liberal Age of the Progressive Movement. The man had become obscured indeed by conflicting myths, his basic philosophy fragmentized and twisted out of context. His states rights symbol as one connoting laissez-faire negativism, opposed to using national power for the national good, was so rigidly established that he was unappreciated by a Woodrow Wilson and despised by a Theodore Roosevelt. Both of these progressives sought to reach goals which in reality were those of Jefferson. Yet both praised not Jefferson but Hamilton, whose nationalistic methods they used to attain their Jeffersonian ends. Wilson thought Hamilton "easily the ablest" of the Founding Fathers. Roosevelt could say nothing harsher of William Jennings Bryan than that he was as "cheap and shallow" as Thomas Jefferson. And Herbert Croly, brain-truster for the Progressive Epoch, likewise condemned his "intellectual superficiality and insincerity." Even darker was his image in the conservative Age of Calvin Coolidge. All too typical was the address given at Mr. Jefferson's University of Virginia in the 1920s by Secretary of State Frank B. ("Nervous Nellie") Kellogg, in which he said that while Jefferson was a great man and all that, his ideas were dangerously radical.

Yet it was in these same 1920s that the day of triumph predicted in 1858 by Grigsby at last began to dawn for his "noble chief of Monticello." That bright dawn was heralded in 1925 by Claude G. Bowers' partisan and popular *Jefferson and Hamilton.* While it glorified Jefferson, it was a refreshing antidote to the many volumes then exalting Hamilton as the hero of an epoch typified by Coolidge's remark that "the business of America is business." A movement then began which has so brightened Jefferson's popular image, not as a partisan hero but as the supreme symbol of democracy, that today he equals, and for many even eclipses, Washington as a national hero. That movement gathered impetus in the New Deal 1930s, reached a peak in the Jefferson Bicentennial of wartime 1943, and still retains its momentum in the cold war 1950s.

Jefferson has been honored by a magnificent memorial in Washington. His Monticello, for a century neglected and its tombstone mutilated, is now restored as a shrine to which come each year over 250,000 patriotic pilgrims. Volume after volume of his writings superbly edited by Julian P. Boyd are coming off the press to be met with critical acclaim. Monograph after monograph by numerous scholars have revealed almost every phase of his many-faceted career. And of the many recent biographies, that in progress by Dumas Malone, by its detailed and judicious scholarship promises to do for our appreciative generation what Randall's classic work of 1858 did for earlier and unappreciative Americans.

Because of this impressive recent scholarship the man as reality rather than myth is much more clearly seen, even though popular adulation tends to obscure that reality. Democratic orators at fundraising Jefferson Day Dinners contribute richly more often to mythology than to history. Partisan writers sometimes have made him more of a New Dealer than Franklin D. Roosevelt. And Isom R. Lamb of California, strangely enough, by a Bridey Murphy hypnotic trance regression has communicated directly with him; from the spirit world he reports that all accounts except his own forthcoming book are inadequate portrayals of the heroic Sage of Monticello. Even more interesting to the historian-detective are the excesses and distortions of conservatives. The popular tide has overwhelmed all their attempts to exploit both his image and a dead past—whether it was the "Liberty Leaguers" of the 1930s, the states rights "Jeffersonian Democrats" of the 1940s, or the pro-segregation "Defenders of State Sovereignty and Individual Liberties" of the 1950s. Most interesting to observe have been today's ineffectual "New Conservatives," who lament the death in our time of a Jefferson shaped in their own antiliberal image. Like Macaulay and their Federalist predecessors they grimly predict that the "New Jefferson" now so popular is a democratic demon who will destroy the republic.

In this latest chapter of The Strange Case of Thomas Jefferson perhaps these present-day Macaulays, in their lefthanded manner, pay him the greatest of tributes. For a vital and living Jefferson has at last triumphed in the long battle waged by his admirers over his detractors. His bright image predominates today because he is so conspicuously a part of our continuing and usable American heritage. It predominates because in our critical epoch, as in his own Age of Anxiety and social upheaval, the democracy he symbolizes has been severely tested, thus far successfully, by economic depression, world war, and today's struggle against totalitarian tyranny. By deepening our knowledge of him, and of the men and events of his Revolutionary Epoch, recent and extensive scholarship has revealed him to be the most contemporary of the Founding Fathers, as best symbolizing the ideals of both the Revolution and of present-day democracy. Jefferson still lives, as John Adams truly said, because he dealt with basic issues as pertinent to free society in our day as in his, and in timeless manner still speaks with inspiring eloquence for that democracy we would preserve and advance.

Our appreciation of him as a contemporary comrade-in-arms is not lessened by seeing him as he really was, a great though fallible man. He himself disliked what he called the "fan-coloring biographers" of his own day who exalted men into gods. We now know that he was very human indeed. Warmly affectionate with family and friends, he had a pervasive kindness, a generous richness of heart and mind, that charmed and enchanted such a Federalist as Margaret Bayard Smith. He was keenly sensitive to criticism, though in public with more than Christian forbearance he turned the other cheek to his relentless enemies. Yet in his warm and unguarded letters he himself was often sharply critical and zealously partisan.

In them he often made such sweeping statements as the tree of liberty from time to time must be manured with the blood of tyrants, or the French Revolution was justified if it left alive only an Adam and an Eve to continue a race of free men. Though in action a moderate, he thus exposed himself to criticism as an extremist. "If he had more of General Washington's reserve," said his admiring friend William Wirt, "he would be less in the power of his enemies than he is." The judicious Madison, most intimate of the "numerous and able coadjutors" to whom he gave such generous credit, did much to temper his impulsive tendencies. As Madison said after his letters were published, "allowances . . . ought to be made for a habit in Mr. Jefferson, as in others of great genius, of expressing in strong and round terms, impressions of the moment."

He was very human in his zealous partisanship which, for example, darkened Patrick Henry's reputation and helped establish the still flourishing myth that Washington's Federalists were "Monarchists." While often indirect in his political tactics, preferring flanking operations to frontal attacks, we now know how untrue was the Federalists' picture of him as a detestable and hypocritical demagogue. We know also how their persistent myth that he was more pro-French than pro-American has been put to scorn by scholars who portray him as the unrivalled "Apostle of Americanism." When most furiously assailed as a "Frenchified Jacobin" for opposing Jay's Treaty with England, the French Minister made this report on him to Revolutionary Paris: today "Mr. Jefferson likes us because he detests England . . . but tomorrow he might change his opinion about us if England should cease to inspire his fear" for America's interests. "Although Jefferson is the friend of" a France dedicated to liberty, equality, and fraternity, above all else "Jefferson, I say, is an American."

We now appreciate better not only how zealous he was but how pragmatically flexible, how amazingly versatile and complex. The complexity of his character and personality explains why biographers find him most difficult to present full-bodied and why rival partisans in exploiting his fame have made him appear inconsistent. It is most naïve, though not uncommon, to be surprised that his views changed from 1769, when as a British colonist he entered public life, to his death on the 50th anniversary of American independence some sixty years later. It would be surprising indeed not to find changes. Like all public men he worked under the pressures of events and of other human beings. And of course there were cleavages between ideals and realities—human gaps between ideal solutions and those he could obtain only through practical politics; between the Sage of Monticello and the party leader; between professions out of power and actions in power; between the humanitarian who often said "Peace is my passion" and the rebel of 1776 who in 1801 fought the pirates of Tripoli and in 1812 approved America's Second War for Independence.

What greatly impresses the historian-detective is Jefferson's remarkable consistency, his lifelong devotion to his basic principles of the freedom and happiness of man—of the liberty of the individual and, since "all men are created equal" and live in society, of the social welfare. Liberty and equality were fundamentally moral principles. They were "self-evident truths" deeply rooted in "the laws of Nature and of Nature's God." Life and liberty were inseparable, he said, for "the God who gave us life gave us liberty at the same time; the hand of force may destroy but cannot disjoin them." And always with Jefferson the measure of an individual was the good he contributes to society: for "Nature has implanted in our breasts a love of others, a sense of duty to them, a moral instinct; in short . . . Nature has constituted *utility* to man the standard and test of virtue." Democracy's great task is to reconcile the individualistic principle of liberty with the social principle of equality.

In the past Jefferson's insistence upon individual freedom has often been distorted into the near-anarchy of a selfish "rugged individualism." In our time his insistence upon the social welfare has been much better appreciated, much more emphasized, by a democratic people compelled to use increasingly its national government in solving problems of national security and of an America urbanized and industrialized. In our time, also, we find perhaps the strangest aspect of The Strange Case of Thomas Jefferson in Communist attempts to capture him as their American symbol. Ignoring his basic principle of individual freedom, they have vainly tried to distort his social principle of "*utility* to man" in a manner most repugnant to The Anti-Totalitarian of Monticello, who had solemnly sworn and had vigorously put into action on many fronts his "eternal hostility against every form of tyranny."

"His history is indeed the history of American liberty," said Hugh Blair Grigsby. And so it is for his long years in the public service. In his youth he successfully led a bloodless social revolution in Virginia, embracing economic, intellectual, and religious liberty. In the very last years of his life, a gallant and indomitable "Old Sachem," he advocated a broad system of public education and established a university "based on the illimitable freedom of the human mind to explore and expose every subject." Always he strove to attain his basic goals: the freedom and happiness of man. It was these goals, it was the "unchangeable . . . inherent and inalienable rights of man," that were of paramount importance. Decidedly secondary were the varied methods or weapons used to attain them. He strove

mightily to attain the maximum of individual liberty, yet he was aware
that man as a social creature must act through his government,
local, state, and national. He was aware also that such slogans, often
attributed to him, as "government is best when it governs least" and
"power is always the enemy of liberty" must not be taken too
literally. He himself had learned one lesson the hard way, as a not
too successful war governor before becoming an effective President.
It was that governmental power strongly asserted is often vital to
win and to maintain liberty.

He changed his methods to meet particular problems. He employed the weapon most effective at the time to gain his liberal and
humanitarian objectives, keeping in mind that majority rule is "the
first principle of republicanism." Again and again Jefferson emphasized these basic ideas: "The Creator has made the earth for the
living, not the dead." Changing conditions in a changing world will
force each generation to change its methods, since "laws and institutions must go hand in hand . . . and keep pace with the times." But
always and eternally unchangeable are man's inalienable rights and
the selfsame democratic goals, man's freedom and happiness. And
this is the hard core of his progressive democratic philosophy; its
living, timeless essence; as applicable in our industrialized America
as in his agrarian America.

Jefferson was the great democratic idealist, yet a practical and
effective one. He was pragmatic, not dogmatic, a shrewd politician
who well knew that in a free society politics is the art of the possible.
He keenly realized that democracy is both a faith in man's capacity
for self-government and an experimental process—a liberal procedure which combines fixed standards with flexibility, and avoids both
radical and reactionary extremes. He called his election "the revolution of 1800." On assuming office, however, he said he would of
course "fall short of effecting all the reformation" he desired. Knowing "how difficult it is to move or inflect the great machine of society,
how impossible to advance the notions of a whole people suddenly
to ideal right, we see the wisdom of Solon's remark that no more
good must be attempted than the nation can bear." Yet with his
habitual optimism he steadily and at times very boldly pushed ahead
on his course of enlightened liberalism. "Sensible that we are acting
for all mankind," setting a hopeful example for oppressed peoples

everywhere, he was determined to advance as best he could America's "interesting experiment of self-government," always "with a single and steadfast eye to the general interest and happiness."

To achieve his goals he used the weapons of states rights and of national rights. In 1798 he employed the Virginia and Kentucky Resolutions, but not to exalt states rights as such. He used them primarily as a weapon to defend basic civil liberties violated by the Alien and Sedition Acts. As President, in 1803 he purchased half a continent in the Louisiana Territory, extending "our empire of liberty" in a "transaction replete with blessings to unborn millions of men." Here he boldly cast aside "metaphysical subtleties." He wisely placed the national good above the strict constructionist view of the Constitution he had earlier used in fighting Hamilton's fiscal policies. In 1806 he suggested a national welfare program in which revenues from a continuing tariff would be spent for a national university and a nation-wide network of canals and highways. In his much-criticized Embargo Act of 1807 against the aggressions of Britain and France, in an unprecedented manner, unparalleled indeed until the Civil War, he exerted the power of the nation's government for the nation's welfare and security.

It was Pickering's Federalists who now upheld the laissez-faire, states rights position. They opposed the national government even more violently than the Jeffersonians did in the 1790s. Jefferson had so "out-Hamiltoned Alexander Hamilton" that John Randolph of Roanoke led the states rights extremists of his own party into opposition. Thenceforth doctrinaire John Randolph, darling of today's "New Conservatives," sneered at his cousin of Monticello as that hypocritical "St. Thomas of *Cantingbury*." He vilified him to the delight of his new Federalist friends. Timothy Pickering admitted that Randolph even outdid himself in vituperation. He wished the Virginian well when he swore to do all he could to make true his prediction that Jefferson's "character on the page of history will appear black as hell."

As "The Noble Agrarian" to many admirers, and as an ignoble one to the mercantile Federalists, he has long been over-simplified. Strong indeed were his loyalties to his Virginia planter's way of life and to that of America's farmers, who were then an overwhelming majority of the population. But as a public servant he strove to advance the economic interests of the whole nation. Federalist businessmen harshly denounced him as a doctrinaire agrarian, hell-bent with his Embargo on destroying their shipping and commerce. But a recent scholarly study more realistically calls him a "Commercial Agrarian Democrat." Early in his career he opposed manufacturing and, in words that are still twisted and distorted, "the mobs of great cities." But he wisely changed these earlier views, since America then lacked manufacturing sufficient even to equip her armies to fight the War of 1812. With his nail factory at Monticello he himself became in a small way a pioneer industrialist.

The uses and abuses of history are many, as The Strange Case of Thomas Jefferson abundantly illustrates. But most persistent and flagrant of abuses are attempts rigorously to limit his usefulness in time and place to the so-called "lost world of Thomas Jefferson," the farmer-republic of an earlier America. Nothing does greater injustice to him and to "the sanctity of history" than to confuse the changing methods he used in his generation with his unchangeable democratic goals; or narrowly to equate his so-called "agrarian democracy" of a dead past with his fundamental principles that are universal, timeless, and very much alive.

Charles M. Wiltse

DEMOCRATIC INDIVIDUALISM AND STATES RIGHTS DOCTRINES

Wiltse argues that the agrarian democracy of Thomas Jefferson, couched upon the principles of decentralization, states rights, and laissez-faire, was more than a modus vivendi, but a social philosophy which delicately balanced the individual and the commonwealth in a workable political system. This Jeffersonian state soon crumbled and diverged into two distinct channels—the one based on an aristocratic theory of class sovereignty, the other on an egalitarian belief in the common man.

From *The Jeffersonian Tradition in American Democracy* by Charles M. Wiltse (New York: Hill & Wang, 1935), copyright 1935, 1960 by C. M. Wiltse, pp. 218–227, 232–236. Reprinted by permission of the author. Notes to the original have been omitted.

I

John Taylor of Caroline was a contemporary and close friend of the three great Virginians who formed the dynasty: Jefferson, Madison, and Monroe. But personal ambition never led him to seek the public stage, and he served his colleagues by word rather than by deed. Though he coupled unparalleled verbosity with a heavy and labored style, yet for all his literary sins, his close logic and his penetrating insight raised his pamphlets to the level of an official body of doctrine for the republican party. It is a doctrine singularly consistent in its championship of individualism, from his first attack on the bank in 1794 to his final philippic against the protective tariff some thirty years later. For Taylor was never called upon, as were his presidential friends, to make the compromises and modifications incident to the administration of high public office. He was able to follow his logic through to the end, unhampered by the dictates of political expediency. It was Taylor who suggested the Virginia Resolutions of 1799 to Jefferson; and it was Taylor who sowed the seeds of nullification, for Calhoun to cultivate and for the South to reap.

The constitutional argument is formulated in Taylor's letter to Jefferson of June 25, 1798, and is expanded, with more or less relevant digressions, in his subsequent writings. The constitution, he contends, is a compact *between the states,* and the parties to it are the various ratifying conventions, these being in turn delegates of the people. It is therefore reserved for the states to determine whether or not the constitution is being infringed, and to declare null and void any unconstitutional act of any branch of the general government. This thesis is most elaborately developed in the *Inquiry into the Principles and Policy of the Government of the United States,* published in 1814, and intended as a belated answer to the constitutional theory of the *Federalist,* and of John Adams's *Defense of the Constitutions of the United States.* This instance alone will serve to show how rare was Taylor's consistency; for Jefferson, who had endorsed both the *Federalist* and the *Defense* in a day in which he had been no more disposed to accept central authority than he was in 1814, yet found no difficulty in taking Taylor's part against Adams.

It was largely the repeated insistence Taylor placed on popular sovereignty that gave him his commanding place in democratic councils. There is no doubt in his mind as to the literalness of delegated power, or the necessity of constant watchfulness on the part of the people lest it be abused. In the early stages of his attack on Hamilton's bank, *An Enquiry into the Principles and Tendency of Certain Public Measures,* published in 1794, Taylor summarizes the fundamental tenets of his creed. If political principles really exist, he argues, and if rights are to be more than mere words, it should be possible to select "a few simple axioms, beyond the reach of polemical artifice, and containing a degree of internal evidence, compelling indubitable conviction." These axioms are not embodied in the constitution, for that may be too readily interpreted by special interests. They are rather results of the constitution, which may be simply stated. The government is to be republican, "flowing from and depending on the people." The right of legislation resides in the people, and is periodically delegated by election to their representatives. The right of election is a substance and not a form, and a legitimate representation "implies an *existing operative* principle, in the representing, impelling them for the good of the represented." Whenever this principle ceases to exist, the government is converted into an usurpation.

Here is individualism with a vengeance! The theory of the American constitution is not, as Adams and Madison had held, to balance interests or orders, but to unite the people in a single interest, and to divide political power between the people and their government, and between the states. There is no room in the system for privilege of any kind. Legislation tending to give to any individual or group power denied to others is therefore unconstitutional. The effect of this principle is to reduce the functions of government to the lowest possible—to confine the activities of the state to those which have earlier been called "repressive" functions. For the moment the line is passed, and government goes beyond the mere preservation of order and liberty, a new source of privilege is created through patronage. The union is a confederation of the people of the various geographical units, and is in no sense a balance of classes or an accommodation of interests.

The three Virginia republicans who administered the government for a quarter of a century did much to carry out these principles, but none of the three went as far as Taylor, who filled the role of self-appointed critic during the first thirty-five years of the constitution. He regarded himself as a Jeffersonian, and Jefferson endorsed his writings without reserve. There are, however, various differences, which might easily go unnoticed by the two men themselves because overshadowed by their larger agreements. Both dreaded the power of capitalism, and fought against it as it manifested itself in the bank scheme and in the tariff, and both opposed the power of the Supreme Court to set aside acts of Congress. But in all these points Taylor's opposition is more thoroughgoing than Jefferson's. The latter accepted the tariff of 1816 on the ground that political independence demanded economic independence. Taylor remained agrarian to the end, holding that agriculture was the only primary and natural source of wealth. He charged that to subsidize manufactures was to create a privileged class, and an artificial opposition of interests. To the doctrine of judicial review, Jefferson opposed constitutional interpretation by the accredited representatives of the people: the federal legislative and executive officers. Taylor offered as a substitute the contract theory of the constitution, and maintained the right of the contracting parties—the states—to refuse to carry out their constitutional obligations if the government overstepped its assigned limits. Both denied the power of the Supreme Court to override the state courts, but Jefferson recognized the validity of an appeal on constitutional questions.

Taylor emphasizes one side of Jeffersonian democracy—the individualistic side; but he deserves none the less the first place in the tradition. His four most important works were published after Jefferson had retired from the presidency, and it was in those years of retirement that Jefferson himself was most inclined to emphasize individualism. It is possible to be more coldly logical and more rigorously consistent in the abstraction of the study than it is in the arena of politics; but it does not follow that the measures best designed to promote good government are those which conform most closely to the abstract principle. It is perhaps for this reason that, though Taylor is more consistent, Jefferson has been more enduring.

The economics of individualistic democracy is an uncompromising laissez-faire theory; and it is such a theory that Taylor expounds in his *Tyranny Unmasked* (1822), an elaborate argument against protection. The protective system creates a monopoly, the proceeds of which accrue to enrich the capitalists, a small minority, at the expense of the great mass of people who must pay more for their manufactured products. This is privilege, and is a plain perversion of the legal equality of the citizens. Moreover, an even greater blow will be struck at agriculture; for the farmer, in addition to paying more for the protected articles, will find the value of his own produce reduced in foreign markets by the restrictions on exchange. The unity of interest which Taylor held to be essential had already been undermined—if, indeed, it had ever existed—and his argument was soon to be echoed by a class as a weapon against the denial of its equal rights.

One further point in Taylor's writings must be discussed, because of its bearing on the later development of the individualistic thesis. In 1820 he published his *Construction Construed and Constitutions Vindicated,* which dealt at length with the two burning questions of the hour: the doctrine of liberal construction, as laid down by Chief Justice Marshall in McCulloch *vs.* Maryland; and the Missouri Compromise. In respect to the former, he reasserts the right of the states to hold the central government within its constitutional limits, and charges that because of the failure adequately to safeguard property against the encroachments of government, a monied class had arisen, and was steadily consolidating the central power at the expense of the community at large. As to the Missouri Compromise, he holds that slavery was merely the excuse, and never the real point at issue. The real question involved was that of preserving the balance of power between the two great sections of the country. The ultimate result of this opposition of interests, he foresees clearly enough; for a balance of power between sections, like that between nations, can lead only to war.

Taylor stands as the link between the democracy of Jefferson and that of Calhoun. With the former, he champions the sovereignty of the people, and denounces class and privilege. With the latter, he regards the constitution as a compact between the states, of the terms of which the parties are to judge. Taylor's doctrine opens the way for nullification and secession just as surely as it was itself grounded on the *Declaration of Independence.*

II

Although the most productive period of his life was its last four years, 1820 to 1824, Taylor belonged, like Jefferson, to an earlier and a simpler age. The younger men who inherited the mantle of party leadership were faced with new conditions. The industrial revolution had arrived; and with the changing social order in America, the economic realism of Calhoun succeeded the humanitarian idealism of the Virginia school. The first meeting of the Twelfth Congress in 1811, saw the appearance in the House of Henry Clay, who had already won his spurs in the Senate, and of John Caldwell Calhoun; while in 1813 Daniel Webster took his seat in the same body. It was these three men, above all others, who determined the course of American government for the next forty years.

It is with Calhoun, perhaps the greatest political thinker this country has yet produced, that we are primarily concerned here. Entering Congress when the country was in ferment and war with England was only a few months away, it was probably inevitable that he should have espoused the cause of nationalism, and he soon came to be the outstanding champion of the war. In 1817, in recognition of his services in Congress, he became Secretary of War in Monroe's cabinet, having just passed his thirty-fifth birthday. Calhoun had not, however, confined himself to military affairs. He had led in the fight for internal improvements, and had gone with Clay to support the so-called "American system"—the protective tariff. In 1816 there was no doubt a genuine need for moderate protection, the manufacturing enterprizes which had sprung up in New England during the war being as yet unable to meet the competition of the older British industrialism. But by 1828 the tariff burden had begun to weigh heavily on the agricultural South. Taylor had accurately forecast the outcome of the Missouri Compromise; and had presented the southern argument against the tariff in the Senate in 1823, while Spencer Roane and Thomas Cooper were actively agitating the question in the states.

It was no longer possible for a southern statesman to hold aloof; and sometime between 1823 and the tariff bill of 1828 Calhoun swung over to the opposition. From that time until his death in 1850 he was the acknowledged leader of the state rights school, and the able champion of democratic individualism. The policy of this later period of Calhoun's intellectual maturity is extraordinarily consistent, bringing him to break party ties again and again, voting sometimes with the democrats, sometimes with the whigs, and not infrequently standing alone. He opposed any form of state subsidy to private enterprize, whether disguised as a tariff, or offered under the form of internal improvements; and he sought to divorce the government from any connection with privately controlled financial institutions. In opposing the recharter of the national bank, he offered as a substitute a bill to make the treasury independent, much as it has since come to be; and during the war with Mexico, he denounced the lavish expenditure on pensions. It was in 1832, however, that the lines were most sharply drawn, and the sectional issue was placed squarely in the center of the stage, where it was to remain until the echo of the guns of Sumter had died away in the smoke of Appomattox.

The steadily rising tariff reached its peak in that year; and with their hopeless minority in the House of Representatives, the southern states were impotent to stem the tide of wealth and privilege flowing under its provisions into the manufacturing states. After fruitless protest, the legislature of South Carolina, under Calhoun's leadership, passed an ordinance of nullification, refusing to permit the enforcement within the state of an act regarded as unconstitutional President Jackson, though himself a South Carolinian, ordered troops to Charleston, and for a time coercion seemed inevitable; but love of union prevailed, and a substantial reduction in the tariff was agreed to in time to prevent military intervention. The method of resistance, however, had been demonstrated successfully, and the tragedy of the Civil War had become all but inevitable.

Calhoun, like Taylor, regarded himself as a Jeffersonian, citing the Kentucky Resolutions of 1799, in which the very word was used, in support of nullification; and as late as 1843 he identified the party divisions of his own day with the breach between Jefferson and Hamilton. Yet Calhoun had gone immeasurably beyond the sage of Monticello; for even while accepting the theory of democracy, he denied the very basis on which the Jeffersonian system had been reared. He too feared centralization; but he feared equally the dominance of the numerical majority. The escape from the former he found in the teaching of Jefferson; the escape from the latter involved a denial of that teaching. Against the dominance of numbers he erected the barrier of class, and based his democracy on a recognized inequality among individuals. Some were by nature inferior, and it was right that they should be held in slavery by those of the superior race. Against the federalist doctrine of centralization he turned the state rights formula, refined and pushed to its logical extreme: nullification. It became in his hands a veto power to be exercised by the states on acts of the national government, and was in effect the germ of the referendum. Sovereignty rests with the people, and the authority of government is a delegated author-ity. Its acts, therefore, are subject to review and repudiation by the people as the ultimate source of power.

But the "people" no longer means, as it meant for Jefferson, the great mass of those living in a given state. By Calhoun the term is restricted to those having a definite economic stake in the govern-ment: the citizen as distinguished from the slave. It is the ideal of the Greek democracy on which this defense of slavery is based; and it is not without its element of humanitarianism. For Calhoun believed, and perhaps rightly, that the life of the southern slave was easier and less brutalizing than that of the New England factory worker.

The most precious possession of the superior race is liberty, and Calhoun would guard it even more jealously than had Jefferson. It is not a thing to be preserved by a bill of rights, but by something more fundamental. The two great threats to liberty are the abuse of delegated power and the tyranny of the stronger over the weaker interests. The safeguard protecting from the first is the suffrage, and the state rights doctrine is the barrier against the second; for by nullification, the smaller groups or interests may compel a recog-nition of their rights from the larger. The conception is one of pro-portional economic representation, the suffrage alone determining the right of the numerical majority, while the vote through consti-tuted organs, such as the legislature, determines the concurrent or constitutional majority, which regards interests as well as numbers.

Calhoun's views are ably presented in his two posthumous works, the *Disquisition on Government,* and the *Discourse on the Consti-tution and Government of the United States.* The latter is a detailed defense of the contract theory of the constitution, and of the state rights doctrine. The former is a brilliant exposition of the philosophy of democratic individualism, which will amply repay more careful analysis.

III

The *Disquisition* was intended both as an independent contribution to political science and as an introduction to the commentary on the American constitution. It sets forth a concise theory of the origin and nature of the state, which is followed by an attempt to interpret the constitution to make it conform to the theory. If the construction is more or less labored, and at times not altogether convincing, it is no fault of the theory, but must be charged to the inadequate work of the convention of 1787. In his broader purpose, that of contributing to the philosophy of government, one must read the *Disquisition* to appreciate the measure of Calhoun's success.

The initial premise is Aristotelian: governments exist necessarily because man is a gregarious animal. His natural desires and inclinations compel him to enter into society, and universal experience shows that no society has ever existed without government. Society is logically prior to government, for its purpose is to preserve and perfect the race, while that of government is to preserve and perfect society; but both follow from the nature of man. The self-regarding are stronger than the social feelings, and the impulse to value one's own safety and happiness more highly than those of others leads inevitably to conflict, and hence to the necessity of some controlling power. This power is government, which, in turn, tends to disorder because administered by men, who are motivated by human selfishness. Their power to prevent injustice must therefore be safeguarded by the constitution or it will be perverted.

Constitution stands to government as government stands to society. Without government, the end of society would be defeated, and without constitution, the purpose of government could not be fulfilled. Government, however, is a matter of divine necessity, while constitution is the work of man. The problem he must solve is summed up in the question: "How can those who are invested with the powers of government be prevented from employing them, as the means of aggrandizing themselves, instead of using them to protect and preserve society?" To establish a power higher than government would be merely to transfer the tendency to abuse to this higher authority; to limit its powers so that they cannot be turned to evil would be to cripple it and defeat its purposes.

The government must be strong enough to command the entire resources of the state to resist external attack, yet must be sufficiently limited to prevent the abuse of this power. Many shrewd devices, such as religion, education, superstition, have been used for this purpose, but all of these Calhoun discards. His aim is to show "on what principles government must be formed, in order to resist, by its own interior structure"—its *organism*—"the tendency to abuse of power." This can be done only by furnishing the governed with the means of effectively resisting any unauthorized extension of the power of the governors: by making the rulers responsible to the ruled, through the suffrage.

*   *   *

The concurrent majority is also best calculated to achieve the end of government, namely, the protection and perfection of society. The mainspring of development is the desire of individuals to better their condition. Liberty and security are both essential to this end, but either extended too far curtails the other. It is the concurrent majority which preserves the proper balance between them. Power is necessary to secure to liberty the fruits of its exertions, and liberty repays by multiplying the gifts of civilization. The sphere of power must always include the means of internal and external protection, and the residuum belongs to liberty. The line between depends on various factors, geographical and economic as well as moral and intellectual, the principle operating to make liberty keep pace with moral and intellectual capacity. It follows that all people are not equally entitled to liberty. It is a reward for the deserving, and to be deprived of it is only justice to the ignorant and the degraded. Liberty and equality of condition are incompatible, and to insist on the latter would be to destroy both liberty and progress. It is the desire of the individual to better his condition that makes progress possible.

The best government is that which most adequately combines liberty and power, and this the concurrent majority does. It is best designed to secure liberty because it best prevents the abuse of power, and entrusts the liberty of the individual to those having like interests with himself. And the progress in civilization which comes from liberty contributes in turn to the development of power. In civilized society the elements of power are discipline, strategy, weapons, money, all of which are increased by the operation of liberty. So also will the concurrent majority operate to augment moral power, by cultivating a disposition to harmony and unanimity, and by giving office to the men best qualified to lead. For each interest, to advance itself, would have to conciliate all other interests; and would therefore select as its representatives men of wisdom, skill, and tact. The individual feelings would be enlisted on the side of the social.

IV

Calhoun's divergence from the Jeffersonian doctrine is fundamental, going back to the very roots of human nature. Man in the abstract is not rational and moral, but selfish and egoistic. Individualism is the primary state, and force alone can preserve the social order. Equality has gone by the board in anything more than a strictly legal sense, and a balance of interests has replaced the agrarian ideal. Calhoun spoke for the party of Jefferson; but it was a party no longer national in its scope. It no longer sought to secure for the individual his own greatest development, and the interest of an economic group had supplanted the dream of a classless society. Humanity was subordinated to cotton.

A more thoroughgoing Jeffersonian was Alexander H. Stephens, of Georgia. But like Calhoun, Stephens identified his philosophy with a lost cause, defending slavery on the ground of a necessary inequality of races. One of the most profound students of the constitution this country has produced, he too harked back to the strict construction view of the pre-Marshall era; and turned the Jeffersonian doctrine of a terminable contract into a legal defense of secession. Like Jefferson, he held the basis of good government to be the small democratic units comprized by the community, and measured the power of the state in terms of the loyalty and devotion of its citizens. He followed the older school, likewise, in his opposition to centralization and his advocacy of state rights, as well as in his insistence that true liberty is the ordered liberty of the legal state. But he too denied the equality of men, and championed the interests of a class rather than the welfare of the whole.

If the Jeffersonian philosophy developed on its aristocratic side through Calhoun and Stephens into a theory of class sovereignty which precipitated the Civil War, it developed also on its egalitarian side through Andrew Jackson. Lacking both the broad cultural background and the trained intelligence of Jefferson, as well as the class ties of Calhoun and Stephens, Jackson spoke for the western pioneer—for the hardworking and largely illiterate masses of laboring men, from which he had himself arisen. His equalitarianism recognized neither economic nor intellectual bounds, and this latter explains, perhaps, the distrust with which Jefferson had regarded him. Honest and inflexible, he belonged to an agrarian world, and could conceive of no other social order. Like Jefferson, he feared the dominance of an aristocratic class, and hated with all the force of his powerful nature the development of a capitalistic system. But where Jefferson had sought to replace the economic aristocracy with an aristocracy of talents, and in the Virginia dynasty had well-nigh succeeded, Jackson was content to substitute for the economic power of a class the numerical rule of the masses.

Jackson had been raised to office through an extension of the suffrage which gave the vote to large numbers of men without property—pioneer farmers in the West, and an urban proletariat created by the industrialism of the East. He reasoned that the source of power lay in the people, and that it was accordingly his duty to reflect their will. The capitalistic system enriched the few at the expense of the many; and since government was the instrument of the many, it must follow that the executive was bound to root out the "hydra of corruption" and to rid the state of capitalism. The National Bank was the only part of the system within his reach, the tariff being beyond his control, so Jackson contented himself with smashing the Bank, which he did with singular directness and remarkable thoroughness. In this he but reflected the will of the numerically superior group to which he owed his office; and it was also in deference to the known will of his constituents that he espoused the cause of nationalism, and scornfully rejected nullification.

A great natural leader, yet utterly without political or social philosophy; independent, honest, domineering, colorful, yet wholly untouched by the finer problems of economic theory; Jackson fired the imagination, and commanded the most devout loyalty of the lower classes, emphasizing in the democratic doctrine everything of which Jefferson and Taylor had sought to purge it. The Jackson era was noteworthy for vigorous administration and for violent quarrels, but left little constructive legislation.

Meanwhile the old federalism of Marshall and Hamilton proceeded under Webster and Clay to develop into a strongly nationalistic party, based on protection for industry and internal improvements at government expense. The Whigs, as they came to be called, learned from Jackson to appeal to the people for votes; but they made no pretence of sharing the perquisites of government with any but the economically dominant class. As Calhoun and Stephens reflected the sectional interests of the South, and Jackson of the West, Webster appealed to the industrial East. Party lines became more sharply geographical, as the clash of economic interests heaped fuel on the fires of party bitterness. The old democratic order was already a thing of the past when the last great Jeffersonian took command.

In a very real sense, Abraham Lincoln was the last great democratic liberal of the school of Jefferson. He too came from the frontier, and had inherited the easy freedom of a pioneer people. He too was the champion of the common man, above all humanitarian. Yet his vision transcended his class, and he saw in the conflict of sectional interests the end of American union. His rejection of the state rights formula followed the slowly maturing conviction that the best interests of the country as a whole could not be reconciled with sectionalism; but in all else he followed admittedly the lead of the great Virginian. In making himself the spokesman of the western farmers, Lincoln harked back to the agrarianism of Jefferson, even while admitting, as Jefferson himself had done, the necessity of manufactures and commerce to the life of the state; and it was from the industrial East as well as the agricultural West that he drew his support.

The Civil War marked the end of the Greek democracy of Calhoun and Stephens, the end of nullification as a corollary of state rights, and the end of the dogma of an inferior race. But it marked also the end of the Jeffersonian state. The planter aristocracy of the South went down to defeat, that government of the people, by the people, and for the people should not perish from the earth; but a hundred new and more powerful vested interests sprang to take its place. Four years after an assassin's bullet had placed the emancipator among the immortals, the railroads had pushed to the Pacific, and the age of big business had begun.

IV THE JEFFERSONIAN POLITICAL SYSTEM

James MacGregor Burns

JEFFERSON AND THE STRATEGY OF POLITICS

Jefferson the politician and pragmatist is as "real" as the philosophical Jefferson and perhaps more relevant to the America of today. Burns ably demonstrates the political prowess of Jefferson in The Deadlock of Democracy. *The elections of 1800, rather than conscious planning, drove the Jeffersonians into the creation of a national political party based on majority rule. The Jeffersonian political system sharply revised the Madisonian model of checks and balances. Jefferson believed that "what is practicable must often control what is pure theory."*

It is ironic that within fifteen years of the adoption of the Constitution, the Madisonian model was suddenly overturned. The man who stood Madison on his head was seemingly the least likely author of such a revolution, Thomas Jefferson. "There are very good articles in it; & very bad," he had said when a copy of the Constitution first reached him in Paris. "I do not know which preponderate." He approved the three coordinate departments, the system of checks and balances, and the indirect election of the Senate. He regretted the absence of a Bill of Rights and the eligibility of the President for re-election. Slowly he warmed up to the charter. "It is a good canvass," he finally granted, "on which some strokes only want retouching."

The Jefferson that feared national power and presidential tenure in the new Constitution is the Jefferson that has emerged most vividly in our national heritage. This was Jefferson the ideologist, who believed that states' rights should be predominant; that the small rural property holder was the foundation of the good society; that large cities were the source of corruption, and city mobs "the panders of vice and the instruments by which the liberties of a country are generally overturned"; that the hope of America lay in an easy, self-regulating system of agriculture that would cultivate

From the book *The Deadlock of Democracy: Four-Party Politics in America* by James MacGregor Burns. ⓒ 1963 by James MacGregor Burns. Published by Prentice-Hall, Inc., Englewood Cliffs, New Jersey. Pp. 25–42. The title of the selection is that of the editor.

the virtues of honest and virtuous yeomen; that the threat to America was urbanization, industrialization, centralized finance, a landless proletariat, and a consolidated national government that would vigorously direct economic development; that that government was best which governed least; and hence that the division of powers between nation and states, and the separation of powers between President and Congress and judiciary, were the great safeguards of the peoples' liberties. Closely akin to this Jefferson was the dreamer and revolutionary who made radical statements about the need of occasional revolutions, for "the tree of liberty must be refreshed from time to time with the blood of patriots & tyrants. It is its natural manure."

There is another, quite different Jefferson that needs to be brought much more sharply into our national vision. This is Jefferson the politician, who grew up in the Virginia tradition of public service; won a seat in the House of Burgesses at twenty-six; led the Virginia reformers in abolishing primogeniture and entail, in disestablishing the Anglican church, and in defending freedom of thought and religion; served unhappily as war governor of Virginia; represented the new nation in France; and became in turn Secretary of State, Vice-President, and President. Closely akin to this Jefferson was the tinkerer and practitioner who devised a leather buggy top, a swivel chair, and a dumb waiter; invented a hemp-beater and the formula for a mold board plow of least resistance; conceived the American decimal system of coinage; and was curious about everything around him. He wrote his daughter: "Not a sprig of grass shoots uninteresting to me."

This second Jefferson, the politician and pragmatist, is, I think, as "real" a Jefferson as the first, and far more relevant to the America of the 1960's.

The First Congressional Republicans

In May 1791, four years after Madison's journey to Philadelphia, Secretary of State Thomas Jefferson took the same road but in the opposite direction. Vexed by the political distempers in the nation's capital, he had persuaded Madison to join him on a long trip through the Northern states. The object was to study the botany of the region, with perhaps a little politicking on the side. For Jefferson was still the naturalist and philosopher as well as statesman and politician. His carriage, equipped with an odometer to measure the distance traveled, had no sooner left behind the noise and bustle of Philadelphia when he was happily breathing the country air and listening for the whippoorwill's cry. His odometer had clicked off over 100 miles when he reached the Hudson ferry and made his way to Madison's house.

New York was no place to escape politics. Local Federalists watched the Republican leaders narrowly. What were they up to? Alexander Hamilton, leader of the New York Federalists, got word that there was "every appearance of a passionate courtship" between the visitors from the Old Dominion and local Republicans Aaron Burr and Robert Livingston. The British consul reported to London that "the Secretary of State's Party and Politicks gain ground here." When Jefferson and Madison, after tarrying in New York only two days, left for Albany by carriage and boat, suspicions did not die. The botanical expedition was just a pretext, it was said; the Republican leaders were travelling to Albany and New England to "sow a few tares" and spread their dangerous doctrines. The fauna and flora that interested them were really political, not natural.

Like most politicians the Federalists were, in a way, too suspicious. Although the travelers probably visited Governor Clinton in Albany and one or two other Republican leaders along the way, what actually excited them most were the flowers and fish, the trees, game, insects, soil, streams, lakes, scenery, and battlefields. They were congenial travelling companions, though the two men contrasted sharply. Jefferson was tall, loose, rangy; he usually had a relaxed, lounging air about him, compared to the younger man's bounciness and vigor. But philosophically they were twins. And as they made the long journey up Lake George to Champlain, down through Vermont to Bennington (where they were stranded for a whole Sunday by a law against Sabbath travel), then overland to the Connecticut Valley and down to Hartford, and finally across the Sound to Long Island, the two men had a chance to compare notes on Republican politics in the Northern states and across the nation. And word seeped out to the surrounding countryside that the famous Virginians had come through.

So in a most fundamental sense the Federalists had every right to worry about the Virginia tourists and their travels. Powerful political currents were loose in America, and the two men were in the middle of the turbulence.

How does a great party get started? Some historians have pictured the founding of the first Republican party as a stroke of genius on Jefferson's part. Like a commander surveying the battlefield, it is said, he rallied people and politicians behind him, built a mighty national machine, and swept on to win the presidential battle of 1800. What really happened was more complicated but no less instructive for understanding American politics, nor less testimonial to Jefferson's key role. Actually, the first Republican party grew out of a series of gropings and blunderings, small ambitions and great issues, petty politics and superb national leadership. And it originally grew up in Congress, not around the Presidency.

Most Americans in the early 1790's did not want parties. Not only the exalted George Washington, who was trying to be President of all the people, but Jefferson, Hamilton, and Madison railed against the spirit of party. "If I could not go to heaven but with a party," Jefferson exclaimed, "I would not go there at all." An anonymous Philadelphian spoke for many Americans when he wrote in a local paper: "We want no *Ticket Mongers:* let every citizen exercise his own judgment, and we shall have a good representation—intrigue, favoritism, cabal and party will be at rest." Party stood for selfish faction and petty maneuver. But the impulse toward political organization was inexorable. As Madison said, men tend to be selfish and aggressive; they attach themselves to one another and to ambitious leaders; and they find plenty of things to quarrel about, sensible and silly. Factions spring up behind leaders contending for place and power. Much of the fighting occurs on a darkling plain of ignorance, but not all is confusion. What gives order to the combat is the structure of political and governmental offices. Around every desired position, administrative, legislative, judicial, develop little clusters of aspirants and their circles of supporters.

Since the Constitution of 1787 set up a new system of national offices—President, Senator, and so on—it might be expected that the first tendencies toward national parties would focus on contests for national offices, especially for Congress and the Presidency. Such was the case. But since Washington was "above politics," the first national party contests revolved around battles for seats in the House and Senate. During most of Washington's first term, congressional politics was personal, fluid, placid on the surface, and sometimes vicious underneath. Politicians ran for Congress and voted in Congress on their own. Such a wholly individualistic politics could not last; inevitably politicians would join forces with like-minded men in order to concert and broaden their power. The only question was when and how.

The man who unwittingly threw down the gage of party battle was Washington's Secretary of the Treasury, Alexander Hamilton. While his chief denounced politics, Hamilton went about the tricky business of organizing congressional support for the Administration's measures—for the national bank, assumption of state debts by the national government, federal subsidies, and the other parts of Hamilton's famous "system." For the New Yorker saw that his program could not be enacted without pressure and persuasion and hard bargaining from the top. If Washington would not provide political leadership, Hamilton would. He forced through his program, but only at the price of uniting the opposition.

The heart of that opposition was the Virginia delegation in Congress, and the head of it was James Madison. As Washington's first term came to an end, the alert Virginian was busy converting the anti-Federalist irregulars in Congress into an organized phalanx. People even spoke of the "Madison party." The anti-Federalists were not content simply to oppose Hamilton's measures. They organized forays against his position in the Administration. They set up a Ways and Means committee in the House to clip his financial powers. They backed Jefferson's successful effort to have the Mint shifted from Hamilton's department to his own. They swore they would topple Hamilton from his "fiscal throne."

Foreign affairs widened the breach. During the mid-1790's Americans were taking sides over the French Revolution. The fall of the Bastille set off a wave of sympathy in revolution-minded America, checked later by news of the execution of Louis XVI and of other excesses. As hostilities flared up betwen Paris and London, Republicans tended to attach themselves to the French cause, Federalists to the English. And both domestic and foreign conflicts were interlaced with disputes over the very style of government. Republicans charged their foes with secretly wanting monarchy under Washington and Adams; Federalists denounced the Republicans for seeking to subordinate the executive to a radical legislature.

Soon the political winds were full of epithets. The Republicans charged that the Federalists were not really Federalists but Monarchists (or Monocrats), Tories, Royalists, aristocrats, the British party. Federalists countered that Republicans were not really Republicans but Democrats, Jacobins, and Frenchified. By early 1797, when Washington gave his farewell speech against parties, the language of party dialogue was complete.

It was a time of numerous newspapers—Philadelphia alone had twelve—and many of these threw themselves into the party battle. Some were the kept organs of a party leader. Hamilton gave printing patronage to the Federalist *Gazette of the United States* and loaned money to its editor, John Fenno. Disgusted by the "hymns & lauds chanted" by this "paper of pure Toryism," Jefferson, with Madison's help, asked a New York journalist, Philip Freneau, to set up a Republican newspaper in Philadelphia. Jefferson sweetened his bid with the offer of a clerkship for Freneau, official advertising for the paper, and inside information from the State Department. Soon the *National Gazette* was fulminating against Hamilton, who complained indignantly to Washington about Jefferson's hireling.

Alarmed at Hamilton's influence, tired by political abuse and squabbles, Jefferson quit Washington's cabinet at the end of 1793 and returned to the tranquillity of Monticello. He left Madison in full command of the Republican party in Congress. During the mid-nineties, with the expected departure of the nonpartisan Washington from the presidency and the likelihood of a party fight over the succession, the Republicans in Congress were becoming more organized. Although party unity was still rough, party lines were tightening in Senate and House. "No disciplined Prussians or enthusiastic French, adhere more firmly to their ranks than the differing members of Congress to their respective standards," a South Carolinian complained, with some exaggeration. Madison was a brilliant congressional tactician, keeping in touch with Jefferson and other Republican leaders outside Congress, planning parliamentary strategy, holding his ranks firm through persuasion and bargaining, occasionally calling his men into caucus.

But the Republican party was not just a group in Congress; gradually during the 1790's it built electoral strength in the states and districts. Earlier members of Congress had won office through small, informal groups of friends and neighbors, with no extensive organization in the modern sense. As the party cleavage widened, members of Congress sent out increasingly partisan circulars to their constituents. In 1796 congressmen in several states campaigned on party tickets. Sometimes the tickets bore partisan labels, sometimes not, but the party groupings behind the ticket were made clear to all. Madison gave some direction to the effort; one of his best grass-roots organizers and reporters was House Clerk John Beckley (who was promptly sacked when the Federalists regained control of the House). Even more, the Republican party in Congress dominated the party's presidential effort in 1796. Meeting in informal caucus, its leaders easily agreed on Jefferson as their presidential nominee. The sage of Monticello was not consulted.

By the end of Washington's second term, in short, America had its first national party in the Republicans. Significantly, it was a congressional party, organized in Congress, around members of Congress and candidates for Congress, with rough party discipline, and reaching out to embrace networks of followers in the constituencies. The Federalists had identity and some organization too, but it was limited; the Federalists were more likely to assume their right to office and less inclined to hustle at the polls. (After the fatal Federalist setback of 1800 Hamilton proposed that the party organize local clubs, debate issues, and set up real party machinery, all under national party control, but by then it was too late for both Hamilton and the Federalists). It was the Republican party in Congress under Madison that pioneered in America's early experiments in nationwide organization.

At this point Jefferson's role was uncertain. As Secretary of State he had quietly led the Republican cause: not only had he got the *National Gazette* started under Freneau, but he had encouraged Republican politicians to seek office; he had stimulated Republican pamphleteering against Hamilton; and on his own he had disseminated Republican philosophy and policies. But when he quit Washington's cabinet in 1793 he also quit his role as party chieftain and left everything to Madison. He wanted Madison to run for President in 1796; Republicans feared, however, that their congressional leader could not carry the crucial mid-Atlantic states. So they ran a reluctant Jefferson who, after sitting the campaign out at Monticello, came in second to John Adams and hence became the new Vice-President. The congressional Republicans were not yet strong enough to elect a President.

Like vice-presidents ever since, Jefferson found his position an awkward one for directing a national party. But now he was back in the swirl of politics, and he could not escape the rising political temper. "Men who have been intimate all their lives," he noticed, "cross the streets to avoid meeting, and turn their heads another way, lest they should be obliged to touch their hats." Madison had retired from Congress, so political intelligence between the two men ran in the opposite direction. In Philadelphia Jefferson led the Republican congressional opposition to Adams and tried to get a new paper started; in Monticello he talked with state politicos that passed by, and corresponded with others.

That Jefferson still had no clear idea where he and his party were headed, however, was shown by a sharp change in his political strategy in 1798. This was his leadership in drafting the Virginia and Kentucky resolutions. A protest against Adams' alien and sedition laws, these resolutions by state legislatures declared the Federalist measures unconstitutional and—far more important—affirmed the right of states to judge for themselves the constitutionality of acts of Congress. There was even the hint of a right of secession. The resolutions failed; to most informed Americans they were a long step backward toward the weak Articles of Confederation that the Virginians had taken the lead in abandoning. They were the Madisonian formula but carried to such an extreme as to be a caricature. They were the reverse of the strategy of party opposition, which assumed that the way to overcome a bad national administration is not to play the politics of Chinese warlords and pull out but to win enough votes at the next election to drive the administration out of power.

The Jeffersonians were still floundering. It was not conscious political planning but the election of 1800 that impelled them to create a great national party.

Jefferson Builds a Party

When Jefferson returned to Philadelphia shortly before New Year's, 1800, he was already planning to run for President. Gone were the doubts and vacillations of earlier days. Bombarded by the Republicans and undermined by Hamilton and his anti-Adams guerrillas, the Adams administration was an easy target. But to Jefferson the Federalists still seemed formidable. To be sure, he considered them inferior in numbers, comprising mainly, he said, "old refugees & tories," British and American merchants, speculators in public funds, federal jobholders, a "numerous and noisy tribe" of office hunters, and "nervous persons, whose languid fibres have more analage with a passive than active state of things." But the Federalists, he noted, were concentrated in the cities and hence could influence government in a way that the Republicans, dispersed in the back country, could not easily overcome.

Jefferson did not campaign across the country, as presidential candidates do today. Stumping was against his nature, and against the custom of the day. Indeed, the masses of voters often did not need to be approached directly, for in some states the presidential electors were not chosen directly by the voters, as they are today, but by state legislatures. Jefferson's presidential campaign was in large part an effort to elect state legislators who would choose the right electors to pick the right man for President.

During 1800 Jefferson decisively asserted control over the Republican party. He had already drawn up a set of party policies—frugal government, reduced national debt, smaller national defense, "free commerce with all nations" but "political connections with none," freedom of religion, press, and speech—and during the year his followers used these policies as a rough party platform in their own campaigns. Jefferson did not answer Federalist charges, however, "for while I would be engaged with one," he said, "they would publish twenty new ones." His tactic was to out-organize the Federalists, not merely out-debate them.

Jefferson's main strategy, however, was simply being Jefferson—Jefferson the revolutionary, the framer of the Declaration of Independence, the author of the Virginia statute for religious freedom, the intellectual leader and symbol of the Virginia Republicans, the great successor to Franklin in Paris, the Secretary of State, the philosopher and politician. Actually Jefferson was a complicated man, so mixed and shifting in his point of view as to appear irresolute to his friends, arrantly hypocritical to his foes, and a puzzle to later historians. But at the time the Jefferson image was glowingly clear, especially to the back-country people living in a long crooked swath from the interior of Maine through the Green Mountains and the Berkshires down the long uplands to his own Virginia country and then on to the inland South and the Southwest.

But Jefferson realized—and this was his supreme achievement as a party leader—that it was not enough to solicit the old centers of Republican support. He must broaden his appeal in order to reach into the cities. He played down his earlier warnings about the city mobs, while his Republican supporters in the cities played up his opposition to speculation, high taxes, usury, British seizure of American ships, and similar matters that vexed mechanics, sailors, and other city dwellers.

Indeed, the first great election test, according to Jefferson's calculations, would come in the nation's largest city, New York. At the end of April 1800, New York state would elect its legislature, which in turn would choose a slate of electors that might hold the balance of power between Jefferson and Adams in the electoral college. Sizing up the political terrain, Jefferson sounded much like any political analyst a century and a half later: "If the city election of New York is in favor of the Republican ticket," he wrote Madison, "the issue will be Republican; if the federal ticket for the city of New York prevails, the probabilities will be in favor of a federal issue because it would then require a Republican vote both from New Jersey and Pennsylvania to preponderate against New York, on which we could not count with any confidence." In charge of the Republican group in Manhattan was Aaron Burr. Jefferson had always been a bit dubious about the slick New Yorker, but this was no time for squeamishness. During the winter Burr made a quick trip to Philadelphia and the two men discussed strategy.

In the next three months Burr staged a masterly political campaign. He faced severe odds, for the Federalists were ably led by his old adversary, Alexander Hamilton, who had won the previous election decisively, and the Republicans were divided. Burr quietly persuaded the older party leaders to unite on one ticket of eminent local Republicans; shrewdly waited to announce his ticket until after Hamilton had pieced together an inferior one (Hamilton had shortsightedly chosen his own satellites instead of eminent Adams supporters); organized his lieutenants solidly on a ward-by-ward basis; card-indexed the voters, their political history, attitudes, and how to get them to the polls; set up committees to canvass for funds from house to house; put the heat on wealthy Republicans for bigger donations; organized rallies; enlisted in his cause the members of the Tammany Society, then a struggling fraternal group; debated publicly with Hamilton; and spent ten hours straight at the polls on the last day of the three-day election.

A superb local tactician behind a great strategic leader—Burr could hardly fail. The entire Republican ticket for the assembly carried by an average of almost 500 votes, and there was a good deal of straight-ticket voting. Word was dispatched to Jefferson in Philadelphia: "We have completely and triumphantly succeeded." Such a hubbub rose in the Senate that it had to adjourn. Federalists were downcast; Republicans exclaimed that the New York returns presaged Jefferson's success nationally.

They were right. During the summer Republican candidates for state legislature and the electoral college toured their districts and talked to crowds wherever they could find them—even "at a horse race—a cock fight—or a Methodist quarterly meeting." The Federalists, solidly based in New England, fought hard to retain the balance-of-power states, but in vain. Although nowhere else did the Republicans have an organization rivalling New York's, the backwoods seemed alive with Jeffersonian politicians who were acting with unprecedented unity and who seemed to have a bottomless supply of pamphlets and printed lists of nominees.

It was well for the Republicans that they fought as hard as they did, for in the end they gained only a narrow victory over the divided Federalists: Jefferson and Burr both won 73 electoral votes, Adams 65, General Charles Pinckney 64, and Jay one. The Jeffersonians' elation was dimmed by the tie vote between their leader and Burr. They had produced party regularity in the elections without really understanding it; now party regularity was playing a mean trick on them. The election was thrown into the strongly Federalist lame-duck Congress. For thirty-five ballots the House was stalemated. Only because the Congressional Republicans stuck together while the Federalists were divided, and because Burr dared not connive with the Federalists, while Jefferson (evidently) indicated through intermediaries that he would carry on certain Federalist policies, was the Virginian able to win out on February 17, 1801.

So Jefferson was President. But would he really be *President?* He had made the Republican party into a tool for winning a presidential election. Could he continue to run the party, or would the party run him? Everything seemed to point to a period of executive weakness. No one had preached with more unction than Jefferson about the sanctity of the separation of powers and checks and balances. He had seemingly looked on his party as something to win through, rather than as something to rule through. And now he faced the Republican majority in Congress, enlarged by the election, prepared to carry out their doctrines of congressional supremacy in a weak national government. Independent, divided, jealous of their legislative powers, the congressional Republicans, after years of carping at Washington, Hamilton, and Adams, had now come into their own.

So they thought. But they underrated the steel in Jefferson's gangling frame and his knack for overlooking general principles when faced with practical politics. "What is practicable must often control what is pure theory," he said blithely, "and the habits of the governed determine in a great degree what is practicable." Not only did Jefferson accept much of the Federalist policy, such as the Bank. He went far beyond Federalists in broadening executive power. And in the Louisiana Purchase he took a step that he considered unconstitutional, telling Congress that it must ratify the agreement with Napoleon, "casting behind them Metaphysical subtleties," and throw themselves on the country for approval of the step at the next election.

What astonishing doctrine! Here was the first Republican President saying in effect that his party should support his unconstitutional act because the voters would sustain the party at the next election. It was a daring move, and wholly successful. Not only was the Louisiana Purchase magnificently vindicated in history, but Jefferson was vindicated in the presidential election of 1804, winning by 162 electoral votes to 14, while the congressional Republicans enlarged their already big majority.

Above all, it was in his leadership of Congress that Jefferson upset old Republican notions of the executive-legislative balance. Considering himself the national head of the party, he gave close and constant leadership to his forces in Congress; he personally drafted bills and had them introduced into Congress; saw to it that the men he wanted took the leadership posts in Congress; induced men he favored to run for Congress by holding out promises of advancement; made the Speaker and the floor leader of the House his personal lieutenants; changed the leadership as he saw fit; used Ways and Means and other committees as instruments of presidential control; dominated the Republican caucus in the House. In short, he took the machinery that the congressional Republicans had built up against Federalist Presidents and turned it to his own uses.

Some Republicans complained bitterly, but they were helpless. Jefferson followed every measure with a hawk's eye, applied pressure where necessary, wined and dined the legislators, and used his Cabinet members and other subordinates as his agents on the Hill. He did not crack the whip publicly, nor did he need to. He simply threw into the balance every ounce of his political, administrative, and moral power—power all the greater because Jefferson had created the electoral foundations of the party.

And he knew how to deal with his enemies, by attacking them from the rear, on their own ground. One of his foes—or so Jefferson thought—was his Vice-President, Aaron Burr. Jefferson not only denied patronage to Burr and his friends; he set out deliberately to destroy the dapper little New Yorker's power in his home state by giving patronage to Burr's adversaries there. Then Jefferson denied him re-nomination for the Vice-Presidency, completing Burr's isolation and helping, in the end, to make an adventurer out of him. John Randolph was another Republican run over by Jefferson's party machine. At first a rising star, a parliamentary leader and chairman of the potent Ways and Means Committee, the stormy young Virginian turned against the President. At the right moment Jefferson simply eased him out of the chairmanship, and then out of the leadership. A few years later Jefferson's lieutenant and son-in-law, John W. Eppes, took up residence in Randolph's district and defeated him for Congress; whether Jefferson's fine hand was behind this *coup de grâce* is for once hard to say.

There were, of course, limits to Jefferson's power. Before leaving office John Adams had carefully packed the judicial branch with staunch Federalists. The enemy had taken refuge in the courts, Republicans noted, but how much power would they have? The right of judicial review had not yet been established in the national government; if the courts tried to invalidate good Jeffersonian measures, Republicans calculated, the President would simply defy the Federalist judges. But the Republicans underestimated the new Federalist Chief Justice, John Marshall—surprisingly, since he was a Virginian. In the famous case *Marbury v. Madison,* he invalidated not a great Republican measure but a minor part of a bill that had given certain technical powers to the Supreme Court. It was a brilliant stroke, for Marshall set forth the vital precedent of judicial review, but in such a way that Jefferson could not retaliate, for there was not even a specific court order that he could refuse to obey. The President had no better luck in his impeachment of Supreme Court Justice Samuel Chase, an intemperate Federalist propagandist. Conviction of Chase would have prepared the way for an attack upon Marshall, but the Senate Republicans could not muster the necessary two-thirds vote to convict Chase.

Marshall himself had astutely predicted at the outset that Jefferson would repudiate old Republican principles of congressional supremacy. "Mr. Jefferson appears to me to be a man," Marshall wrote Hamilton, "who will embody himself with the House of Representatives . . . and become the leader of that party which is about to constitute itself the majority of the legislature." What Marshall did not see was that in doing so Jefferson would augment rather than weaken the Presidency. Because Jefferson repudiated the anti-national ideas of the old guard of the Republican party, because he adopted the strong legislative methods of the "presidential" Federalists, because he built a new Republican party to win a presidential election and then governed through it—because of all this Jefferson was the father of the first truly national Republican party, as Madison had been of the Constitution, and again like Madison, one of the grand strategists of American politics.

The Theory of Majority Rule

Timid ladies in Boston, so it is said, had hid their Bibles under their beds on the eve of Jefferson's Inauguration. They had been frightened by Federalist alarms that March 4, 1801, would usher in a hideous new revolution with "the loathesome steam of human victims" offered in sacrifice to a new Goddess of Reason. As steady a man as the new Chief Justice, John Marshall, had written on Inauguration morning that the democrats were divided into "speculative theorists & absolute terrorists," and he was not sure in which class to put the new President. But Marshall, unlike the ladies in Boston, would attend the Inaugural, since he had to administer the oath. By the afternoon of March 4 he was feeling much relieved, for the Inaugural speech had struck him as judicious and conciliatory.

Despite the fierceness of the election contest, Jefferson had told the crowd, all would now abide the result. "All, too, will bear in mind this sacred principle, that though the will of the majority is in all cases to prevail, that will to be rightful must be reasonable; that the minority possess their equal rights, which equal law must protect, and to violate would be oppression. . . ." Events abroad had divided Americans, he granted. "But every difference of opinion is not a difference of principle. We have called by different names brethren of the same principle. We are all Republicans, we are all Federalists. If there be any among us who would wish to dissolve this Union or to change its republican form, let them stand undisturbed as monuments of the safety with which error of opinion may be tolerated when reason is left free to combat it."

"We are all Republicans, we are all Federalists"—these words must have fallen like soothing music on Marshall's ear. And ever since, the famous phrase has been quoted as a lofty and patriotic expression of nonpartisanship. Actually, Jefferson was making a partisan gambit. Recognizing that his election majority had been perilously thin, he saw that he must detach moderate Federalists from the extremists, keep the support of his own party, and thus consolidate his position. He was not pretending that he would follow Federalist principles or even neutral ones; most of his speech called for good Republican measures. He was arguing that no deep division of principle separated him from moderate Federalists.

The Inaugural speech was, indeed, an almost perfect expression of the practical operation of majority rule. The will of the majority must always prevail, Jefferson said, but it must be and would be reasonable. The Republicans would not press extreme party doctrines. Opponents—even those preaching disunion—would be left free. Jefferson was implying that in order to hold and expand his majority, he must embrace policies so broad and so moderate that no minority party or group would be imperiled. We do not need to infer Jefferson's strategy only from his public speeches. In letter after letter he made his plan crystal clear—to bring over moderate Federalists into the Republican camp and thus to create an invincible majority behind the new Administration. Jefferson had an ingenious nomenclature for this strategy. Moderate Federalists he termed "Republican Federalists," and the radicals in his own party he called "Sweeping Republicans." Jefferson served as umpire, connector, and ultimately as unifier of the two groups, as the 1804 triumph proved.

It was Jefferson's actions, however, more than his words, that revealed the anatomy of majority rule. On the one hand he carried on many of the more moderate Federalist policies; and despite Republican grumbling he left in office Federalists who were not extremely partisan or "monarchical." On the other hand, he put good Republican measures through Congress and saw to it that his own loyal followers were rewarded as much as possible. But the high point of Jefferson's majoritarianism, as we have seen, came in the Louisiana Purchase. When the chips were down, when a great decision had to be made and pressed quickly, Jefferson violated congressional rights, by-passed accepted constitutional processes, refused to go through the long process of a constitutional amendment, and threw himself and his party on the mercy of the new popular majority that he was building up.

From both Jeffersonian words and practice, then, we can draw some basic elements of the strategy of majority rule:

1. Majority rule in a big, diverse nation must be moderate. No majority party can cater to the demands of any extremist group because to do so would antagonize the great "middle groups" that hold the political balance of power and hence could rob the governing party of its majority at the next election. A democratic people embodies its own safeguards in the form of social checks and balances—the great variety of sections and groups and classes and opinions stitched into the fabric of society and thus into the majority's coalition.

Since "tyranny of the majority" has long been a term to scare little children with, we must note again that the Jeffersonian system had internal checks and balances, just as Madison's formula had. But the two types differ radically. Madison's formula turned on the "Swiss watch" concept, as Saul K. Padover has aptly termed it, of checking government through major "opposite and rival" interests, any one of which, through its branch of government, could stop extremist action by the majority. Jefferson's system assumed that in a nation like the United States, where sectional, economic, and other group lines cut across parties in a maze of overlapping memberships, and hence where neither major party could abuse any major interest without alienating people in its own ranks—that a governing majority in such a nation could not afford politically to be immoderate, because it could not afford to alienate moderate voters holding the balance of power.

2. The Jeffersonian formula of majority rule allows more government action than the Madisonian model of checks and balances. Once a majority party had been pieced together—no easy job—and its leaders had taken over the three branches of the national government, the majority could govern rather freely and vigorously within its broad mandate, as Jefferson did. But the Madisonians would require that even after a majority had thus won power, strong minority interests—farmers, say, or Southerners or creditors—would still have a veto power over government action. In a sense the difference between the two systems was quantitative—the Jeffersonian formula required leaders to gain and keep the support of a simple majority of the people—say 55 per cent—behind federal action, while the Madisonians demanded clearance with a far larger pro-

portion of the people (since any major group held a veto power). But this was one of those differences in degree that became a major difference in kind when it came to the capacity of government to act.

3. Jeffersonian majority rule had a more popular, egalitarian impetus than the Madisonian. To win majorities a party leader must reach out to embrace new voters, while holding on to his present supporters; otherwise the opposition party might get the jump. It did not matter if the new voters were poor or ignorant, if they were aliens or even women—every effort must be made to enfranchise more voters and to get the warm bodies to the polls. Madisonian politics lacked this impulse. Whether or not the "veto groups" had wide popular backing was not crucial; such groups could often get their grip on some lever of government whether or not they had broad support among the voters.

To operate properly majority rule required a reliable mechanism: a vigorous, competitive party, under strong leadership. To be sure, majority rule in one sense is not the same as a strong two-party system; the liquid, ever-changing majorities, embracing different coalitions, that form and re-form in a New England town meeting, a city council, or the French Assembly, can do so apart from durable party lines. But effective majority rule on a national scale in a continental nation demands a durable popular majority organized by a leader who can depend on his following in moments of need, as in Jefferson's case. This makes the national majority something more than a mere expedient, a mere holding company for a collection of minorities. Moreover, the majority party—and the opposition that hopes to supplant it—must be competitive; if either one forsakes victory in order to stick to principle, as the Federalists did after the turn of the century, it threatens the whole mechanism of majority rule. Majoritarian strategy assumes that in the end politicians will rise above principle in order to win an election.

Madison's system demanded a reliable mechanism too: interlocking gears of government, each one responding to different thrusts originating in different groups of the electorate. To get the gears to mesh demanded endless bargaining and adjusting among the groups who had their hands on the gears—and hence demanded high-level negotiators who could deal with group leaders. It also meant that government action could be feeble and halting, as agreements among hostile groups might be overly compromised and meaning-less. Madison's formula, like Jefferson's, could be abused—espe-cially if one group became so adamant and rigid that it refused to bargain.

So much—for the moment—for the competing formulas. The im-portant point is that by the end of Jefferson's second term the nation was trying to operate both systems. Would such a hybrid work?

William Nisbet Chambers

JEFFERSONIAN REPUBLICANS AND THE DEVELOPMENT OF THE MODERN PARTY SYSTEM

"The party of Jefferson in the 1790's was a new political engine, the first of its kind in modern history." It was the archetype of the modern party based on a broad electorate. Unlike the Federalist organization, which failed to develop popular participation and responsiveness to public opinion, the Republican party of Jefferson relied upon an extended popular following and encouraged popular participation and initiative in party action. The elitist Federalists sought to mobilize or manipulate popular opinion, rather than to be guided by it, says Chambers.

I

The establishment of the Republicans as a full-blown party was only one aspect of a general movement in the new republic to solve its basic political problems. These included questions of democracy and national stability, and issues of economic development, as well as the establishment of political parties. Over-all, the national de-velopment constituted steps toward political modernization.

From *Political Parties in a New Nation: The American Experience, 1776–1809* by William Nisbet Chambers. Copyright © 1963 by Oxford University Press, Inc. Reprinted by permission. Pp. 95–112.

Indeed, American development after the Revolution of 1776 was almost a classic instance of political modernization. Thus, we find a constitution on the rationalist model, and Washington serving as a charismatic focus of acceptance and legitimacy in the transition to fully rational, legal foundations of authority; an open politics of conflicting interests; orderly administration, particularly as exhibited by Hamilton; free, formal associations of individuals on a rational basis for political action, as in the Democratic or Republican Societies, and the gradual displacement of family or fluid-faction "connexions" by the open, rationalized, stable connections of party; innovations in policy or inventions in political methods not only by Hamilton, but by men like Madison or Gallatin, and emphasis on rational discussion as typified by Jefferson and practiced by thousands; mass communication and propaganda in the two *Gazettes,* the *Aurora,* and other papers; the rise of "new men" like Beckley and Burr to labor at the "new careers" of methodical politicians as contrasted with notables in politics; and a tendency toward national outlooks and co-ordination as against parochial patterns and localism.

There were special and significant features in the American experience in modernization. As contrasted with European nations, American political shapers were not confronted with a protracted conflict to overthrow a closed, traditionalistic, or hierarchical social and political structure, for such a structure was never firmly fixed in America. Unlike most emerging nations of the twentieth century, where modernization has entailed an intense race from a slow start to bring an underdeveloped society to the level of modernity seen in alien Western societies, the new America worked from an already comparatively favorable position. It was thus able to achieve modernization as a development of existing elements and trends, rather than a forcing of alien patterns. Furthermore, in comparison with both European and latter-day underdeveloped nations, the American republic was fortunate in that it enjoyed crucial preconditions for a democratic polity. Nonetheless, the American experience followed typical paths of modernization, from the rationalization of authority to the development of political parties.

The passage from clique, faction, or junto politics to party politics has, in general, been an important aspect of political modernization.

Certainly, it was so in America. As compared with factionlike formations, parties represented rationalized, comparatively ordered, and methodical ways of performing crucial political functions, even when they showed aspects of disorder on their own. Also, their public and continuing character made them less dependent than cliques or factions on particular persons, families, or "connexions," and virtually required leaders and active workers in a modern style. Yet the development of American parties also depended on national political stability and national economic development. Without these, the new America might not have continued as a democratic polity, and the first experiment in modern parties might have died with it.

II

An infant democracy, if it is to survive, must evolve modes of carrying on political conflict without destroying national order and unity. To Washington or to Hamilton, as to many who shared their views, such national unity was paramount, and opposition was a threat to stability. Unity and order were a delicate web which must not be strained.

To other shapers of American politics, however, democracy implied criticism, free access to politics, real options in elections. Thus Madison, Jefferson, and the Republicans fought for the right to construct open yet peaceful competition between parties for power.

The Federalists had a cogent cause in their concern for stability, a cause which the Republicans in their way shared. An opposition may indeed tear asunder the untried fabric of a new democracy if it runs to conflict over fundamentals of social and political order, or utilizes the methods of violence. If conflict is to go on without disrupting national unity, it must stay within agreement on certain basic values of the society, or at least on certain underlying rules of the political game. Where social cleavage is deep and broad, and political issues are basic and intense, it is difficult to generate shared attitudes or secure agreement on rules for politics. Yet viable democratic politics involves a paradox: at once agreement and disagreement, consensus on fundamentals and cleavage on issues.

In dealing with this vital paradox young America drew heavily on its colonial background and early experience. It had at hand the strong threads of English law, Locke and the eighteenth-century Enlightenment, and republican precepts, or what Louis Hartz has called the "liberal tradition." Furthermore, it wove the central threads of this tradition (with some modification) into the durable republican cloth of the Constitution of 1789. Early conflict over the Constitution gave way to a remarkable acceptance of it, particularly after the addition of the ten amendments called the Bill of Rights in 1789–1791; and acceptance gradually became a strong emotional attachment to the Constitution as symbol and instrument—though patriotic men could still disagree over what particular provisions of the document should mean in operation. Thus the new nation developed a set of central faiths, commitments, and loyalties woven around a concept of individual liberty, and a widespread acceptance of basic republican rules for the conduct of politics. It did so within a society which could readily develop in a liberal direction because it was not bound to a feudal fabric of graded estates, or of aristocracy against bourgeoisie, submerged masses, or peasantry. It arrived, in Tocqueville's phrase, "at a state of democracy without having to endure a democratic revolution," or without having to endure the breaks in the social texture which social revolution may bring.

Conflict generally remained within the moderate borders of the liberal tradition. Even Shays's Rebellion in 1786–1787 and the Whiskey Insurrection of 1794 were movements of small property owners to protect their property rights, not instances of primitive communism threatening all property, of the sort Babeuf represented during the French Revolution. Cleavages between the Federalist and Republican parties did not really shake the fundamentals of liberty or property, the rules of republican politics, or the social order. Furthermore, early proposals that the nation should take George Washington as a dictator or even as King George I also foundered on the liberal tradition and the developing republican consensus. To be sure, some men favored the interests of one kind of property, others those of another; some men wanted a more elitist, restrictive, "English" republic, others a more democratic, libertarian, "French" republic; some distrusted The People, others relied on them—and consensus was subjected to strains, or questioned, or accepted half-heartedly in certain quarters during its years of formation. Yet, generally, conflict did not become so serious that groups or parties clashed over fundamentals.

The strength of the new national fabric was repeatedly tested. One danger that may threaten a new nation is the possibility that particular conflicts may explode into national disruption. In Shays's Rebellion, the Whiskey Insurrection, the intimations of disunion in the Jay treaty controversy—or in the later Fries Uprising in eastern Pennsylvania in 1799, or proposals for separation by New England in the early 1800's—such threats stained the early American experience. The grave issue in each case was whether partial conflicts would lead to general violence or to secession of part of the nation from the whole. Yet in the event, no national leader or party was ready to extend local dissent to general disruption. Faith in the republic, attachment to orderly decision-making, and abhorrence of violent methods were too strong in the nation's leaders, people, and parties to permit them to indulge in insurrection or in schemes of disunion. In each case, a loyal opposition valued national survival above immediate concerns. In each case, national unity and the emerging national consensus prevailed.

III

The progress of a nation's economy may both provide support for political modernization and democracy and also be affected by them. In the West, historically, the emergence of democratic politics has been associated with the rise or existence of segments of the population which constitute a substantial middle class, with inclinations toward middle-class modes of life and attitudes among other segments of the society, and with a considerable sharing of economic well-being. In its earliest manifestation at least, the liberal-democratic tradition has been a middle-class tradition, although in certain kinds of social development middle-class groups may not pursue democracy as a goal.

In a more general sense, the emergence of the democratic spirit has been associated with certain preconditions of economic and social advancement. Such conditions do not automatically produce democracy; but they have, in general, constituted prerequisites for full democratic participation and practice. Four such preconditions have been suggested by Seymour Martin Lipset: high or rising levels in national wealth, in economic development, in urbanization, and in education. High indices in these areas have been closely correlated with the rise and continued stability of democracies, low indices with dictatorships or with unstable democracies. National wealth, in an economy which is relatively advanced, can lay foundations for economic well-being and economic security. If economic well-being is widely diffused, the probability increases that the society will escape broad social cleavages between haves and have-nots, and that political conflict and party cleavage will occur within a moderate range. With the increased contacts and communication among men which urban centers bring, and also with the tools of political understanding and administration which widespread education makes available, the chances for democratic development are further increased. The existence of such features in a society means, in effect, the existence of a "modernized," generally middle-class way of life.

All of these preconditions may be discerned in early American history. The new nation was a relatively wealthy one compared to its contemporaries. Property—particularly agricultural property—and economic well-being were unusually broadly diffused among its people. To be sure, its economy was not "advanced" in terms of latter-day industrialization. Out of a total national income of $668 million in 1799, agriculture accounted for an overwhelming $264 million, while manufacturing produced only $32 million; the nation bought most of its manufactured goods abroad. Nor was the United States in the 1790's characterized by the urbanization that accompanies a manufacturing economy. The first census in 1790 showed 3,727,559 rural dwellers out of a total population of 3,929,214; and the 201,655 urban dwellers lived in only two centers larger than 25 thousand (a total of 61,653), and were otherwise dispersed in 22 so-called "urban places" of 2.5 to 25 thousand. Yet, for its time, the United States was no provincial, peasant economy. It was not significantly "backward" by European standards of the eighteenth century, and it was certainly not so in comparison to many markedly underdeveloped new nations of the twentieth century, whose road to democracy is thereby more difficult. Although manufactures remained small, commerce and other kinds of enterprise accounted for much more of the total national product: miscellaneous enterprises and finance for $60 million; transportation, including overseas shipping, for a substantial $160 million; construction, including shipbuilding, for another $53 million; service and service trades for $64 million; and trade for $35 million. Indeed, shipping, shipbuilding, and related commerce made up in considerable part for the infant standing of manufacturing; and, in addition, a significant portion of American agriculture was involved in the market economy. Furthermore, the nation's modest but lively urban centers did produce urban middle-class intellectuals and intellectual ferment and also exerted powerful influences over the countryside. Literacy and educational levels, while not readily measurable, were by all accounts high, and they extended to the great rural population as well as to town dwellers.

In short, many crucial social prerequisites were present for the development of democracy and the parties that depended on it— while at the same time the variety of groups, sections, and regions stimulated modernization in national politics and the emergence of parties. Only the purposes and energies of *homo politicus* remained as necessary to establish democratic institutions, and these had been forthcoming.

The direction the economy of a new nation takes inevitably becomes embroiled in its politics. A common tendency has been positive government action toward industrial growth. In one sense, this was Hamilton's approach to political economy, even though his policy ran counter to the path many later emerging nations have taken—the path to government control, substantial government ownership, or socialism. To Hamilton the proper role of government in the economy was to promote, rather than control, capitalist enterprise. Indeed, his program of a funded national debt as a source of capital, a national bank to provide venture credit, excise and other taxes to service the debt, and high tariff duties to protect native industry, rehearsed the steps which Karl Marx's analysis decades later described as the standard pattern of forced capitalist accumulation. The ultimate result was a long stride toward economic advance for the American nation. One immediate effect, however, was gain for a few special interests through hothouse government sponsorship.

There was of course another possible direction. This was the political economy Jefferson and most Republicans came to represent: a course looking toward a continuing planter's and freeholder's Arcadia, a predominantly agricultural life in which merchandising and manufactures widely diffused among small units would serve as handmaidens to husbandry. The political economy of this direction, as it developed in America, was characterized by a strong equalitarian stress mixed with *laissez faire*. The proper role of government, Jefferson thought, should be to secure property in as many hands as possible. It was time, he wrote in 1795, "to provide by every possible means that as few as possible shall be without a little portion of land. The small land holders are the most precious part of a state." More generally, Jefferson looked to the widest possible diffusion of human well-being as the most favorable soil for maintaining the dignity of the individual personality. Yet, given the conditions of the times, the Republican agrarian economic prescription would, ironically, have entailed a slow pace of economic growth for the new nation and limited standards of living for its population.

There was indeed irony in the positions of both parties. The general ideological theme of the Federalists was conservative and traditionalist, whereas new parties in later emerging nations have been radically innovative and anti-traditionalist. On the other hand Federalist economic policy was highly innovative and modernist, emphasizing government action toward an advanced, industrial, capitalist society—again, however, contrary to the often anti-capitalist attitudes of new nations in the twentieth century. The Republicans were post-Enlightenment and anti-traditionalist in political ideology, but still largely wedded to agrarian economic conceptions in a pre-industrial economy—conceptions that the American nation with its already comparatively prosperous agricultural economy could afford, but which stand in sharp contrast to the intense drives for industrialization in new nations today. Thus in both parties political outlooks ran in some sense in contradiction with economic policy, and in crossed or atypical ways as compared with the course of later emerging nations.

Yet cleavage on economic policy was not total. Both the Federalist program, stressing government innovation and promotion with elitist consequences, and the Republican direction, emphasizing a minimum of government intervention and equalitarian norms, were consistent with the values of individual property ownership and with republican methods. In an ultimate sense, furthermore, the purposeful direction Hamilton espoused and the values Jefferson represented are not necessarily incompatible: planning and promotion need not serve elitist purposes or narrow group interests, and equalitarianism need not be tied to agrarianism, or pay the price of a slow rate of economic development and a modest standard of living.

One virtue of modern political parties is that they can facilitate rational or democratic decisions on such matters, by providing—as Hamilton and the Federalists and Jefferson and the Republicans were doing—reasonably clear choices on policy, including issues of political economy.

IV

The party of Jefferson in the 1790's was a new political engine, the first of its kind in modern history. It exhibited little continuity with antecedent formations, and it developed political relationships which carried it well beyond the Federalists as an archetype of a modern, "popular" party. In the long process of learning and inventing in the face of need and opportunity, it had pioneered in rationalized or modernized political practices, which observers abroad later referred to as "American methods." Such practices, from the caucus to mass electoral appeals, were nonetheless frequently reproduced as democracy made its way in other nations.

Early Republicans were often stigmatized as "Anti-Federalists," a reference to the opposition to the Constitution of 1787. The idea was a plausible one, and it is true that most of those who favored the new Constitution at the convention of 1787 became Federalists in the 1790's, while those who refused to sign became Republicans. It can also be argued that many districts (and thereby presumably interests) which voted against the Constitution in the ratification controversy also stood as Republican bastions in succeeding years. Thus, for example, the argument runs that the districts which opposed the Constitution in New York in 1788 were the same as those which opposed the Federalist Jay for governor in 1792, or that the

forces which had fought ratification in western Pennsylvania re-
appeared in the whiskey tax protests of 1793–1794 and in later
Republicanism. Parallels may also be found between the elitist,
"energetic" government ideas of many pro-Constitutionalists and
of the Federalists, while beliefs in popular, limited government were
shared by many anti-Constitutionalists and Republicans.

**Party Attachment of Members of Constitutional
Convention Living in 1791**

Position on Constitution	Party Attachment in 1791		Not Known
	Federalist	Republican	
Supporters, 43	25	12	6
Opponents, 6	0	6	0

Compiled from Charles A. Beard, *Economic Origins of Jeffersonian Democracy*
(New York, 1915), 34–74.

Nevertheless, serious difficulties attend the assumption of clear
continuity from anti-Constitutionalists to Republicans. While most
leaders who had opposed the Constitution became Republicans,
so did many who had favored it, including Madison and Jefferson.
At the state ratifying convention in New York, for example, representatives of the powerful Livingston and Van Cortlandt families
and even Melancton Smith voted for the Constitution and yet all
later supported the Republican cause—as did the anti-ratification
Clintonians. Of Pennsylvania's two initial senators, both staunch
supporters of the Constitution, one became a Federalist while the
other, Billy Maclay, rebelled against the Hamiltonian *"high-flying*
Federalists" of 1790–1791. Among Pennsylvania's first delegation
to the House, four leading members followed a similar course from
support of the Constitution to Republican affiliation, though the
later Republican leader Gallatin was an "Anti-Federalist" in 1787,
at least in his insistence on the addition of a Bill of Rights to the
Constitution as a condition for its adoption. In Virginia the "philosopher of the Constitution," Madison, was joined in the Republican
cause by anti-Constitution men like Patrick Henry (at the outset),
George Mason, and James Monroe, and also (soon or late) by such
pro-Constitutionalists as Wythe and Giles. Indeed, Giles was described by the anti-Constitutionalist Mason at the ratifying conven-

tion in Richmond as "a stripling of a lawyer at the Hotel this morning who has as much sense as one-half of us, though he is on the wrong [pro-Constitution] side." Another strong friend of the Constitution, Henry Lee, helped Madison to recruit Freneau for the *National Gazette* and proselytized for subscribers in Virginia, although he, like Patrick Henry, later turned Federalist. All told, of the twenty-two anti-Constitution members at the Virginia convention whose careers can be traced, thirteen became Republicans and nine became Federalists. Of the leading quartet of South Carolina Republicans in 1795–1796, Pierce Butler and Charles Pinckney had supported the Constitution, Hampton and Sumter had opposed it.

Similar catalogues could be made for other figures in the national or state arenas. Over-all, far too many pro-Constitutionalists became Republican leaders or cadre workers to sustain the notion that the "Anti-Federalists" simply metamorphosed into the Republican body of the next decade.

The point is highlighted in the Congressional divisions over Hamilton's proposals. In the House, where the stongest resistance to Hamilton's measures emerged, not more than a half-dozen members had been active against the new frame of government. Yet, in broaching federal assumption of the state debts, Hamilton touched off a stiff and continuing Congressional resistance which included friends of the Constitution. Insofar as there were lines from proponents or opponents of the Constitution to Federalists or Republicans, they were broken or badly bent in the debt assumption controversy. The party conflict Hamilton sparked was a new conflict.

Yet the crucial difficulty lies even beyond such questions as these. The argument of continuity oversimplifies the actual politics of ratification, particularly as it relates to parties. It persists in seeing the controversy as a single national battle, even a battle between "Federalist" and "Anti-Federalist" parties, each based on a broad and continuing cleavage of "business"-mercantile interests on the one side and "populist"-agrarian interests on the other. In fact, however, as we have seen, the question was not fought out on such clear, dualistic, national lines; and certainly the controversy was not fought out between national parties as we have defined parties. It is possible to trace important continuities (as well as discontinuities) between the alignments of interest groups and opinion aggregates for and against the Constitution on the one hand, and the alignments for the Federalists or the Republicans in the 1790's on the other. If parties are distinguished from other, looser political formations in terms of structure, function, and ideology, however, alignments of groups and bodies of opinion are only elements in the followings of parties, while parties as such are the durable structures of national leaders, local leaders or cadre, and actives, who perform the manifold functions of party. These functions, to be sure, include mobilizing followings as the foundations of party power, but the followings which parties mobilize are not the parties themselves. Thus, parties as structures had to be built new in the 1790's.

It is in terms of relationships between structure and following that the Republicans may be thought of as a new kind of political institution. The Federalists achieved party structure earlier and found a substantial popular power base; and yet they never quite transcended their ministerial, English-oriented, elitist origins. They represented interests, shaped opinion, and offered choices to the electorate; but they were not given to encouraging intraparty popular participation. They always depended on a comparatively close nucleus of leaders in government, and their attitude toward the public and electorate was always an uncertain mixture of condescension and fear. The Republicans on the other hand, although slower to form, finally established a close rapport between leaders and followers.

The difference is manifest in various facets of the Republican formation. Like the Federalists, the Republicans built out from a nucleus at the center of government, many of their early leaders also were notables, and Jefferson frequently showed at least a trace of condescension in his attitude toward the people, despite his republican philosophy. Yet the coruscations of republican sentiment in currents of opinion, in the Democratic and Republican Societies, and in the furor over foreign policy, before there was a Republican party, gave the party a broad potential power base in advance. Furthermore, from the outset the Republican leaders, cadres, and actives included a large number of "politicians," of men who made their careers and achieved prominence in politics, as contrasted with notables; and the Republicans were very nearly a "party of politicians," in Max Weber's term. In this situation, the party's leaders came to look to public opinion and to the electorate as vital powers to which the party should be responsive or responsible. Thus the Republican outlook developed in terms of leaders not only acting on their following but also interacting with it. The Republican founders were the first modern party-builders to conceive of a party in a distinctively democratic role, and thus the first to create a genuinely "popular" party.

The distinction between popular and other parties raises the important question of relationships between leaders and followers which facilitate intraparty democracy. A popular party may be thought of as an open modern party which combines substantial stability in structure with responsiveness to an extended popular following and with encouragement of popular participation or initiative in party action. Not all modern or successful parties are popular parties. Thus the Federalist formation remained a semi-elitist party in a democratic context. It never developed strong ties of popular participation or responsiveness to popular opinion, and it continued to look upon elections as referendums or plebiscites on its established policies rather than as expressions of popular influence. In short, it operated as a plebiscitarian rather than as a democratic or popular party, as many parties in other new nations were to operate in later years. As a plebiscitarian party, the Federalists were less concerned with popular participation or initiative than with popular mobilization or manipulation, less sensitive to popular opinion than determined to mold it.

The character of the Republican formation as a popular party may be seen in its tripodal foundations. At the center of government was the party "point," exercising or seeking to exercise governmental power and providing national leadership and co-ordination. In the localities were ranged the component units of party structure proper, composed of local leaders, local cadres, and local actives, together with such local organization as they may have achieved. Also in the localities were the varied elements of the party following. Between men at the point and local leaders, and also between local party workers and their followings, there were strong lines of direct, often face-to-face, or primary interaction. Between point and following, there was a more distant, secondary relationship of action, by leaders impinging on or influencing followers. The interaction between central leaders and following, which was so important to intraparty democracy, depended heavily on indirect relationships between leaders at the "point" and the popular following by way of local party units.

Tripodal Foundations of Developing Republican Party Structure

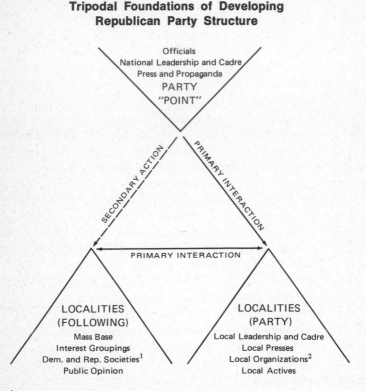

Officials
National Leadership and Cadre
Press and Propaganda
PARTY
"POINT"

SECONDARY ACTION

PRIMARY INTERACTION

PRIMARY INTERACTION

LOCALITIES
(FOLLOWING)
Mass Base
Interest Groupings
Dem. and Rep. Societies[1]
Public Opinion

LOCALITIES
(PARTY)
Local Leadership and Cadre
Local Presses
Local Organizations[2]
Local Actives

[1] In the period of activity or survival, 1793 to 1795/6.
[2] In development from 1796 to 1805.

Thus understood, Republican party structure was not only more modern and more complex than Federalist structure but also characterized by deeper and more varied foundations, which rested on broader segments of the population as a stable substructure or following. As "a body of men," in Burke's language, the Republicans were remarkably "united," determined to promote "the national interest" in terms of the principles on which they "agreed," and blessed with a degree of "popular confidence" which old-style faction politics could never have provided.

V

The popular character of the Republican party is related to another aspect of the role of parties in a democracy. This is their potential to redress imbalances of power by counteracting the advantages which social elites or favored interest groups would otherwise enjoy.

The problem is a persisting one. At the constitutional ratifying convention in New York in 1788, Melancton Smith had raised the issue sharply. The general "influence of the great," and their superior opportunities to join together for political purposes, he warned, would give them preponderant power over men of "the poor and middling class." In the Massachusetts convention Amos Singletary touched on the same idea, in a blunt, less-tutored way, when he declaimed against "these lawyers, and men of learning, and moneyed men," who would "get all the power," and "swallow up all us little folks, like the great *Leviathan*." So also did Jefferson in 1791, when he looked toward a greater "agricultural representation" to counter Hamilton's forces, and Madison in 1792 when he called for two parties in "balance."

There are many possible sources of power or influence which men or groups can draw on in politics. Two important ones are wealth and direct economic control over others, with the political ways and means which may follow. Another factor is superior social status or position, which can command deference from lesser members of the population or provide ready access to authority in the political system. Still further possible sources are learning; aptitude at such political skills as associations, legislation, or administration which lawyers so often display; and the quality of leadership that various groups can muster. In addition, consciousness of interests and awareness that these interests can be served through politics may enhance power or influence, as may the opportunity or ability to associate or organize for political action, and the unity or cohesion a group may achieve within its ranks. Moreover, wealth, established status, and education, taken together, tend to compound chances for acquiring leadership experience or ability, and those who hold such resources are also likely to generate strong political consciousness, find ready opportunities for association, and develop substantial unity of purpose and action. Against these sources is a factor for power which is basic to democracy, the superiority of numbers—and yet numbers by no means always prevail.

One after another of these sources of power was touched on directly or by implication in the forebodings of early Republicans. They saw them operating, as a general rule, to the advantage of persons of established privilege, or notables, who could command deference from the populace. Thus, Melancton Smith argued:

> *If the elections be by plurality . . . it is almost certain none but the great will be chosen, for they easily unite their interests: the common people will divide, and their divisions will be promoted by the others. . . I do not mean to declaim against the great . . . [but] will anyone say that there does not exist in this country the pride of family, of wealth, of talents, and that they do not command influence and respect among the common people?*

Without parties, such fears might indeed have been realized in America. Over the years, the advantages of those who enjoyed established property, position, and power were bound to be mitigated by the decline of deference patterns and by the rise of public opinion as an influence on government. Yet Jefferson himself was to find public opinion insufficient, and the discovery convinced him of the necessity of party action. The abstract notion of a popular majority in a pristine conception of democracy was one thing, the exigencies of partical action and results were another.

In the realm of such action, parties may serve as democratic counterforces to advantages in power. Only through time can they affect the economic and social conditions of "the poor and mid-dling class." They can exert a more immediate impact on other factors of power potential, however, if certain minimal conditions obtain in the populace, such as awareness of interests, some propensity for political participation or initiative, and receptivity to association or organization. Parties may offer leaders and leadership; and through their structure they may diffuse knowledge and skill in political tasks, stir the sense of political consciousness and efficacy, promote cohesion in their followings, and develop tools of association or organization. They may also counteract the weakness of "divisions" among "the common people," in Melancton Smith's words, by drawing them together into popular partisan combinations. Thus they may call forth and mobilize the latent strength of numbers. In open party systems, they may also clarify the options presented for decision by numbers in elections. Finally parties, as agents or catalysts for substantial segments of the populace, may effect transfers of power in government by peaceful, democratic means.

The first dozen years of American party politics witnessed such a transfer of power. At the outset the Federalists, with their power-favored components, were dominant. The course of elections from 1792 to 1804, however, showed a steady reduction in the effect of

Reversal of Federalist and Republican Power Positions

	Electoral Votes for President, 1792–1804			
	1792	1796	1800	1804
Federalist	77[a]	71	65	14
Republican	55[a]	68	73	162

[a] Electoral vote for vice-president; Republican vote as the total for George Clinton (50), Thomas Jefferson (not a candidate, 4), and Aaron Burr (1).

Taken from Bureau of the Census, *Historical Statistics of the United States, Colonial Times to 1957* (Washington, 1960).

their advantages as the Republican party brought its battalions to full strength. Without the development of a popular party or popular parties, such a transfer in government power could hardly have occurred.

The potential of parties for bringing about a balance of power is increased in two-party situations. Where two parties contend, the electorate can choose between readily understood, either-or options of personnel or policy—either Federalists or Republicans, either this policy bent or that, either this set of leaders or the other. Even in relatively free one-party systems, options are likely to be less open and clear than they are in two-party systems. In multifactional or multiparty situations, elections are more likely to be by plurality, with the frustrations for democratic choice Melancton Smith feared, and less likely to be by a majority, as Jefferson would have had it. Two-party systems, on the other hand, strengthen the fulcrum of popular choice on which leverages against imbalances of power may rest.

In any system, however, the ability of party to offset special advantages in power remains a potentiality which is not always realized. Whether it is depends not only on the responsiveness of the populace to parties, but also on the responsiveness of parties to the wishes of their followings. It varies, furthermore, with the significance of the options parties offer in elections and with their ability to carry choices made by the electorate into effect in government. In years to come, in sharply contended struggles, the Republicans were to labor to prove the democratic potentiality of a party in action.

Richard P. McCormick

THE FIRST AMERICAN PARTY SYSTEM

The organization of the national government under the Constitution stimulated the development of national political parties. But the key to party organization and identity became the contest for the Presidency. In contrast to the later party systems the Federalist and Republican direction came from the top down. Their organizations began in Congress and surrounded the Presidency. Federalist failure to fully exploit the presidential elections on a national basis contributed to the party's decline. Ultimately, Republican success, which undermined party unity, discipline, and partisan zeal, coupled with the changing political environment, brought the rise of the second, and differently structured, American party system.

The relationship between what I have chosen to call the first and the second American party systems requires some explanation. The parties that developed within the states and throughout the nation after 1824 were new parties. They did not have their origins

From *The Second American Party System* by Richard P. McCormick (University of North Carolina Press, 1966), pp. 19–31. Reprinted by permission.

in the same types of circumstances that had produced the first party system, they reflected the fact that significant alterations had taken place since 1820 in the environment of politics, and they differed in many characteristic respects from the early parties. There are, at present, divergent interpretations of the history of political parties, and because this study derives in part from my conception of what happened, I feel obliged to try to state very briefly my general understanding of the course of party development down to 1824.

Before the establishment of the new government under the federal Constitution, politics in the several states was conducted on a non-party basis. Throughout the colonial period, despite the vitality of representative institutions in all of the colonies, it has not yet been established that parties, in any acceptable sense of that term, can be said to have existed. Something approaching party politics can be detected In Rhode Island, Connecticut, New York, and Pennsylvania at certain periods, but the formations were either vague or transitory and bore little resemblance to the parties of the early federal era. The movement for independence gave rise to the elaborate organization of what might be considered a "Whig" party, but once the issue of allegiance—or independence—had been settled, this party became identical with the state, and the opposition, which had never possessed a comparable organization, was identified with treason. Meanwhile, under the new state constitutions, with their modest provisions for an expanded electorate and for new categories of elected officials, politics was conducted much as before. Candidates were self-nominated, or were put forward by "friends," and voters responded as individuals rather than in terms of any party identities.

Political interest generally was centered on contests for seats in the legislatures or on the claims of rival candidates for local offices. The township and the county—rather than the state—constituted the arena of electoral politics, and at those levels politics could be managed informally by the candidates themselves or by loose cliques of influential citizens. Within the legislatures groupings often existed, based on sectional, economic, or other factors, and there were leadership juntos that exerted a powerful influence on the course of legislation, on appointments, and perhaps on the selection of favored candidates in gubernatorial elections. But even in such states as New York and Pennsylvania, where factional groupings are most discernible, parties had not yet appeared.

The form of government instituted under the federal Constitution added new dimensions to American politics and stimulated the formation of political parties within the states and throughout the nation. The provisions that were made for choosing the president were to give a national scope to politics and encourage cooperation among political leaders in the several states in behalf of particular candidates. In quite a different way, the creation of a House of Representatives elected from the states by popular vote served to relate state politics to national politics. Whereas in 1790 parties had not been formed in any state, by 1800 in most of the states politics was being conducted on a party basis.

How these early parties emerged and what they represented remain subjects of controversy. My own view would be that a cleavage first developed within the administration, that is, within the circle closest to the president; that in due course a comparable cleavage manifested itself in Congress; that the formation of these congressional factions encouraged the building of parties in the states; and that the successive contests for the presidency in 1796 and 1800 contributed further to focus and heighten party feelings. The first American party system is distinguishable from the second in that parties seem to have formed within Congress before they formed in the states and before the contest for the presidency became the dominant consideration. The studies of Dauer, Charles, and Cunningham are all in general agreement on the fact that by 1795 the members of Congress had become aligned in two opposing groups, each with recognizable leaders, consistent positions on public issues, and—at least in the case of the Republicans—a mechanism, the caucus, for managing party affairs. These "interior-type parties," to use the terminology of M. Duverger, did not reflect pre-existing party alignments in the states nor were they created directly in response to the exigencies of presidential politics.

After parties had become delineated in Congress, a stimulus was given to the formation of similar party alignments in the states. But in 1796 a new factor was introduced into the situation with the contest for the presidency between Jefferson and Adams. Their candidacies served to dramatize the partisan cleavage that was emerging and to extend party strife beyond the bounds of the congressional districts to encompass an entire state. Although it is quite impossible to differentiate them at this time, it would appear that two very different national influences now became operative in party formation, the one emanating from the interior-type congressional parties and the other from the contest over the presidency.

Party formation proceeded rapidly during Adams' administration, nurtured by spectacular clashes over foreign policy as well as by intense controversy over domestic issues. As party lines became drawn ever more sharply, party leaders both within Congress and in the states viewed the issues of the day from a new perspective, that of party advantage. They also became increasingly engrossed, as 1000 approached, with mobilizing their forces for the presidential election. The area of party politics was broadened to include not only the struggle for control of Congress and the presidency but also contests at other levels of government. National alignments established a framework for conducting party politics within the states, and even within counties and townships.

By 1800, or shortly thereafter, two-party situations are observable in most of the states. These parties had to perform a variety of functions, depending in large part on the character of the constitutional and legal framework within which they operated. In general, they competed in the election of congressmen, presidential electors, governors, members of state legislatures, and other officials. But their functions, and their organizational structures, varied according to whether governors and presidential electors were chosen by the legislature or by popular vote, whether congressmen were elected from districts or from the state at large, whether the county was the major electoral unit or whether there were many different electoral units, and whether the balance between the parties was close or uneven.

The Republicans soon established themselves as the dominant party. Although the Federalists retained control of most of the New England states until after the War of 1812, they were confronted by a formidable opposition even in that region. Their position in the Middle States was weak, except in Delaware and Maryland, and they were unable to maintain their enclaves in the state of the Old South or to acquire a foothold in the newer states of the West. The presidential elections of 1804 and 1808 resulted in lopsided victories for the Republicans and demonstrated that they were in a dominant or competitive position in every state except Connecticut.

The Federalists were quite ineffectual outside New England and certain of the Middle States. The War of 1812, and the events leading up to it, occasioned a reversal in the declining fortunes of the Federalists. They increased their dominance in New England, won impressive triumphs in Maryland, Delaware, and New Jersey, and even threatened the control of the faction-ridden Republicans in New York. Rallying behind De Witt Clinton of New York in 1812, they nearly achieved victory. Had Pennsylvania not remained faithful to Madison, he would have been defeated in his bid for re-election. But this resurgence was short-lived, and it did not extend to the South or to the West. By 1817 the Federalists had lost all of the Middle States, except Delaware, and all the New England states, except Massachusetts. Indeed, after 1819 the only New England state in which the Federalists continued to compete on a state-wide basis with their opponents was Massachusetts, which finally succumbed to Republican control in 1823.

As parties formed within each state, more or less elaborate machinery was developed, chiefly for the purpose of securing agreement on candidates. It was recognized very early that if a party did not concentrate its entire vote behind a single candidate for each office it would dissipate its strength and risk defeat. The elaborateness of the party apparatus varied and was generally related to the intensity of party competition. Where the Federalists were non-existent or weak, as in Tennessee or North Carolina, little or no formal machinery was required to insure a Republican victory. But throughout most of New England and the Middle States, where the parties were often closely balanced, parties became highly organized at all levels of government.

It is probably significant that in most states the management of party affairs at the state level was ostensibly assumed by the caucus, made up of party members in the legislature and, in most instances, co-opted party leaders. New Jersey and Delaware were exceptional in that they pioneered in the use of the delegate state convention, and in Maryland, where there were no state-wide elections, there was apparently no formal machinery for managing state party affairs. Elsewhere, from Massachusetts to North Carolina, the legislative caucus held sway.

In New England, where the caucus type of party management was most highly developed and was used by both parties, nominations were made for state-wide elective offices and, in addition, a central committee was appointed to exercise supervision over local party committees. The result was a centralized, well-disciplined party apparatus. In New York and Pennsylvania, and probably Ohio as well, the caucus was a regular feature of party machinery but it did not wield so great an influence as it did in New England. In Virginia and North Carolina, because Federalist opposition was weak and the state was not an important unit of electoral activity, the caucus had very limited functions. Kentucky, Tennessee, and Georgia were so overwhelmingly Republican in sentiment that they developed little in the way of formal party machinery.

Below the state level, where some device was needed to make nominations for congressmen, members of the state legislature, and county officials, there was extensive use of delegate conventions. By around 1810 such conventions were commonly employed throughout New England and the Middle States and also in Ohio and, on rare occasions, in Kentucky. Elsewhere in the South and West such party management as there was in the counties and congressional districts was informal. The convention machinery, which was very complex in those states that had several different types of electoral units, was devised and used almost exclusively for the purpose of securing agreement on party candidates. It was not contrived for the purpose of formulating party policy. The legislative caucus, on the other hand, might concern itself with party policy and customarily adopted an address that served as a party platform.

It would be extremely important to be able to evaluate the degree to which both caucuses and conventions were subservient to party leaders and were "used" to lend a kind of sanction to decisions previously determined by the leaders. Were the caucuses and conventions genuine decision-making bodies, or were they, rather, cosmetic devices designed to give a color of popular authority to the leaders' decisions? Was the Virginia Junto—or the Essex Junto—

the agent of the caucus or its master? Such questions have been the subject of little investigation and would doubtless be difficult to answer, but they are crucial to any understanding of the nature and operation of parties.

The construction of a party apparatus was not the exclusive work of the Republicans, as has so often been suggested. On the contrary, the Federalists in a number of states vied with the Republicans in building elaborate party mechanisms. In New England, Republicans and Federalists employed essentially the same kind of party machinery. Elsewhere, conspicuously in Delaware and Maryland, the Federalists employed party machinery with as much energy and success as their rivals. Although the Federalists generally did not have an aversion to organizing, they were disposed—especially in New England—to favor a secret type of apparatus and were less inclined than were the Republicans to embrace the delegate-convention system.

Zealous as the Federalists were in developing party machinery in those states where they were strong enough to compete with the Republicans, they lacked effective organization at the national level. The Republicans used the device of the congressional caucus to secure agreement on candidates for the presidency and vice-presidency. The caucus had come into existence in 1796, and in 1800 it was convened secretly to endorse Aaron Burr as Jefferson's running mate. Subsequently it met openly every four years to perform its nominating function. The Federalists made similar use of the caucus in 1800, and they may have held some kind of secret caucus in 1804, but thereafter they abandoned the device, presumably because their congressional forces were so numerically weak and geographically concentrated as to give little authority to their pronouncements. In 1808 and 1812 Federalist leaders met in "convention" in New York City for the purpose of concerting their forces in the presidential campaigns, but by 1816 they had abandoned any hope of mounting an effective opposition in national politics.

The failure of the Federalists to sustain themselves as a national party brought about the decline and eventual disintegration of the first American party system. Many explanations of the unsuccessful career of the party could be advanced. It could be argued that they lacked effective leadership, that they espoused unpopular policies, that they were too strongly identified with the Northeast, and that they represented the outmoded survival of aristocratic traditions in an increasingly democratic society. There is certainly merit in all of these contentions. But in an admittedly narrow political context, the failure of the Federalists could be attributed to the fact that they did not appreciate the importance of the contest for the presidency in the American party system and did not fully exploit the potentialities of that event. Except in 1812, they virtually permitted the presidency to go to the Republicans by default; they made no determined, imaginative, or far-ranging efforts on behalf of their poorly selected candidates.

The Republicans, once they had won the presidency and dominance in Congress, obviously possessed many advantages over their rivals. In their efforts to achieve power, they had been stimulated to organize an offensive against the Federalists and had created the rudiments of party machinery and a strong *esprit de corps* among their adherents. The congressional caucus, the leadership assumed by the president, the availability of federal patronage, and the relationships that were established among prominent party figures all operated to strengthen and perpetuate the party. Of decided importance, too, was the availability of the successive members of the "Virginia dynasty"—Jefferson, Madison, and Monroe—whose prestige was sufficiently great to forestall the kind of crippling conflict over the succession that was to ruin the party in 1824. The early formation of the Virginia–New York alliance, despite the occasional restiveness of the junior partner, gave the party a strong base in the Middle States and by moderating its sectional character conferred on the Republicans a national appeal that the Federalists could not match.

Indeed, the party ultimately became the victim of its success. As the Federalists weakened, both at the national level and within individual states, the Republicans found it increasingly difficult to maintain the fiction that unity and discipline were essential to the party. Unity was destroyed by factionalism, partisan zeal subsided, party machinery fell into disuse, and even party identification came to have little meaning.

A cursory survey of the condition of parties in the states before the presidential election of 1824 reveals the extent to which the first

American party system had disintegrated. There were fourteen states, exclusive of South Carolina, in which at some time politics had been organized on the basis of competition between Republican and Federalist parties. In only five of these—Maine, Massachusetts, New Jersey, Delaware, and Maryland—were elections still being contested in terms of the old party designations. In seven other states—Vermont, New Hampshire, Connecticut, Rhode Island, Pennsylvania, Virginia, and North Carolina—the Federalists had either "retired" from electoral combat or had become so weakened through loss of members or fusion with Republican factions as to leave the Republicans virtually unchallenged. Only in New Hampshire and Pennsylvania were there major contests in elections, and these were between rival factions within the old Republican party. Elsewhere, elections were dull affairs that gave unopposed victories to Republican candidates, except when local personal rivalries aroused voter interest. Two other states—New York and Ohio—can be treated as special cases. In New York after 1820 the Bucktails and the Clintonians represented a distinctive type of party formation that had no counterpart elsewhere. In Ohio few vestiges of partisanship survived; even the Republican party had all but lost its identity and politics was conducted essentially on a personal basis.

There were nine states in which politics had never really been organized on the basis of the old party distinctions. In seven of these —Indiana, Illinois, Tennessee, Missouri, Alabama, Mississippi, and Louisiana—elections featured contests among personalities, local factions, and ethnic or sectional groupings rather than parties, although all of these states expressed a nominal Republican allegiance in presidential elections. Here, again, two other states presented special situations. In Georgia the curious alignment that pitted the Troup party against the Clark party bore no relationship to national parties and was so loose and informal in organizational structure as to constitute a kind of quasi-party. Kentucky offered a unique instance of state-oriented parties arising out of the agitation of a specific issue, the "relief" legislation that followed the Panic of 1819, and its Old Court and New Court parties endured until 1826. Most of the "no-party" states, as they may be vaguely designated, were not to experience genuine party formations until late in the

Jackson era. They form an interesting category, among other reasons, because they illustrate how politics could be conducted over a long period of years on a no-party basis.

The first American party system had been influenced by the constitutional and legal environment that prevailed during its formative years. By 1824, when we can begin to observe the formation of the second American party system, that environment had altered, and the party system was to reflect these new conditions. Most important of all was the gradual change that had taken place in the method of choosing presidential electors. In 1800 electors were chosen by the legislatures in ten states; in only two states were they chosen by popular vote of the state at large. By 1824 only six states still clung to the legislative choice, and after 1832 South Carolina was the only state that did not choose electors by popular vote from the state at large.

The significance of this change in the method of conducting presidential elections has been too little appreciated. The general adoption of the popular, state-wide voting procedure gave a popular dimension to the presidential contest, created or enhanced the need for state party machinery, weakened the political authority of legislative caucuses, occasioned the development of national party conventions, and made the presidential election the dramatic focal point of American politics. What most differentiated the Jackson elections from those in which Jefferson was involved was this change in the method of choosing electors.

Between 1800 and 1824, too, suffrage qualifications were liberalized in several states—notably Connecticut, New York, New Jersey, and Maryland—with the result that nearly all adult white males were eligible to vote by 1824 in presidential elections, except in Rhode Island, Virginia, and Louisiana. Voting was also facilitated by refinements in election machinery. In most states polling units—or election districts—were reduced in area in order to enable voters to exercise their franchise with a minimum of inconvenience. *Viva voce* voting, with its lack of secrecy and its cumbersomeness where long slates of officials had to be elected, was steadily replaced by the ballot, and—indeed—by the printed ballot. As state constitutions were revised, more and more offices were made elective, instead of appointive. The custom of holding state elections at different times from presidential elections persisted, however, and before 1832 only New York held both elections on the same day.

Whereas the first American party system had been effectively limited to fourteen states—in four of which the Republicans quickly achieved lopsided dominance—the second American party system would embrace twenty-three states by 1835. In the sense, then, of geographic and sectional extension, the party system acquired a new dimension, and the difficulties inherent in operating national parties was compounded. One of the remarkable achievements of the second party system was to be the extension of party politics to these newer states.

In many other respects, the political environment had altered between the age of Jefferson and the age of Jackson. As long as politics could be managed informally, without the agency of elaborate party apparatus, those who were recognized at the time as "the gentry" wielded decisive influence. But the role of the gentry declined when politics was organized on a party basis. The management of the party type of politics required considerable manpower, demanded the expenditure of large amounts of time on routine or trivial matters, called for talents that were by no means restricted to the gentry, and offered tangible rewards in the form of patronage and prestige to attract men from many ranks and callings. For increasing numbers of men, politics, or more specifically the operation of party machinery, was to become a vocation.

The new politics was also to reflect the revolution that was under way in communication and transportation. The vast multiplication of newspapers and magazines facilitated the transmission of news of politics, and the intense zeal of partisan editors was a potent factor in molding and heightening party spirit. The steamboats, canals, and ultimately the railroads enlarged the dimensions of the political community, making it feasible to hold state and national party conventions, stage "monster" rallies, conduct extensive campaign tours, and generally to manage politics on a grand scale.

The new brand of politics was to differ from the old, then, in part because of these changes in the environment. Politics was not to be conducted under the same conditions in 1830 as in 1800. The sum effect of new conditions was to give an increasingly popular tone to politics. Campaigns and elections assumed the aspect of folk festivals. Candidates and voters indulged themselves in a moving, engrossing, and satisfying dramatic experience. As many foreign observers astutely noted, politics in the United States filled a need that was met in many European nations by the pomp, ceremony, and pageantry of the great established churches. The opportunity to participate in spectacular election contests gave the humble citizen a sense of identification that was intensely important to him. No account of American politics can ignore this "dramatic" appeal, although we have scarcely begun to appreciate its peculiar force and its powerful consequences.

The second American party system derived in part from the experience acquired during the era of the first party system, in part from the changes occasioned by the altered environment of politics, and in part from the imagination and zeal of the leaders who were to give a new form to the party system. The transition from the old to the new system occurred at different times and under particular circumstances in each state, but throughout the nation as a whole the major influence on the development of parties was to be the contest for the presidency. With these general considerations in view, we can proceed to examine the course of party formation in the New England states, and subsequently in the Middle States, the South, and the New West.

V JEFFERSON AND THE AMERICAN DEMOCRATIC TRADITION

Vernon L. Parrington

JEFFERSON THE DEMOCRAT

Vernon L. Parrington's three-volume classic, Main Currents in American
Thought *(1927–1930), portrays American history with a pronounced sympathy
for the liberal Jeffersonian tradition that characterizes other Progressive
historical works. In Parrington's view Jefferson is the progenitor of the
American liberal tradition and American history is depicted as a continuing
struggle between Jeffersonian liberalism and Hamiltonian conservatism.*

The years following the great defeat were disastrous to the party of
agrarian democracy. Under the brilliant leadership of Hamilton the
Federalists went forward confidently, gaining daily a firmer grip on
the machinery of government, and establishing their principles in
far-reaching legislative enactments. Their appeal to the wealthy
classes, to those who made themselves audible above the clamor,
was electrical. Hamilton was the hero of the hour, and the effusive
approval that augmented with every added profit to the money
brokers, seemed to indicate that the country was enthusiastically
behind the Federalist policy. To what despondency the democrats
were reduced is revealed in Maclay's *Journal*, with its caustic com
ment on political measures and motives. But the tide was already at
the turn. The ideas let loose by the French Revolution were running
swiftly through America, awakening a militant spirit in the democracy. Antagonism to the aristocratic arrogance of Federalism, and
disgust at its coercive measures, were mounting fast. If that inchoate
discontent were organized and directed by a skillful leader, it might
prove strong enough to thrust the Hamiltonian party from power. To
that work Thomas Jefferson devoted himself with immense tact and
untiring patience. A master of political strategy, he spun his webs
far and wide, quietly awaiting the time when the bumbling Federalist
bees should range too carelessly in search of their honey. Accepted
at once as the leader of agrarian America, he was to prove in the

From *Main Currents in American Thought,* Vol. I, pp. 347–362, by Vernon L. Parrington, copyright, 1927, by Harcourt, Brace & World, Inc.; renewed, 1955, by Vernon
L. Parrington, Jr., Louise P. Tucker, Elizabeth P. Thomas, and reprinted by permission of the publishers. Notes to the original have been omitted. The title of
the selection is that of the editor.

course of a long life the most original and native of the political leaders of the time.

Despite the mass of comment that has gathered about Jefferson, the full reach and significance of his political philosophy remains too little understood. Uncritical praise and censure have obscured or distorted his purpose, and allied his principles with narrow and temporary ends. Detraction will not let him alone. The hostility of his enemies, as a recent biographer has remarked, has frequently taken "the peculiar form of editing his works or writing his life." For this distortion there is, perhaps, more than usual excuse. Certainly Jefferson is the most elusive of our great political leaders. Apparently inconsistent, changing his program with the changing times, he seemed to his enemies devoid of principle, a shallow demagogue who incited the mob in order to dupe the people. One of the most bitterly hated and greatly loved men in the day when love and hate were intense, he was the spokesman of the new order at a time of transition from a dependent monarchical state, to an independent republican state. Back of the figure of Jefferson, with his aristocratic head set on a plebeian frame, was the philosophy of a new age and a new people—an age and a people not yet come to the consistency of maturity, but feeling a way through experiment to solid achievement. Far more completely than any other American of his generation he embodied the idealisms of the great revolution—its faith in human nature, its economic individualism, its conviction that here in America, through the instrumentality of political democracy, the lot of the common man should somehow be made better.

From the distinguished group of contemporary political thinkers Jefferson emerges as the preeminent intellectual, widely read, familiar with ideas, at home in the field of speculation, a critical observer of men and manners. All his life he was a student, and his devotion to his books, running often to fifteen hours a day, recalls the heroic zeal of Puritan scholars. He was trained in the law, but he was too much the intellectual, too curious about all sorts of things, to remain a lawyer. For such a man the appeal of political speculation was irresistible, and early in life he began a wide reading in the political classics that far outweighed Coke and Blackstone in creative influence on his mind. He was equally at home with the English liberals of the seventeenth century and the French liberals of the eighteenth; and if he came eventually to set the French school above the English, it was because he found in the back-to-nature philosophy, with its corollary of an agrarian economics and its emphasis on social well-being, a philosophy more consonant with Virginian experience and his own temperament than Locke's philosophy of property. But he was very far from being a narrow French partisan, as has been often charged; rather he judged old-world theory in the light of its applicability to existing American conditions, and restrained his love of speculation by immediate practical considerations. The man of affairs kept a watchful eye on the philosopher in his study.

In the major doctrines of his political philosophy Jefferson was an amalgam of English and French liberalisms, supplemented by the conscious influence of the American frontier. That fusion early took place in his mind. The first bill that he introduced into the Virginia Assembly, at the age of twenty-six, was a bill to permit slave-owners to manumit their slaves; and his first published pamphlet, issued in 1774, rejected the legal reasoning of John Dickinson and Daniel Dulaney—supporting the parliamentary right to impose external taxation—and took its stand on the doctrine of natural right to local self-government and freedom of trade. When two years later he drafted the Declaration of Independence the fusion was complete. The strong influence of French humanitarianism is revealed in the passage on slavery that was stricken out on the floor of Congress, and more significantly in the change in the familiar phrasing of the several natural rights. Samuel Adams and other followers of Locke had been content with the classical enumeration of life, liberty, and property; but in Jefferson's hands the English doctrine was given a revolutionary shift. The substitution of "pursuit of happiness" for "property" marks a complete break with the Whiggish doctrine of property rights that Locke had bequeathed to the English middle class, and the substitution of a broader sociological conception; and it was this substitution that gave to the document the note of idealism which was to make its appeal so perennially human and vital. The words were far more than a political gesture to draw popular support; they were an embodiment of Jefferson's deepest convictions, and his total life thenceforward was given over to the work of providing such political machinery for America as should guarantee for all the enjoyment of those inalienable rights. If the fact that he set the pursuit of happiness above abstract property rights is to be taken as proof that Jefferson was an impractical French theorist, the critic may take what comfort he can from his deduction.

That Jefferson was an idealist was singularly fortunate for America; there was need of idealism to leaven the materialistic realism of the times. It was a critical period and he came at the turn of a long running tide. He watched the beginnings of the political shift in America from isolated colonial commonwealths to a unitary sovereign state; and his wide reading and close observation had convinced him that the impending change was fraught with momentous issues for the common man. He had meditated much on the social results of the slow oscillations in western civilization between social decentralization and centralization, with their contrasting political and economic structures; and he understood how the movement from simplicity to complexity—from freedom to regimentation—creates a psychology and an institutionalism that conducts straight to the leviathan state, controlled by a ruling cast, serving the demands of exploitation, heedless of the well-being of the regimented mass. This great lesson in social drifts he brought home to America. There had been created here the psychology and institutions of a decentralized society, with a corresponding exaltation of the individual and the breakdown of caste. In the broad spaces of America the old-world coercive state had dwindled to a mere police arrangement for parochial duties; the free citizen refused to be regimented; the several communities insisted on managing their affairs by their own agents. Such was the natural consequence of free economics; but with the turning of the tide would not the drift towards centralization nullify the results of earlier American experience and repeat here the unhappy history of European peoples?

To the philosophic mind of Jefferson, such a question was not academic, but urgent and vital. He had been bred in that older world, he believed passionately in the excellence of its virtues, and his political and social philosophy was determined by that experience. He sprang from a society deep-rooted in an agrarian economy, and he wished to preserve that society. Born on the Virginia frontier, he had never seen a hamlet so large as twenty houses before his eighteenth year; his neighbors and associates were capable and vigorous frontier democrats, who managed the affairs of local government with the same homespun skill that went to their farming. "It is not difficult," remarks an acute critic, "to see how the great principle of Jefferson's life—absolute faith in democracy—came to him. He was the product of the first West in American history; he grew up with men who ruled their country well, who fought the Indians valiantly. . . . Jefferson loved his backwoods neighbors, and he, in turn, was loved by them." This early conviction of the excellence of a freehold order was confirmed by later experience; wide observation and much travel convinced him that no other people was so favored by circumstance as the American, or so vigorously self-reliant. That such well-being resulted from a plastic economics, he regarded as self-evident; and from this economic freedom came political freedom. In his European travels he saw everywhere want and wretchedness dwelling in the shadow of the aristocratic state, and he could not dissociate the two. Political tyranny was the outward and visible sign of greater tyrannies that ran down to the very roots of society; the leviathan state was the convenient instrument through which those tyrannies took their heavy toll of the common well-being. America was a land of free men; it was exploited neither by an aristocracy nor a plutocracy. Surely there could be no greater or nobler ambition for an American than to assist in preserving his country from the misery that must attend a change from the present happy condition of democratic industry, to the serfdom of the European wage-taker and peasant.

To a mind imbued with such conceptions the appeal of the Physiocratic theory of social economics would be irresistible. The ground was prepared for the sowing of the seeds of the liberal French thought. With its emphasis laid upon agriculture, its doctrine of the *produit net*, its principle of *laissez faire*, and its social concern, the Physiocratic theory accorded exactly with his familiar experience, and it must have seemed to Jefferson that it was little other than a deduction from the open facts of American life. He had read much in the works of the Physiocratic group, and was intimately acquainted with DuPont de Nemours; and the major principles of the school sank deep into his mind and creatively determined his thinking, with the result that Jeffersonian democracy as it spread through Virginia and west along the frontier assumed a pronounced Physiocratic bias. The sharp struggle between Jefferson and Hamilton must be reckoned, in part at least, a conflict between the rival principles of Quesnay and Adam Smith, between an agrarian and a capitalistic economy. Much as Jefferson feared the ambitions of an aristocracy, he feared quite as much the creation of a proletariat. As he looked into the future he saw great cities rising to breed their Roman mobs, duped and exploited by demagogues, the convenient tools of autocracy; and counting the cost in social well-being, he set his face like flint against the rising capitalism. A free yeomanry he regarded as the backbone of every great people, the producers of the real wealth, the guardians of manly independence; and the number of factory workers measured for him the extent of social disease. It is this Physiocratic conception that explains his bitter hostility to protective tariffs, national banks, funding manipulations, the machinery of credit, and all the agencies of capitalism which Hamilton was skillfully erecting in America. Not to have hated such things Jefferson must first have emptied his mind of the teachings of experience and the lessons of the social philosophers.

In the *Notes on Virginia* there is a well-known passage that amplifies his favorite thesis that a sound American economy was an agrarian economy:

> *The political economists of Europe have established it as a principle, that every State should endeavor to manufacture for itself; and this principle, like many others, we transfer to America. . . . But we have an immensity of land courting the industry of the husbandman. Is it best then that all our citizens should be employed in its improvement, or that one half should be called off from that to exercise manufactures and handicraft arts for the other? Those who labor in the earth are the chosen people of God, if ever he had a chosen people, whose breasts he has made his peculiar deposit for substantial and genuine virtue. It is the focus in which he keeps alive that sacred fire, which otherwise might escape from the face of the earth. Corruption of morals in the mass of cultivators is a phenomenon of which no age nor nation has furnished an example. It is the mark set on those, who not looking up to heaven, to their own soil and industry, as does the husbandman, for their subsistence, depend for it on casualties and caprice of customers. Dependence begets subservience and venality, suffocates the germ of virtue, and prepares fit tools for the designs of ambition. . . . Generally speaking the proportion which the aggregate of the other classes of citizens bears in any state to that of its husbandmen, is the proportion of its unsound to*

its healthy parts, and is a good enough barometer whereby to measure its degree of corruption. While we have land to labor then, let us never wish to see our citizens occupied at a work-bench, or twirling a distaff . . . for the general operations of manufacture, let our work-shops remain in Europe. It is better to carry provisions and materials to work-men there, than bring them to the provisions and materials, and with them their manners and principles. . . . . The mobs of great cities add just so much to the support of pure government, as sores do to the strength of the human body. It is the manners and spirit of a people which preserve a republic in vigor. A degeneracy in these is a canker which soon eats to the heart of its laws and constitution.

Such was his attitude in 1782, an attitude identical with Franklin's. Thirty-four years later he had modified his views of industrialism. The bitter experience of the Napoleonic wars, with the hardships and losses visited upon neutral shipping, had convinced him of the need of domestic manufactures, and he was then deeply interested in improved machinery, new methods, original ventures. "We must now place the manufacturer by the side of the agriculturist," he conceded, or remain in economic dependence. But how much further the country should be industrialized, whether it "shall be proposed to go beyond our own supply" to compete in foreign markets, was not yet clear to him; the problem remained still to be determined whether "the *surplus* labor" would be "most beneficially employed in the culture of the earth, or in the fabrications of art." In such commentary Jefferson failed to measure the thrust of economic determinism that drives every people to go through with the Industrial revolution, once it is begun; but if we recall the primary principle of his political philosophy, that the "care of human life and happiness, and not their destruction, is the first and only legitimate object of good government," we may perhaps judge what would have been his attitude towards a centralized industrialism. He would have judged its desirability, not by the balance sheet of corporate business, but by the social ledger. As a social economist he could not think in terms of the economic man, nor simplify human beings to labor commodity, nor reduce the social tie to the cash nexus. It is inconceivable that he should have shared Hamilton's satisfaction at the contemplation of women and children—and many of the latter "of tender age"—wasting away in the mills; he was too social-minded for that, too much an idealist, too human in short. Though necessity might force him away from a simple agrarian economy, it does not follow that he would become partisan to a centralizing industrialism, with control vested in banking credit.

It is a common charge that Jefferson was consumed with suspicion, and it is set down against him as the mark of a mean and ungenerous nature. That in later years he was suspicious of fair-spoken advocates and plausible programs was as true of Jefferson as of Sam Adams; he had learned like the Boston democrat the virtue of the saying, *felix qui cautus,* and with so much at stake he would practice caution. He feared many things, for he was acutely aware of the incapacity of the heedless majority to defend itself against an able and instructed minority. As a child of an aristocratic age he fell into the mistake of visualizing that minority in the guise of a landed gentry, rather than in the guise of plutocracy; but in his quick fear of a minority he had all history as counselor. When he took his seat in Washington's cabinet his suspicions of the Hamiltonian program were quickly aroused. He believed that a monarchy was aimed at, and if that proved unattainable, then a highly centralized state designed to hold in check the democratic tendencies. His line of reasoning may be summarized thus: In consequence of the republican enthusiasm of the early years of the Revolution, democratic reorganization of the several state governments had been successfully achieved. Very great progress towards democracy had been made. Certain legislative acts of agrarian assemblies were now being turned against democracy, to invalidate it as a working system of government. But if agrarian majorities had used their power to enact laws beneficial to their interests, they were only applying a lesson learned from long experience with aristocratic legislatures. Such acts were no serious indictment of the democratic principle, and to make partisan use of them to justify curtailing the powers of the majority, was a betrayal of popular rights. And this, Jefferson believed, was the deliberate purpose of the Federalist leaders. Unable to stem the popular tide in the several commonwealths, the wealthy minority had devised a plan to superimpose upon the sovereign commonwealths a centralized federal government, so hedged about as to lie beyond the reach of local majorities, and hence able to override and nullify the democratic will. Once safely established, this federal government would gather fresh powers into its hands, until there emerged a rigorous machine, modeled after the British system, and as little regardful of the common interests. If this were not the Federalist purpose, why all the praise of the British system as the ripe product of experience, exactly adapted to the political genius of the English race?

In the matter of appeal to past experience, which provided the staple of Federalist argument, Jefferson discovered fresh grounds of fear. The past he looked upon as evil, and the record of experience was a tale of injustice and bitter wrong. He would not have America follow the trodden paths, for whither they led he knew too well. He would countenance no entangling alliances with old-world upper-class systems of statecraft, for such systems would reproduce in America the evils it should be the chief business of America to prevent. There must be erected here no counterpart of the European state; there must be no king, no aristocracy, no plutocracy; but a new democratic organization of government, in which the welfare of the whole people should be the sole concern.

> When I left Congress in '76 [he wrote as an old man] it was in the persuasion that our whole code must be revised, adapted to our republican form of government, and now that we had no negatives of Councils, Governors and Kings to restrain us from doing right, that it should be corrected in all its parts with a single eye to reason and the good of those for whose government it was planned.

Not past experience but present need should instruct America in drawing the plans of a new system of government and a new code of law. In analyzing the evils of European systems Jefferson came to certain conclusions that dominated all his later thinking, and that may be phrased thus: The political state tends inevitably to self-aggrandizement, the logical outcome of which is a political leviathan, too big and too complex for popular control. With sovereign powers vested in the hands of governmental agents, those agents lie under a constant temptation to corruption and tyranny, and in the end they align the powers of the state on the side of the most ambitious and capable. The greater the power of government, the ampler its revenues, the more energetic its administration, the more dangerous it may become to the rights of men; for where the prize is greatest, men struggle most ruthlessly, and what prize could be greater than the privilege of exploiting society in the name of the state? History knows no objective more tempting to the will to power, than the control of the absolute state. A government adequately socialized, intent solely upon furthering the common well-being, Jefferson would have been unanxious about. But such governments existed only in the dreams of Sir Thomas More and the Utopians; he could discover none such either in the past or present. Everywhere strong governments were little more than efficient tax-machines to support armies and provide subsidies and places for the minority. Against such forces of corruption the people struggle in vain.

If such was the common testimony of old-world experience—and no man who knew the inner workings of government there would deny it—what reason was there to expect that like causes would work unlike results in America? To what purpose was the talk of strong government encouraged amongst the holders of the public debt? To what end had lobbyists for the funding bill invaded the floor of Congress? It was idle to expect in America a nullification of the law, that where power sits within, corruption waits without. The love of power is universal. Most men are potential autocrats, the strong and capable may become actual autocrats. No man is good enough, no group of men, to be trusted with unrestrained powers —in America any more than in Europe. A centralized government in control of the tax-machine, and secure from popular restraint, would undo the results of the Revolutionary War. The movement to consolidate power, Jefferson asserted, was "but Toryism in disguise." "The generalizing and concentrating all cares and powers into one body . . . has destroyed the liberty and the rights of men in every government which has ever existed under the sun."

> Our country is too large to have all its affairs directed by a single government. Public servants at such a distance, and from under the eye of their constituents, must, from the circumstance of distance, be unable to administer and overlook all the details necessary for the good government of the citizens; and the same circumstance, by rendering detection impossible to their constituents, will invite the public agents to corruption, plunder and waste.

The practice of local home rule had grown up in America in response to native conditions; it had resulted from democratic needs; and Jefferson was too thoroughly American, too instinctively democratic, to overlook the significance of local sovereignties in a democratic philosophy. From the sharp contrast between American and European practice he deduced a cardinal principle, namely, that good government springs from a common interest in public affairs, and that such common interest is possible only when the field of activities is circumscribed. Set government apart from the people, or above them, and public interest is lost in a sense of futility. The danger of an encroaching tyranny by a superimposed sovereignty is made easy by the public lethargy in respect to distant and unfamiliar things, and establishes itself through the psychology of custom. Jefferson was never greatly concerned about stable government; he was very much more concerned about responsive government—that it should faithfully serve the majority will. He made no god of the political state. He had no conventional reverence for established law and order; he inquired rather what sort of law and order he was asked to accept, was it just or unjust. Changing conditions make ancient good uncouth, and established institutions tend to fall into dry-rot, or to become tyrannical. Men are more important than constitutions, and the public well-being is more sacred than statutes. An occasional revolution, he commented grimly apropos of the hue and cry over Shays's Rebellion, is salutary; if it does not come of itself it might well be brought about. Progress in government results from experiment; and it is easier and safer to experiment on a small scale than on a great. Inertia increases with size, and the more consolidated the government, the more unyielding it becomes. The longest delayed revolutions are the gravest.

In asserting the principle of the majority will, Jefferson like other democratic thinkers of the time, found himself countered by the argument of abstract justice. Vehement denunciation had greeted Paine's doctrine that what a nation chooses to do, it has a right to do. There can be no rights, it was confidently asserted, superior to the right. The people may legislate, but it remains to determine the validity of statutes in the light of justice; that which is unjust is *ipso facto* null and void. It was Coke's doctrine of judicial review, set up in America after its repudiation in England, and Jefferson's hostility to it was bitter. As an intellectual he had none of the lawyer's complacency with legal principles, or conceit of the law's sufficiency; and as a democrat he would not yield sovereignty into the hands of the judiciary. He had no veneration for the Common Law of England: it had grown up by slow accretions during centuries of absolutism; how should it be expected to answer the needs of a freer age? It must be purged of outworn elements, imbued with democratic sympathies. The Revolution had been fought in defense of rights that are broader and more human than legal principles; and to hand over those rights to be interpreted away by lawyers, seemed to him moonstruck madness. It was the law of Blackstone rather than of Coke that he feared most—that "elegant" canonization of the malign influences of Tory reaction, and that was so cried up by the smatterers and "ephemeral insects of the law" in America; whereas Coke "was as good a Whig as ever wrote":

> *Blackstone and Hume have made tories of all England, and are making tories of those young Americans whose native feelings of independence do not place them above the wily sophistries of a Hume or a Blackstone. These two books, and especially the former [Blackstone], have done more towards the suppression of the liberties of man, than all the million of men in arms of Bonaparte, and the millions of human lives with the sacrifice of which he will stand loaded before the judgment seat of his Maker.*

As Jefferson grew older his fear of judicial encroachment on the popular will became acute, but it shifted from distrust of the Common Law to concern over the Supreme Court. A strong and outspoken hatred of the Federal judiciary runs through all his later writings, and he lost no opportunity to popularize the thesis—"It is a misnomer to call a government republican, in which a branch of the supreme power is independent of the nation."

> *The great object of my fear is the Federal Judiciary. That body, like gravity, ever acting, with noiseless foot, and unalarming advance, gaining ground step by step, and holding what it gains, is engulfing insidiously the special governments into the jaws of that which feeds them.*

> *It is a very dangerous doctrine to consider the judges as the ultimate arbiters of all constitutional questions. It is one which would place us under the despotism of an oligarchy. . . . The Constitution has erected no such single tribunal, knowing that to whatever hands confided, with the corruptions of time and party, its members would become despots.*

As Jefferson watched Chief Justice John Marshall gathering all things within the purview of the Federal judiciary, preparing future strongholds by the skillful use of *obiter dicta,* legislating by means of judicial interpretation, nullifying the will of the majority, and with the power of repeal made nugatory by the complexity of the process, he saw clearly what the outcome would be. Surely that was no democracy where judge-made laws were enforced by bench warrants, and where the sovereign power lay beyond the immediate reach of the popular will. The government that he desired would not rest on the legal fiction of an abstract justice above statutes and constitutions, whereof a group of judicial gentlemen were the repositories and guardians. It would be like Paine's, "a plain thing, and fitted to the capacity of many heads"; for "where the law of the majority ceases to be acknowledged, there government ends; the law of the strongest takes its place."

Granted the truth of Jefferson's premises that power tends to contract to the hands of a few, and that all government of the few is vicious, then democracy is the only form of government under which an approximation to justice can be realized. A class will serve class interests. Government by an aristocracy is government in the interest of the aristocracy. For the staple argument of the Federalists, that gentlemen of principle and property alone may be intrusted with affairs of state, Jefferson had a quiet contempt. "I have never observed men's honesty to increase with their riches," he remarked. On the contrary, he regarded the "better sort of people" as a chief hindrance to the spread of social justice. The past had been evil because the past had been exploited by gentlemen of principle and property. They had kept government away from the people, and with their secret councils and secret diplomacy they had plundered the taxpayers and drenched nations in blood. Their selfish rivalries everywhere exacted a heavy toll of society and left behind a trail of poverty and wretchedness. The future would be better in the degree that mastery passed into common hands.

From the conclusions of his democratic premise he did not shrink. If it were indeed true that the people were beasts, then the democratic government of the future would be a bestial government— and even that might be better than the old arrangement of masters and slaves. But the American people whom Jefferson trusted were very far from beasts; he was convinced that they were honest and well-meaning; and if government were brought close to them, kept responsive to their will, a new and beneficent chapter in human history would open. The populistic laws passed by the legislatures of Rhode Island and New Hampshire, about which such an uproar was raised by fearful creditors, and which were urged as an argument against popular government, gave him no concern. He understood the ways of propaganda, and he never accepted judgment of the American people from the mouths of their enemies. The cure for the evils of democracy, he believed, was more democracy. The whole are far less likely to be unjust than the few; and if sovereignty does not rest in the majority will, where shall it lodge?

> Hume, the great apostle of toryism, says "the Commons established a principle, which is noble in itself, and seems specious [i.e., pleasing], but is belied by all history and experience, that the people are the origin of all just power." And where else will this degenerate son of science, this traitor to his fellow men, find the origin of just power, if not in the majority of the society? Will it be in the minority? Or in the individual of that minority?

The America of Jefferson's day was a simple world, with a simple domestic economy. More than ninety per cent were plain country folk, farmers and villagers, largely freeholders, managing their local affairs in the traditional way. There were no great extremes of poverty and wealth, no closely organized class groups. With its sharp restrictions on suffrage and the prestige accorded the gentry, it was still far from a political democracy; but it was hastening towards a more democratic order. Remote from the cesspools of European diplomacy, and not yet acquainted with imperialism, it had no need for a leviathan state. Economic conditions sanctioned a *laissez-faire* government, simple and unambitious. In such a world the well-known words of Jefferson's first inaugural address, justified themselves to all who did not seek to use the state for personal advantage.

> A wise and frugal government, which shall restrain men from injuring one another, which shall leave them otherwise free to regulate their own pursuits of industry and improvement, and shall not take from the mouth of labor the bread it has earned. This is the sum of good government, and this is necessary to close the circle of our felicities.

In one significant direction he would extend the scope of government—the encouragement of education. An intelligent people is necessary to a democracy; free schools are a sign of a free society. Tyranny thrives on ignorance and superstition, and every exploiting group fears popular education. Free himself in thought and action, believing in the unshackled commerce of ideas, hating all censorships, Jefferson accounted the founding of the University of Virginia his largest contribution to the well-being of his native commonwealth.

To all who profess faith in the democratic ideal Jefferson is a perennial inspiration. A free soul, he loved freedom enough to deny it to none; an idealist, he believed that the welfare of the whole, and not the prosperity of any group, is the single end of government. He was our first great leader to erect a political philosophy native to the economics and experience of America, as he was the first to break consciously with the past. His life was dedicated to the service of freedom, and later generations may well recall his words, "I have sworn upon the altar of God eternal hostility against every form of tyranny over the mind of man." Europe made Jefferson wholly American. From his studies in France he came to see that where men enjoy free access to the sources of subsistence, government is likely to be simple and honest, and society free and content; but where a policy of preemption has run its course, the function of government is seduced from its social purpose to perpetuate the inequalities which spring from the progressive monopolization of natural resources, with augmenting corruption and injustice. To preserve government in America from such degradation, to keep the natural resources open to all, were the prime desire and object of his life. That such an effort was foredoomed to failure, in presence of imperious forces that shape society beyond the capacity of political means to change or prevent, cannot detract from the nobility of his ideal, or the inspiration of his life. Among the greater thinkers of the constitutional period Jefferson remains by far the most vital and suggestive, the one to whom later generations may return most hopefully.

Richard Hofstadter

JEFFERSON THE PRAGMATIST

Changing, modern America, says Hofstadter, has "emptied the practical content out of Jefferson's agrarian vision of democracy," a process which was under way even in Jefferson's time. Did Jefferson then resolutely defend a dying society, a lost cause? No, says Hofstadter, rather because of his basic pragmatism and flexibility Jefferson "yielded a good part of his agrarian prejudices without sacrificing his democratic preferences," and the line between the Jeffersonians and the Hamiltonians, to be sure, was not that between two kinds of philosophy, but between two kinds of property.

Thus far Jefferson, with his faith in the farmers, his distrust of the urban classes, and his belief in the long-range value of rebellions and social disturbances, seems at the opposite pole from the Constitution-makers—and so he might have been if his political theory had been elaborated into a coherent system. But he had more in common with the conservative thinkers of his age than is usually recognized. His differences with the political theory of the Constitution-makers were differences of emphasis, not of structure. He shared their primary fears. He did not think that political constitutions could safely rely on man's virtue. In a letter to Mann Page in 1795 he declared that he could not accept the idea of the Rochefoucaulds and Montaignes that "fourteen out of fifteen men are rogues." *"But I have always found that rogues would be uppermost,* and I do not know that the proportion is too strong for the higher orders and for those who, rising above the swinish multitude, always contrive to nestle themselves into the places of power and profit." It was the upper, not the lower orders of society that he thought especially unregenerate—but it was Jefferson, too, who could use words like "canaille" and "swinish multitude." [1]

From *The American Political Tradition*, by Richard Hofstadter. Copyright 1948 by Alfred A. Knopf, Inc. Reprinted by permission of Alfred A. Knopf, Inc., and Jonathan Cape Ltd. Pp. 28–39. The title of the selection is that of the editor.

[1] Not long after the first edition of this volume was published, Mr. Charles Carroll Ransom, Jr., was kind enough to call to my attention that the phrase "swinish multitude" was in very common use among the Federalists in 1795, in connection with the controversy over Jay's treaty. Mr. Ransom suggests—I believe correctly—that Jefferson's own use of the phrase was ironic rather than literal. My original construction of his meaning seems therefore to have been incorrect. R.H.

Jefferson, of course, accepted the principle of balanced government and the idea that the people must be checked. "It is not by the consolidation, or concentration of powers, but by their distribution that good government is effected," he wrote in his autobiography. He designed a constitution for Virginia in 1776 which employed the principle of checks and balances and required property qualifications of voters.[2] Of the two houses of the legislature, only the lower was to be elected by the people: the senate was to be chosen by the house, as was the governor, so that two of the three parts of the lawmaking body were at one remove from the citizens. Five years later, criticizing the Constitution that had been adopted by Virginia instead of his own, he complained primarily of its lack of checks: the Senate and the House of Delegates were too much alike because both were chosen by the voters in the same way. *"The purpose of establishing different houses of legislation is to introduce the influence of different interests or different principles."* He continued:

> All the powers of government, legislative, executive, and judiciary, result to the legislative body. The concentrating these in the same hands is precisely the definition of despotic government. It will be no alleviation that these powers will be exercised by a plurality of hands and not by a single one. One hundred and seventy-three despots would surely be as oppressive as one. . . . As little will it avail us that they are chosen by ourselves. An elective despotism was not the government we fought for, but one which should not only be founded on free principles, but in which the powers of government should be so divided and balanced among several bodies of magistracy, as that no one could transcend their legal limits without being effectually checked and restrained by the others.

This would have been accounted sound doctrine at the Philadelphia Convention of 1787. A government that does not divide and balance powers in a system of checks is precisely what Jefferson means by despotic; the fact that the governing body is chosen by the people does not qualify his complaint; such a government, without checks, is merely "an elective despotism." Jefferson, then,

---

[2] And yet in his *Notes on Virginia* he voiced his displeasure with the limited suffrage of the state: "The majority of the men in the State who pay and fight for its support, are unrepresented in the legislature, the roll of freeholders entitled to vote not including generally the half of those on the roll of the militia, or of the tax-gatherers."

refused to accept simple majority rule, adopting instead the idea that "different interests or different principles" should be represented in government.

All this sounds close to the theories of Madison and Adams. In fact, Jefferson did not differ with them strongly enough to challenge their conservative writings of the constitutional period. In 1788 he wrote to Madison praising the *Federalists* as "the best commentary on the principles of government which ever was written." Two years later, advising his nephew Thomas Mann Randolph on a course of reading, Jefferson praised Locke's work as being "perfect as far as it goes," and then added: "Descending from theory to practice, there is no better book than the Federalist." In 1787 he told John Adams that he had read his *Defence* "with infinite satisfaction and improvement. It will do great good in America. Its learning and its good sense will, I hope, make it an institute for our politicians, old as well as young." [3]

When the text of the federal Constitution of 1787 reached him in France, Jefferson confessed to Adams that he was staggered at what had been attempted, but soon recovered his composure. He informed Madison that he saw many good features in it, but objected strongly to two things: the absence of a bill of rights (later included in the first ten amendments), and the eligibility of the president for more than one term. In the end he gave it a substantial endorsement: "It is a good canvas, on which some strokes only want retouching." His regard for it grew with the years.

As much as Madison or Morris, Jefferson disliked the idea of city mobs—"the panders of vice and the instruments by which the liberties of a country are generally overturned"—but he believed that they would not emerge in the calculable future because America's lands would be open to make substantial farmers of the ragged and discontented. In his First Inaugural he said that the land would last the American people "to the hundredth and thousandth generation"! The United States would be a nation of farmers, tilling their own soil, independent, informed, unexcitable, and incorruptible. Such a na-

---

[3] Later he also endorsed heartily John Taylor's *An Inquiry into the Principles and Policy of the Government of the United States* (1814), which was in large part a headlong assault on Adams's theories. This of course was after the Federalist-Republican antagonism had ripened.

tional destiny, he must have felt, would be secured by the Louisiana Purchase.

The future, then, would be founded on a propertied class in a propertied nation. Jefferson leaned strongly to the idea that a propertied interest in society is necessary to a stable political mentality. In 1800 he wrote a friend that he had always favored universal manhood suffrage; but this was one of those theoretical notions to which he was not firmly wedded. "Still I find some very honest men," he added, "who, thinking the possession of some property necessary to give due independence of mind, are for restraining the elective franchise to property." His 1776 draft of a constitution for Virginia had required that voters own either a freehold estate of twenty-five acres in the country or one fourth of an acre in town, or pay taxes within two years of the time of voting. Never did Jefferson try to introduce universal manhood suffrage anywhere.[4]

The outstanding characteristic of Jefferson's democracy is its close organic relation to the agrarian order of his time. It seems hardly enough to say that he thought that a nation of farmers, educated, informed, and blessed with free institutions, was the best suited to a democratic republic, without adding that he did not think any *other* kind of society a good risk to maintain republican government. In a nation of large cities, well-developed manufactures and commerce, and a numerous working class, popular republicanism would be an impossibility—or at best an improbability.

Certainly the balance of Jefferson's good society is a tenuous thing: the working class is corrupt; merchants are corrupt; speculators are corrupt; cities are "pestilential"; only farmers are dependably good. Sunder human nature from its proper or "natural" nourishment in the cultivation of the soil and the ownership of real property, and he profoundly distrusts it. Sunder democracy from the farm and how much more firmly does he believe in it than John Adams? Yet this is just what the relentless advance of modern indus-

[4] It is important to add, however, that in 1776 Jefferson proposed that Virginia grant fifty acres of land to every white of full age who had less than that amount. This would have made suffrage practically universal. It also illustrates his belief in broadening economic opportunities where free land made the policy possible, as well as the vital linkage in his mind between landed property and democracy. He was, at this time, more democratic in his conception of the economic base of government than in his conception of the structure of government.

trial capitalism has done: it has sundered four fifths of society from the soil, has separated the masses from their property, and has built life increasingly on what Jefferson would have called an artificial basis—in short, has gradually emptied the practical content out of Jefferson's agrarian version of democracy. This process had its earliest beginnings during Jefferson's lifetime, and, as we shall see, he yielded a good part of his agrarian prejudices (like the pragmatic, undoctrinaire soul that he was) without sacrificing his democratic preferences. But although he clung to his humane vision of democracy, he left it without the new economic rationale that it required.

In after years Jefferson declared that the struggle between his party and the Federalists was one between those who cherished the people and those who distrusted them. But he had been associated with a number of men like Elbridge Gerry, Pierce Butler, Charles Pinckney, and Edmund Randolph who did not cherish the people in the least, and the differences in abstract principle were hardly intense enough to account for the fierceness of the conflict or for the peculiar lines along which it was drawn. Although democratically minded Americans did stand with Jefferson, the line of division was essentially between two kinds of property, not two kinds of philosophy.

The Federalists during Hamilton's service as Secretary of the Treasury had given the government a foundation of unashamed devotion to the mercantile and investing classes. Through his method of funding the national debt, through his national bank, and through all the subsidiary policies of the government, Hamilton subsidized those who invested in manufactures, commerce, and public securities, throwing as much of the tax burden as possible on planters and farmers. The landed interests, however, were in a majority, and it was only a matter of time before they could marshal themselves in a strong party of their own. Jefferson's party was formed to defend specific propertied interests rather than the abstract premises of democracy, and its policies were conceived and executed in the sober, moderate spirit that Jefferson's generation expected of propertied citizens when they entered the political arena.

When Jefferson was elected in 1800, the more naïve Federalists, frightened to the marrow by their own propaganda, imagined that the end of the world had come. Fisher Ames anticipated that he would soon scent "the loathsome steam of human victims offered in sacrifice." Among those who knew the President-elect, however, there was no such hysteria—especially not among insiders who had private knowledge of the circumstances under which he had been chosen.

The election of 1800 was unique in American history. Because no distinction had yet been made in the Constitution between ballots cast for presidential and vice-presidential candidates, Jefferson and his running mate, Aaron Burr, won the same number of votes in the electoral college. The tied contest was thrown into the House of Representatives, where it fell to Federalist Congressmen to choose between two Republicans. To some this seemed merely a choice of executioners; others, looking upon Jefferson as their supreme enemy, gravitated naturally toward Burr. Not so Alexander Hamilton, who had long been Burr's political rival in New York. In a remarkable letter to a Federalist Representative, Hamilton gave a shrewd estimate of Jefferson's character. He admitted that his old foe's views were "tinctured with fanaticism; that he is too much in earnest with his democracy." But it is not true, he continued, in an appraisal that is as penetrating in substance as it is unfair in phrasing,

> that Jefferson is zealot enough to do anything in pursuance of his principles which will contravene his popularity or his interest. He is as likely as any man I know to temporize—to calculate what will be likely to promote his own reputation and advantage; and the probable result of such a temper is the preservation of systems, though originally opposed, which, being once established, could not be overturned without danger to the person who did it. To my mind a true estimate of Mr. Jefferson's character warrants the expectation of temporizing rather than a violent system. . . . Add to this that there is no fair reason to suppose him capable of being corrupted, which is a security that he will not go beyond certain limits.

Not entirely satisfied with Hamilton's advice, Federalist leaders sought for assurance from Jefferson. The Virginian refused to commit himself in response to direct approach, but a friend who sounded him out informally was able to convey to the Federalists the comforting knowledge that Jefferson's intentions were moderate. That Jefferson abandoned any of his original plans, and in that sense bargained away any principles to win the office, is extremely unlikely; but when he entered the White House it was after satisfying the Federalists that he and they had come to some kind of understanding.

A little thought on the difficult position in which Jefferson now found himself should convince anyone that for a man of his moderate temperament there was small choice in fundamental policy. The Hamiltonian system, now in operation for twelve years, had become part of the American economy. The nation was faring well. To unscramble Hamilton's system of funding, banks, and revenues would precipitate a bitter struggle, widen the breach between the classes, and drive moderates out of the Republican ranks; it might bring a depression, perhaps even rend the Union. And when the strife was over, there would always be the need of coming to terms with the classes that carried on commerce and banking and manufactures. Further, even if the landed interests were charged with the burden of Hamilton's debts, there was always the probability that they were better off when the system was working smoothly than they would be after a ruinously successful assault upon it. Jefferson, in short, found himself in a position much like that of modern social-democratic statesmen who, upon attaining power, find themselves the managers of a going concern that they fear to disrupt. Just as they have been incapable of liquidating capitalism, so Jefferson found himself unable to keep it from growing and extending its sway over the agrarian masses. Instead he wisely confined himself to trimming carefully at the edges of the Hamiltonian system.

Jefferson's First Inaugural Address was a conciliatory document contrived to bind up the wounds of the bitter period from 1798 to 1800 and to attract moderate Federalists to his support. "We are all republicans—we are all federalists," he declared. Soon the President was writing to Dupont de Nemours in words that show how well Hamilton had taken his measure:

> When this government was first established, it was possible to have kept it going on true principles, but the contracted, English, half-lettered ideas of Hamilton destroyed that hope in the bud. We can pay off his debts in 15 years: but we can never get rid of his financial system. It mortifies me

to be strengthening principles which I deem radically vicious, but this vice is entailed on us by the first error. In other parts of our government I hope we shall be able by degrees to introduce sound principles and make them habitual. What is practicable must often control what is pure theory.

Jefferson kept his promises to friends and enemies alike. So successfully did he whittle away at the Federalist machinery by reducing expenditures that he was able to abolish the hated excise duties that had stirred up the Whisky Rebellion and still make great inroads on the public debt. He tried hard to tame the federal judiciary—the last arm of the national government still under Federalist control—but to little effect. Through the Louisiana Purchase he widened the area for agrarian expansion. In 1811, two years after his terms were over, his party also allowed the First Bank of the United States to die upon the expiration of its charter.

But no attack was made upon other vital parts of the Hamiltonian system. No attempt was made to curb such abuses as speculation in public lands; nor did the well-organized Republican machines try hard to democratize the mechanics of government in the states or the nation. Limitations on the suffrage, for example, were left untouched. Professor Beard observes that the Republican states were "no more enamored of an equalitarian political democracy" than the Federalist states. Had Jefferson suggested a broad revision of the suffrage, many of his state leaders who had no use for theoretical democracy would have looked at him askance; if he had been the crusading democrat of Jeffersonian legend he could not have been so successful a machine leader.

Since his policies did not deviate too widely from those of the Federalists, Jefferson hoped to win over the moderates from their ranks and planned to use the patronage in doing so. "If we can hit on the true line of conduct which may conciliate the honest part of those who were called federalists," he wrote to Horatio Gates soon after taking office, "and do justice to those who have so long been excluded from [the patronage], I shall hope to be able to obliterate, or rather to unite the names of federalists and republicans."

In politics, then, the strategy was conciliation; in economics it was compromise. Soon the Republican machines began flirting with the financial interests they had sworn to oppose. Republican state legislatures issued charters liberally to local banks, which, in turn, tended to cleave to the Republican Party in politics. Jefferson gave his benediction to this process of mutual accommodation. When the Bank of Baltimore applied to the administration for assistance, he wrote to Secretary of the Treasury Albert Gallatin:

> *It is certainly for the public good to keep all the banks competitors for our favors by a judicious distribution of them and thus to engage the individuals who belong to them in support of the reformed order of things or at least in an acquiescence under it.*

And:

> *. . . I am decidedly in favor of making all the banks Republican by sharing deposits among them in proportion to the disposition they show. . . . It is material to the safety of Republicanism to detach the mercantile inter- est from its enemies and incorporate them into the body of its friends. A merchant is naturally a Republican, and can be otherwise only from a vitiated state of things.*

John Adams, in the quiet of his retirement at Quincy, might have been amused to see a new elite, closely linked to the fiscal interests, emerging in the heart of the Republican Party, but the militant agrarian John Taylor was deeply discouraged. In 1811 he wrote:

> *. . . those who clearly discerned the injustice and impolicy of enriching and strengthening the federalists by bank or debt stock, at the publick expense, will seldom refuse to receive a similar sinecure. In short, a power in the individuals who compose legislatures, to fish up wealth from the people, by nets of their own weaving . . . will corrupt legislative, executive and judicial publick servants, by whatever systems constituted.*

The inability of the Republicans to follow a pure policy of demo- cratic agrarianism was matched by their inability to fashion a posi- tive theory of agrarian economics. The predominant strain in their economic thinking was laissez-faire, their primary goal essentially negative—to destroy the link between the federal government and the investing classes. Acute and observant, their economic writing was at its best in criticism, but it offered no guide to a specific agrarian program. They had no plan; indeed, they made a principle of planlessness.

Jefferson has been described as a physiocrat by many writers—among them V. L. Parrington—but there is little more substance to this notion than there is to the preposterous idea that he was influenced chiefly by French thought. He was naturally content to remain an eclectic in economics. "No one axiom," he wrote to J. B. Say in 1815, "can be laid down as wise and expedient for all times and circumstances." Their defense of free trade was responsible for whatever appeal the physiocrats had for Jefferson; but after he read *The Wealth of Nations* he became a convert to the doctrines of Adam Smith.[5]

Like other theorists of the "natural law" era, Jefferson was quite ready to believe that the "natural" operations of the system of self-seeking private enterprise were intrinsically beneficent and should not normally be disturbed by government. In his First Inaugural he called for "a wise and frugal government, which shall restrain men from injuring one another, *which shall leave them otherwise free to regulate their own pursuits of industry and improvement,* and shall not take from the mouth of labor the bread it has earned."[6] In a letter to Joseph Milligan, April 6, 1816, in which he discussed the proper limits of taxation, he concluded that the state ought not be aggressive in redistributing property:[7]

> *To take from one, because it is thought his own industry and that of his fathers has acquired too much, in order to spare to others, who, or whose fathers have not exercised equal industry and skill, is to violate arbitrarily the first principle of association, "the guarantee to everyone a free exercise of his industry and the fruits acquired by it."*

John Taylor, perhaps the cleverest of the agrarian writers, likewise believed that "it is both wise and just to leave the distribution of property to industry and talents."

This conception of state policy was not anti-capitalist but anti-mercantilist. Jefferson and his followers had seen the unhappy ef-

[5] Ultimately he came to prefer J. B. Say's adaptations of Smith as more lucid and readable, and showed much admiration for the work of Destutt de Tracy.
[6] In his Second Inaugural, when he listed the things government should do, he asserted that it should maintain "that state of property, equal or unequal, which results to every man from his own industry or that of his fathers."
[7] He added that if an individual's wealth becomes so overgrown that it seems a danger to the State, the best corrective would not be discriminatory taxation but a law compelling equal inheritance in equal degree by all the heirs.

fects of British governmental interference in American economic affairs, and they regarded Hamilton's system of state economic activity ("the contracted, English, half-lettered ideas of Hamilton") as merely a continuation at home of English economic ideas. Hamilton had set the government to helping the capitalists at the expense of the agrarians. The Jeffersonian response was not to call for a government that would help the agrarians at the expense of the capitalists, but simply for one that would let things alone. Where modern liberals have looked to government interference as a means of helping the poor, Jefferson, in common with other eighteenth-century liberals, thought of it chiefly as an unfair means of helping the rich through interest-bearing debts, taxation, tariffs, banks, privileges, and bounties. He concluded that the only necessary remedy under republican government would be to deprive the rich of these devices and restore freedom and equality through "natural" economic forces. Because he did not usually think of economic relationships as having an inherent taint of exploitation in them, he saw no necessity to call upon the state to counteract them. It was not the task of government to alter the economic order: the rich were not entitled to it and the poor would not find it necessary.

Jefferson rejected from his political philosophy the idea that one man has any intrinsic superiority over another; but he implicitly and perhaps unwittingly took it back again when he accepted competitive laissez-faire economics with its assumption that, so long as men were equal in law, and government played no favorites, wealth would be distributed in accordance with "industry and skill." Such a philosophy seemed natural enough to American farmers and planters who were in their own rights entrepreneurs, businessmen, exporters, and often, in a small way, speculators with a weather eye on land values—men accustomed to stand on their own feet.

In due time, of course, Jeffersonian laissez-faire became the political economy of the most conservative thinkers in the country. Fifty years after Jefferson's death men like William Graham Sumner were writing sentences exactly like Jefferson's and John Taylor's to defend enterprising industrial capitalists and railroad barons from government regulation and reform. And one hundred years after the Jeffersonians first challenged John Adams at the polls, William Jennings Bryan, leading the last stand of agrarianism as an independent

political power, was still striving to give his cause the color of
respectability by showing that, after all, the farmer too was a
businessman!

Merrill D. Peterson

TWENTIETH-CENTURY DEMOCRACY AND THE CRISIS OF JEFFERSONIAN PHILOSOPHY

Peterson's The Jefferson Image in the American Mind *is, as he puts it, "not
a book on the history Thomas Jefferson made but a book on what history
made of Thomas Jefferson." As have Parrington, Hofstadter, and so many
other contemporary historians and public figures, Peterson seeks to evaluate
the applicability of the Jeffersonian ideal in the twentieth century. Did Jefferson dream the American dream and then betray it? Have Jefferson's
egalitarian principles been "grafted on a greedy, middle-class Hamiltonian
capitalism?" Why has the "disintegration of the Jeffersonian philosophy of
government" brought about the "ultimate canonization" of Thomas Jefferson?*

> *Jefferson's objects have not fallen out of date. They are our own objects,
> if we be faithful to any ideals whatever; and the question we ask our-
> selves is not, How would Jefferson have pursued them in his day? but
> How shall we pursue them in ours? It is the spirit, not the tenets of the
> man by which he rules us from his urn.*
>
> Woodrow Wilson, Jefferson Day Address
> New York City, April 16, 1906

The crisis of American democracy in the twentieth century has been
at heart a crisis in the Jeffersonian philosophy. Its economic base
in a simple agrarian order of small property owners was gone. Some
of its ruling principles—private property, economic freedom, limited
government—were appropriated by the corporate powers of industrial capitalism. The Jeffersonian philosophy defined liberty largely

in terms of the absence of governmental restraint. The conception seemed not only useless but positively harmful in a society where the aggressions against the individual were economic rather than political, begging to be met by more rather than less government. Other Jeffersonian ideas were similarly turned upside down: for example, "trust the people." Experience seemed to prove that the more power was diffused among the people, the more oligarchical and irresponsible the governing authority became. In this topsy-turvy political universe, the inherited philosophy could not readily clarify the great issues of the time or serve democratic progress.

Traditional concepts were thus called up for review and revision, first in the Progressive Movement at the beginning of the century and later in the New Deal. Progressivism, although it lacked unity of theory or of program, possessed an underlying critical spirit which justified Parrington's characterization, "a great stock-taking adventure." Walter Weyl captured this spirit in the opening sentences of *The New Democracy,* in 1912. "America today is in a somber, soul-questioning mood. We are in a period of clamor, of bewilderment, of an almost tremulous unrest. We are hastily revising all our social conceptions. We are hastily testing all our political ideals. We are profoundly disenchanted with the fruits of a century of independence." Disenchantment with "our old time democracy" involved for Progressives like Weyl a large measure of disenchantment with Jefferson. To hasten the advance toward the New Democracy, wherein the state would become the overlord of many rights previously held to be private, Americans must escape from the thralldom of the individualistic tradition. "Our hand is stayed by ancient political ideas which still cumber our modern brains; by political heirlooms of revered—but dead—ancestors," Weyl said.

The political idiom of these advanced Progressives was distinctly Hamiltonian. Many of them were, in fact, admirers of the impetuous adventurer whose administrative exploits at another time of crisis they hoped to see duplicated. But other Progressives spoke in the Jeffersonian idiom without, however, suffering the constraints of inherited doctrine. The difference between Bryan, who epitomized the code-Jeffersonian, and Woodrow Wilson, the new evangel of the Democratic party, was in this respect the difference between the leader for whom Jefferson was the father of a set creed and the leader for whom Jefferson represented the "spirit of democracy." The two idioms of Progressive thought clashed most significantly in the presidential contest of 1912. The debate between Wilsonian New Freedom and Theodore Roosevelt's New Nationalism carried the traditional dialogue of Jefferson and Hamilton to the crossroads of American democracy in this century.

For reasons that are generally well known, the nation retreated from Progressivism after the First World War. The extent of the retreat, so far as it affected public policy, is usually exaggerated; but the fact that during the nineteen-twenties Hamilton was a saint of Republican reaction and Jefferson was torn between agrarian and urban Democrats suggests the reversion to an earlier ideological configuration. The Democratic party, crushed and broken, once again commenced the search for a "new Jefferson," and seemed to find him at last in the person of Franklin D. Roosevelt. The Roosevelt New Deal replaced the party's tradition of individualistic democracy, which had ended in its own negation, with a shapeless Progressive synthesis accenting a pragmatic approach to grave national problems. The New Deal's importance for Jefferson's reputation was twofold. First, the voice of its opposition was Jeffersonian. The alternate Hamiltonian road to progressive democracy was not reopened; conservatives on the right and, to a lesser degree, radicals on the left, sought the support of the Jefferson symbol the New Deal claimed as its own. Second, the New Deal killed the Jeffersonian philosophy as a recognizable and usable tradition in American government and politics. As if in acknowledgment of the act, some said in requital for it, the Roosevelt administration built a great national temple to Jefferson's memory. In the death of the political tradition, the *American* hero was full-born at last.

Every society needs a sense of continuity with its history, a set of commonly diffused symbols rooted out of the past to manifest its modes of action and evoke its ideals. But the symbols, unless they are constantly revised to meet the tests of an ever changing national life, may drag the society down to disaster. The proposition of Alfred North Whitehead may be taken as self-evident:

The art of free society consists in the maintenance of the symbolic code; and secondly in fearlessness of revision, to secure that the code serves those purposes which satisfy an enlightened reason. Those societies which cannot combine reverence to their symbols with freedom of revision, must ultimately decay either from anarchy, or from the slow atrophy of a life stifled by useless shadows.

In the American polity, Jefferson and Jeffersonian philosophy consistently furnished important elements of the "symbolic code." They survived the great ordeal of the nineteenth century. Would they survive the ordeal of the twentieth century? They would not unless made serviceable to a society far different from the one Jefferson knew. Despite the restored prestige of Jefferson symbol and precept in 1900, there were alarming signs of that atrophy Whitehead mentions and, partly because of it, general uneasiness with Jeffersonian concepts. The possibility presented itself of a social and political reconstruction under Hamilton's star rather than Jefferson's. But this was not destined to be. The process of revision, although it was more than political, was completed during the Roosevelt era. It was fearless; much that had always passed as Jeffersonian dropped out of the symbolic code. Whether the progressive synthesis of the New Deal satisfied "an enlightened reason" is a question about which men may still differ. But it is irreversible. And the fact that the Jefferson Memorial rose from the Potomac in 1943 testifies to the artistry with which the New Deal combined reverence for the symbol and freedom of revision.

*   *   *

Jefferson and the New Deal

The New Deal lacked a consistent philosophy, but it possessed a sense of tradition, a faith in democratic ideals, a set of symbols and conventions, which served some of the purposes of a philosophy. Addressing the Jefferson Day dinner at St. Paul, Minnesota during his pre-convention campaign in 1932, Franklin D. Roosevelt called for the renewal of the old social contract on the new terms of American life. The "long and splendid" day of Jeffersonian individualism was over, Roosevelt announced. Americans who shared Jefferson's faith in the ability of free men to work out their own destiny might safely undertake to plan and direct their social and economic life. "Government with him was a means to an end, not an end in itself; it might be either a refuge and a help or a threat and a danger, depending on the circumstances." To make the national government "a refuge and help," in the present circumstances, was not to negate but to affirm the tradition. "If Jefferson could return to our councils," Roosevelt thought, "he would find that while economic changes of a century have changed the necessary methods of government action, the principles of that action are still wholly his own." The Roosevelt Revolution, as it has been called, went forward within a fixed structure of "principles" to which the changed methods of action were *not* answerable, except in the pragmatic sense of justifying the traditional faith by its works for human welfare.

In speeches and writings, in party ritual and in commemorative acts, the New Dealers consciously sought to give a Jeffersonian face to the revolution. The Jefferson symbol was one device by which the New Deal satisfied what Thurman Arnold defined as the crucial need of intelligent statesmanship: "a formula which is capable of dramatizing our ideals, and at the same time of giving us freedom to progress along the road of experiment and discovery."

The New Deal was to be, in Henry Wallace's words, "a twentieth century model of Jefferson's principles of government." If nearly all that had been known for over a century as Jeffersonian principles was missing from the new model, it could still be argued that new modeling itself—"the earth belongs to the living"—was the one sacred principle in the philosophy. Jefferson, an administration spokesman said in 1934, "was fixed in adherence to the principle that the administration of government at any given time should be controlled by conditions then existing, so as to promote the interests and opportunities of the people." *Administration* was not a matter of fundamental principle. The ideal was to be realized by radiant cooperation with reality. While this could be said to have saved the ideal it also killed the political philosophy. State rights: it could not be taken seriously after the Prohibition repeal, and the Roosevelt administration was the most centralizing in American history. Free trade: the Democratic platform of 1928 abandoned the "tariff for revenue only" doctrine and, despite the reciprocal tariffs program of a Jeffersonian Secretary of State, New Deal trade policy was nationalistic. The "least government" principle: New Dealers even denied that Jefferson ever uttered the familiar axiom attributed to him.

Equal rights: the deliberate policy was no longer to abolish but to spread and balance privileges. Public economy: Roosevelt soon retreated from his Jeffersonian position of 1932. The primacy of the legislative branch: the President became "chief legislator," and old fears of executive tyranny were pushed aside. And so on, down the page, the list of principles pushed aside could be stated. The effect of the New Deal on the Jeffersonian philosophy of government was not changed by calling the principles *methods.*

Nevertheless, it was deceptively easy to see in Roosevelt a "new Jefferson" and in his administration a "new model" of the old Democracy. Democrats were prepared to witness the new evangel. The search was fulfilled in Roosevelt. Some were quickly disillusioned. But with the mass of Democrats the illusion remained convincing. If, as the scholar Dumas Malone said in 1933, the New Deal could not possibly be Jeffersonian, if Jefferson's armory was strong in defensive weapons and weak in offensive ones, if his own Presidency proved the disastrous consequences of negativism, it was still likely, Malone thought, that his flexible mind would devise new methods to combat today's tyrannies and that "he would bestow his apostolic blessing on Franklin D. Roosevelt, as the new President buckles on his Hamiltonian sword." Tying up to Jefferson—what could be simpler? Jefferson, the aristocratic champion of the common man; Roosevelt, the patrician champion of the underprivileged. Jefferson who drove the "paper and stock interest" from the government; Roosevelt who drove "the money-changers from the temple." Jefferson assailed the Supreme Court; so did Roosevelt. Jefferson distinguished between "human rights," which were natural, and "property rights," which were civil; the New Deal interfered with the latter in order to strengthen the former. The essence of Jeffersonian Democracy was hostility to every form of oppression; the New Deal's attack on the "economic royalists" was in the spirit of Jefferson's attack on the "corrupt monarchists." Whenever in any country there are unemployed lands and unemployed poor, Jefferson had said, "legislators cannot invent too many devices for subdividing property." Was not social welfare legislation a modern application of Jefferson's teaching? The political scientist, Charles E. Merriam, labored to prove that Jefferson preceded Roosevelt as a "national planner." Deliberately and systematically, he wrote, Jefferson "planned to put a floor under equality and liberty" by a free public land system, a broadly conceived transportation network, and a democratic educational system. "Jefferson planned not only liberty *from* evils but also liberty *for* something—for the pursuit of happiness."

The pragmatic element in Jefferson's statesmanship, so often obscured in the past, established another link between the historic symbol and the New Deal. He was no reverential worshipper of constitutions, it was said, and his administration was notably free of dogma. The Embargo represented a greater interference with individual liberties than the National Recovery Administration. The Louisiana Purchase mocked every Jeffersonian of niggardly constitutional views. Speaking at Little Rock, Arkansas in 1936, Roosevelt interpreted the Louisiana Purchase so as to make Jefferson appear to be the author of the constitutional theory it assumed. Not Jefferson but his advisers, according to Roosevelt, thought the acquisition unconstitutional. (He was equally ingenious in 1940, when he cited the Louisiana Purchase as a precedent for the executive agreement on the exchange of destroyers for bases with Great Britain, conveniently ignoring the Senate's advice and consent to Jefferson's treaty with France.) Perhaps as journalist-historian Irving Brant thought, a workable Jeffersonian theory of the New Deal might be built on Jefferson's practice, but not on his theory.

The universal solvent of every difficulty encountered in the translation of Jefferson into a symbol congruous with the New Deal was his faith—"the cardinal element bequeathed by Jefferson to the American tradition," according to philosopher John Dewey—in the right and ability of the people, the *living* generation, to govern themselves. This faith, Dewey wrote in 1940, "was stronger than his faith in any article of his own political creed—except this one." The various articles were thus dissolved in the conviction that democracy constantly vindicates itself in its working. "Democracy is not a goal," said another philosopher, T. V. Smith, with the New Deal's pragmatic slant; "it is a going. Democracy is whatever can be arrived at democratically." He associated this view with Jefferson. So too, with more thoroughness, did Charles M. Wiltse in arguing for the "essentially Jeffersonian" groundwork of the New Deal in *The Jeffersonian Tradition in American Democracy,* in 1935. Jefferson's legacy, this young scholar said, "is not his solution to the political problem, but his realization that the problem must be solved anew in each succeeding era." The residual core of Jefferson's faith was preserved by lopping off the "principles" that inhibited its working.

When the individualistic references of Jefferson's creed were frustrated by the inability to locate the individual in the intricate social maze, when society no longer and largely of itself supported the individual in his inalienable rights, when even the primary value of political freedom must now be maintained, not in the old way as freedom from government, but as freedom to use government intelligently to solve social problems—when these new conditions and assumptions pertained, then Jefferson ceased to represent a particular political design and came to represent instead the going democratic process. Even socialism, reached and maintained democratically, would affirm Jefferson's faith. For socialism was not, according to this logic, a separate *ism* opposed to Jeffersonianism. The latter was infinitely expansible in regard to the relations between government and property, since it conceived of property as an auxiliary value, a civil or legal right, rather than an indefeasible moral right. "Nothing," Jefferson had said, "is unchangeable but the inherent and inalienable rights of man." Viewing the problem in this spirit, Dewey asserted, "it is sheer perversion to hold that there is anything in Jeffersonian democracy that forbids political action to bring about the equalization of economic conditions in order that the equal rights of all to free choice and free action be maintained."

Although the Jefferson symbol was thus radically revised, its essential *moral* basis was unchanged. The belief in inalienable rights, in "trust the people," in consent rather than coercion—the vocabulary Jefferson had used to express these truths was outmoded, as Dewey said, but it was doubtful if democracy could survive unless men unreservedly took "the position Jefferson took about its moral basis and purpose." And, leaving aside for the moment the massive partisan predisposition to apostolic succession in the Jeffersonian line, perhaps the felt need to renew this faith furnishes an important key to why the Roosevelt Revolution occurred under Jefferson's sign instead of Hamilton's. In many respects, the New Deal's prophet was Herbert Croly. Its administrative theory and practice, its fiscal apparatus, its political economy were Hamiltonian. Observing this in 1934, Broadus Mitchell, a Johns Hopkins economist just beginning a life's work on Hamilton, thought it ironical that Jefferson's fancies should have been laid away in lavender by a Democratic administration. "Have our major tendencies been centrifugal or centripetal?" Mitchell asked. "The world over, has the separate citizen preserved his autonomy, economic and political, or has he yielded it up to the central authority?" The answers were self-evident. Hamilton pointed the way to the work of the New Deal in mastering an unruly economy, Mitchell asserted. But in this opinion he had little company; for, like Hamiltonians before him, Mitchell seemed blind to the intransigent ideal, the faith in democratic government, for which the American people remembered Jefferson and, because he lacked it, forgot Hamilton.

The clue of the New Deal's Jefferson image leads finally to the President's desk. Whether or not Roosevelt imagined himself a "new Jefferson," the role was thrust upon him and he seemed to enjoy it. People were constantly trying to interest him in Jefferson mementoes —a letter, a portrait, a silver cup, a gold toothpick. Would the President like to see them? No, the answers came back, he was too busy putting Jefferson's ideas to work to treasure his relics. One portrait in particular, the crayon drawing by the Polish patriot and American revolutionist, Thaddeus Kosciusko, kept turning up at the White House. Admirers, including the Polish Ambassador, were struck by the resemblance to Roosevelt. He was flattered and amused. Finally, the owner of the original portrait offered to sell it to Roosevelt. He, as usual declined.

The incident ties another Jeffersonian thread into the Roosevelt story. The portrait's owner was Mrs. Martin W. Littleton, who had inspired the campaign several decades earlier for the government's acquisition of Monticello. Her pamphlets were in Roosevelt's collection of Jefferson literature, for he had enlisted in the Monticello movement at the start. From 1930 until his death, he served on the Board of Governors of the Thomas Jefferson Memorial Foundation. Stuart Gibboney, its President, was a warm personal friend. Roosevelt did everything he could to help the Foundation improve Monticello. Annually, from 1934 to 1938, he personally saw to the assignment of a Civilian Conservation Corps detail to clean up the woods and fields on the property. Since the Foundation was a private association, the government's assistance had no legal warrant. The President gave the Independence Day address at Monticello in 1936. Monticello showed that Jefferson was a "great gentleman" and a "great commoner." "The two are not incompatible." The statement said as much about Roosevelt as about Jefferson. The President often expressed the hope that Monticello might yet become the property of the United States, entrusted to the care of the National Park Service, like his own Hyde Park estate. Every April 13 of his Presidency, a personal aid placed a wreath at Jefferson's tomb. The last was laid there on April 13, 1945, as his funeral train moved up through Virginia.

Monticello was only one of Roosevelt's works for Jefferson. The Democrats were determined to build Jefferson a memorial in the nation's capital as splendid as Washington's and Lincoln's. The President constantly had his hand in this project. Without his personal intervention, the gigantic National Expansion Memorial in St. Louis would probably never have got off the drawing boards. Beginning in 1938, by authorization of Congress, the President annually proclaimed April 13 in commemoration of Jefferson. In January 1939, the President inquired of the Corps of Engineers if there was any record of a Jefferson memorial tree on the White House grounds. The record showed nothing. So he had the Corps plant a grove of twenty tulip poplars (his favorite tree, though the Lombardy poplar was, in the way of trees, an original Jeffersonian symbol) on Jefferson's next birthday.

There were many ways to work "the Jefferson angle" into the New Deal, and few escaped the President or his subordinates. He named Claude Bowers and William E. Dodd, perhaps the nation's two best known Jeffersonian historians, ambassadors to Spain and Germany respectively. Every executive department or office seemed to have its own Jefferson specialist and project. In Agriculture, Everett Edwards, M. L. Wilson, and others wrote pamphlets on Jefferson as Farmer. In Interior, Saul Padover produced a major study, *Thomas Jefferson and the National Capital*. The Patent Office dedicated a bust to its first superintendent. And the Library of Congress, under Archibald MacLeish, installed an impressive series of Thomas Jefferson Murals in its new annex. The national Democratic boss, James

A. Farley, was an avid Jefferson Day speaker; and nearly every high administration official sooner or later came around to the Jefferson theme.

Roosevelt put Jefferson into many of his speeches. His aids compiled huge files of Jefferson quotations arranged under subject headings. Friends and advisers sent him copies of Jefferson letters, which they hoped he might find useful. Occasionally he directed some subordinate to run down a Jefferson text suited to buttress his position on a delicate question. One instance in which the Jefferson research entered into a major address concerned the diplomatic recognition of the Soviet Union on November 16, 1933. Two weeks before, the Executive Office asked the State Department's historical adviser to make and forward photo-duplicates of certain Jefferson manuscripts relating to United States policy toward Imperial Russia. This was done the following day. In one of the manuscripts, a letter addressed to his Russian friend, M. Dashkoff, on August 12, 1809, Jefferson said: "Russia and the United States being in character and practice essentially pacific, a common interest in the rights of peaceable nations gives us a common cause in their maintenance." The passage was marked, perhaps by Roosevelt, with three red lines. Some days later it was incorporated in a speech memorandum. It appeared in Roosevelt's address at Savannah, Georgia, on November 18, 1933, as a justification of the recognition and an illustration of the spirit in which it was tendered.

If Hamilton was the true father of the New Deal, the administration certainly made valiant efforts to redeem its error by increasing Jefferson's fame. In 1938 both the Jefferson nickel and the Jefferson three-cent postage stamp made their appearance. Jefferson's visage had been on the nation's postage for several decades, but never on the most generally used denominations. The philatelist President decided in 1937 upon a general revision of the postage designs, the first in twenty-five years. The new standard designs should compose a "presidential series," correlating the sequence of American Presidents with the postage denominations. In accordance with this directive, the Post Office Department drew up the specifications and submitted them to the President. Seeing that strict adherence to his original plan would put Jefferson on the scarce one and one-half-cent stamp, Roosevelt picked up a pencil, assigned Benjamin Franklin to the lowest denomination, Washington to the next, inserted Martha Washington in Jefferson's inconspicuous place, added Adams, and thus brought Jefferson out on the three-cent stamp—the carrier of nearly every letter in the first class mail. The Department adopted this amended presidential series. Its publication caused a mild political hassle. Lincoln, after all, had been stricken from the three-cent stamp in favor of Jefferson. A New York congressman charged that the new series was "a scheme to make sure that all Republicans are forgotten." But then the Republicans, in 1929, had relegated Jefferson to the scarce two-dollar bill. The Jefferson nickel replaced the "buffalo nickel" after the expiration of the latter's normal twenty-five-year term. While a no less deliberate maneuver to put Jefferson's name and visage in circulation, it did not receive the same personal attention from the President, nor did it annoy many Republicans.

Roosevelt of course regarded Jefferson as the founder of the Democratic party, and a playful kind of partisanship entered into his decision to put Jefferson on the three-cent stamp and to quote him against the opposition. But he had also come to believe that Jefferson ought to be celebrated nationally, like Washington and Lincoln, as an American hero. So he soft-pedaled the conventional partisan use of the Jefferson symbol, seeming to prefer Andrew Jackson for this purpose. As much as we love Jefferson, he wrote to E. M. House in advance of the Jefferson Day dinners in 1934, we should celebrate him not as the founder and philosopher of the Democratic party but as the supreme spirit of American liberalism and progress. And the accumulated effect of the varied Jefferson enterprise of the New Deal, over which Roosevelt presided, was to enhance Jefferson's reputation in reference to a larger constellation of civilized values than the political tradition comprehended. The partisan symbol was dying even in the house of Democracy.

"This is a very prosperous time for Thomas Jefferson," the newspaper columnist Simeon Strunsky wrote in 1936. "Everybody has a kind word for him. Nearly everybody writes a book about him. Every political party and faction in the end calls him father." The situation was not unprecedented in Jefferson's posthumous history. All American history, it sometimes seemed, represented the effort to discover Jeffersonian answers to the problems encountered in the nation's progress. During the depression decade, Jefferson shaded the entire political spectrum from the American Liberty League on the far right to the Communist party on the far left. "Sacerdotal cults" arose, it was observed, "differing among themselves, but each professing the exclusive validity of its own interpretation of the American scripture according to Thomas Jefferson."

Of these cults, the one called Southern Agrarianism had the most earnest affair with Jefferson. Usually dated from the Twelve Southerners' manifesto of 1930, *I'll Take My Stand,* the agrarian movement of thought came to reflect during the succeeding decade several diverse influences: the aesthetic and cultural ideas of the Fugitive group of Southern writers, first centered at Nashville and then at Louisiana State University; the Southern Regionalism of Howard Odum and his group at the University of North Carolina; the English Distributist school of Hilaire Belloc and others, which especially influenced the work of the National Catholic Rural Life Conference; and the agrarian current in American historiography. All agrarians advocated retreat from the rootless materialism of industrial society and restoration of an integral way of life, the economic basis of which was landed property, with individual ownership and control sufficient for personal independence and family livelihood. The movement arose in the South as an alternative solution to the Southern problem. The liberal evangels of the New South, with their faith in education and industrialism, stood condemned. They had, it was said, betrayed the true Southern heritage of classical thought, Christian religion, and rural life to the Northern ideal.

The agrarians were, on the whole, predisposed to see Jefferson as the father of their faith. Monticello—the Palladian villa of a cultivated country gentleman—in a sense symbolized the best part of the heritage they wished to regain. John Gould Fletcher, one of the Twelve Southerners, attacked the liberals' association of Jefferson's name with their idea of universal education, and called for a return to his, as Fletcher believed, selective system. Jefferson's democratic ideal, another of the twelve wrote, was an "unmixed agrarian society," with local and region autonomy, just enough government to prevent disaster, and—"the keystone of the arch"—broadly diffused ownership of land. Not only was Jefferson a symbol of the agrarian tradition; he was himself a traditionalist, whose ideas and habits of life antedated the modern age not by accident but by choice. But the agrarians, least of all the Southerners, could not embrace Jefferson without serious qualms and reservations. Allen Tate, for example, convicted him of the root American heresy against culture and religion: the idea that the ends of man are sufficiently contained in his political destiny. Nevertheless, the agrarian movement's general effect was a grotesque exaggeration of Jefferson's traditional, Southern, and agrarian features. It made Jefferson into a symbol of ideas and policies which were, under the circumstances, at once futile and reactionary.

As the movement spread beyond the South during the depression, the provincial analysis was shaped into a key to the American problem. By far the most illuminating of Jefferson were the popular historical writings of Herbert Agar. This poet, man of letters, and journalist, New York born of Southern parentage, gradually outgrew the intense conservatism of the Southern Agrarians and, as he did, came to write with more discrimination of Jefferson. But, in the gross, his books on American history, commencing in 1933 with the Pulitzer prize-winning *The People's Choice,* a study of the Presidency, pitched upon a dominant idea: Jefferson dreamed the American dream, betrayed it, and America has been damned ever since.

The dream was an agrarian utopia. A political democracy, a free economy, a native culture, all based upon and infused with the common values and habits of a people living on the land—this was the dream. Why was it, then, that when the opportunity for realization came to him, Jefferson "betrayed the America of his dream"? Why did Jefferson the President fail permanently to secure his principles, broaden the base in landed property, raise up legal bulwarks for its protection, and divert, while there was still time, the industrial revolution into salutary channels? Though Agar's several reports did not always agree with each other, the main points of the diagnosis were clear. First, Jefferson's unfortunate personality: "exaggerated charm," "softness of character," "easy hopefulness," most of all "an alarming wooly mindedness." Second, Jefferson built the Democratic party upon an untenable farmer-labor, rural-urban, combination. Having already, through his Virginia reforms, degraded and impoverished the landed gentry from which the agrarians should have drawn their leaders, Jefferson "then gave a vested interest in the party to the carefree demagogues of New York City," who cared not for principle but for the powers of office. Third, Jefferson, gave up the game by clinging, in the face of invasion, to his principle of the least possible government. "This was a poor principle with which to fight the most dynamic forces in Western history, forces which had just begun to invade our shores from Britain and which Hamilton had been welcoming with open arms." Finally, as Jefferson lost the economic battle in this way, he lost the constitutional battle as well by lowering the defenses against Federalist tactics: liberal construction, centralization, bank and debt. America was thus doomed to become a mere "money-based democracy." Jefferson's democratic ideas grew more and more popular as the actual environment became less and less Jeffersonian. "Democratic, egalitarian principles suitable to the rural world of Jefferson's dream were grafted on a greedy, middle-class Hamiltonian capitalism."

But there was still a way out, Agar thought. Jefferson understood the heart's desire of the American people. They held him in affection, a kind of tragic hero, despite his historical defeat; they constantly returned to "that lost fight." What was required was not merely the restoration of Jeffersonian principles but the restoration of Jeffersonian society. Agar called, with other agrarians, for federal action to break down corporate power, to build up the small propertyholders' democracy and the family-type farming of the Jeffersonian ideal. But lest the means employed to this end become too Hamiltonian, Agar voiced the old Jeffersonian fear of a government empowered to achieve the ideal. Reflecting the teachings of the arch-conservative economist Friedrick Hayek, he denounced government planning and Keynesian fiscal policy. Agar, with the other agrarians, clung to "the noble dream" but could not, any more than the man he arraigned as its betrayer, will the means of realization.

Everybody else was claiming Jefferson, columnist Heywood Broun noted in 1938, so there was "no reason why the Communists should not make the attempt to press a red card upon the sage of Monticello." The claim was as absurd as it was spectacular; yet it was congenial with the New Deal's stress on Jefferson's progressiveness and with the intellectuals' discovery during the decade of a revolutionary past inviting leaps into the future. American radical sects, from the early Owenite Socialists to Marxists Socialists and Communists, had never been strongly attracted to Jefferson. Of course, he was something of a free-thinker, a pacifist, a revolutionist, and an equalitarian. This was good for inspiration; but his crucial role in history was to break the trail for an individualistic capitalism to which there was no return and beyond which his philosophy of government promised nothing. A. M. Simons enunciated this modern Socialist view in his pioneering work of 1911, *Social Forces in American History,* and it was still being repeated in the early 'thirties. "Today . . . it is the struggle of the proletariat which is important and not the struggle of the petty bourgeoisie," V. F. Calverton declared; "the Jeffersonian challenge as a result has become anachronistic."

As the decade advanced, however, the leftists tried to deduce Marx from Jefferson. First the Socialists and then, after 1935, the Communists moved to furnish their creeds with heroes from the American past. "Communism is Twentieth Century Americanism" the party cried. Serious scholars, such as Charles M. Wiltse, had traced the Jeffersonian tradition into democratic socialism, so why should the Communists not take the next step? "We Communists today are continuing the heritage of Jefferson and Lincoln. . . . Jefferson's theory of democracy realized fully that political power can be maintained and extended only when given a solid economic foundation. The essential features of Jefferson's program must be brought up to date." Furthermore, as Jefferson fought the reactionary nations of his day in alliance with revolutionary France, so present-day American foreign policy ought to support revolutionary Russia against the fascist nations. The party's chief, Earl Browder, acknowledged that Jefferson was not Marx; but the Father of Democracy stood at the portal of the mighty torrent of revolution destined to sweep through the world. Jefferson was a "bourgeois democrat" and "the architect of American capitalism"; yet he might serve, it seemed, as a symbol of the proletarian revolution against the order he founded.

Jefferson quite obviously could not be imaged as a proletarian. Using him as a heroic symbol of revolution, the Communists still did not idolize the man or his principles. In the Jefferson Bicentennial of 1943, the weekly *New Masses* paid him handsome tribute; but Howard Fast's historical novel, *Citizen Tom Paine,* published in the same year, furnished a truer reflection of Communist feelings. Jefferson merely played, and rather fearfully, Fast thought, at adoring the common man. Paine *was* the common man, his ideas "closer to those of the average working man than Jefferson's ever could be." Jefferson enjoyed a certain éclat among the Communists; and, of course, there was no comparison between the propaganda value of the two symbols, Jefferson and Paine. As Fast's book indicated, however, the Communists retained the historic preference of radical sects for the Founding Father America rejected.

The much more serious, indeed the only significant, challenge to the New Deal's Jefferson image came from the motley assemblage on the political right: the reactionaries of the millionaire-financed American Liberty League, Old Guard Republicans, liberal intellectuals of the nineteenth-century vintage, and insurgent "Jeffersonian Democrats." From the New Deal standpoint, all these people were *conservative,* though they rallied under Jeffersonian colors. The tactics implied the wholesale transference of conservative allegiance from Hamilton to Jefferson. Hamilton was nearly forgotten as the conservatives hurled Jeffersonian missiles at the Roosevelt administration:

In questions of power, then, let no more be heard of confidence in man, but bind him down from mischief by the chains of the Constitution.

When we must wait for Washington to tell us when to sow and when to reap, we shall soon want bread.

Such were the texts of Liberty League sermons. The titles of a few scattered editorials in Colonel Robert R. McCormick's *Chicago Tribune* suggest the frame of mind: "Jefferson or Marx" (this is the issue), "The Discarded Founder" (the Democrats have repudiated their patron saint), "State Rights and the Constitution" (hurrah for the doctrines of '98), "The Man of Prophesy" (Jefferson predicted the "third term" peril), "Maxims of Jefferson" (isolation, frugality, constitutionalism, and so on). Jefferson was quoted in the letter against the finer distillations of his spirit. What he had said in 1800, he would have repeated were he present in the flesh in 1936.

The Republican trend is Jeffersonian, William Allen White wrote from the National Convention at Cleveland in 1936: "We may easily have the Democrats defending Hamiltonian principles in the campaign of '36 and the Republicans presenting a program calling for Jeffersonian home rule." The Republicans rediscovered the party's lost Jeffersonian origins in the slavery crisis. Party Chairman John D. M. Hamilton kept up the "back to Jefferson" cry several years after the terrible defeat in 1936. At a Lincoln Day dinner in 1938, he raised his glass to Jefferson and Lincoln, entwined in the party's history and memory. "Jefferson was the hero of the Lincoln Republicans. The Republican party is more Jeffersonian today than those who pay mere lip service to his name." On July Fourth 1938, both Hamilton and New Deal Senator Claude Pepper acclaimed Jefferson as the father of their respective parties before a record audience at the University of Virginia's Institute of Public Affairs. "This afternoon," newspapers reported, "a wreath, sent by President Roosevelt, was laid on Jefferson's tomb at Monticello by Senator Pepper, at 2:30 o'clock and at 3:30 o'clock another was placed there by Mr. Hamilton."

Whatever may be said of the logic of the Republican appeal to Jefferson, it had certain practical values, not the least of which was to sever dissident "Jeffersonian Democrats," mostly Southerners, from their party allegiance. Roosevelt's "court packing" plan in 1937 and his later decision to seek a third term helped to make the self-styled Jeffersonians a formidable faction in 1940. Fighting the "nine old men," the administration drew upon Jefferson's well-furnished armory of "anti-judicialism," which had seen service in every major offensive mounted against the Supreme Court from the last years of Jefferson's life down to Robert LaFollette's valiant campaign in 1924. Distinguished authority supported the New Deal contention that Jefferson had denied the Court's ultimate power and gone to great lengths to control it. Neither Jefferson's theory nor his practice, Charles Beard reported, yielded any comfort to conservatives who regarded the Court as the sacrosanct palladium of American liberty. Indeed, conservative elements had always deplored Jefferson's "anti-judicialism." But now the stage revolved and Jefferson the Constitutionalist held their attention. The "Jeffersonian Democrats," unlike the Republicans, could at least make a case for their consistency in this matter. Constitutionalism had always been an article of Democratic orthodoxy. No less an authority than Claude Bowers had recently pronounced the idea of Jefferson's hostility to the judiciary a myth. Concededly, as Virginia's Senator Carter Glass said, Jefferson hated Marshall and feared *his* Court; his complaint, however, was that the Court was too liberal, too centralizing, too casual in regard to constitutional limitations. Even then, alarmed as he was, Glass said, Jefferson never proposed to remedy the condition by *packing* the Court.

Jefferson's position on the "third term" was seemingly less equivocal than his position on the judiciary. As far back as 1880, when Grant threatened to upset the two-term tradition, prominent Democrats had appealed to Jeffersonian opinion and precedent. Grant Republicans had then answered that Jefferson's real reason for declining a third term had nothing to do with the high principle he stated, but rested on the certain knowledge he could not be re-elected. No Jeffersonian could ever believe that canard! Yet Harold Ickes had to be satisfied with it in his attack on "The Third Term Bugaboo." As Fred Rodell showed in his careful analysis, "Thomas Jefferson had plenty to say about perpetual presidential reeligibility, and all of it was decidedly unfavorable." For historical witness, the Democrats in 1940 were forced to rely almost entirely on Hamilton's seventy-first *Federalist* paper, while Republicans were amply supplied with Jefferson texts, all "the reasoned result of deeply felt political principles." Here, if anywhere, in the Roosevelt years was a conclusive Jeffersonian principle. It did not admit of exception on the plea of changing circumstances, since the circumstances in this instance were essentially those that had caused Jefferson to declare against re-eligibility. In fact, the new capabilities of the Presidency would seem to have made Jefferson's principle more urgent in 1940 than in 1800. New Dealers might say re-eligibility was merely a question of mechanics. "Jeffersonian Democrats" were not put off by this ruse. There must be fundamental principles somewhere! Of course there were; but not in the old sense of unchanging Jeffersonian principles of government. The new model Jeffersonian Democracy not only discarded old methods; it discarded old principles as the need arose.

James M. Beck, a long-time worshipper at Hamilton's shrine and peerless exemplar of constitutional fetishism in the decade or so prior to the New Deal, struck one of the keynotes of the conservative discourse in a dramatic speech in Congress on April 18, 1934. The administration, he declared, "is realizing beyond any dream of Alexander Hamilton his ideas as to the nature of our government and what its desired form should be." The principles of Jefferson?— "they are virtually non-existent for any practical purpose." The future?—"a unitary socialistic state." The nation should, by all means, build a towering monument to Jefferson; nevertheless, the portentous reality, Beck insisted, was that Jefferson is "the 'forgotten man' in the philosophy of American politics."

Is Jefferson the Forgotten Man? Nicholas Murray Butler asked in a widely publicized address in 1935. That Butler could even raise the question, let alone answer it in the affirmative, was a revelation. He grew up in Paterson, New Jersey, which traced its beginnings to Hamilton's Society for the Establishment of Useful Manufactures; he was a delegate, often a very influential one, to every Republican Convention from 1880 to 1932; and as President of Columbia University from 1902, Butler did as much as any man of his time to perpetuate Hamilton's fame, locally, nationally, and internationally. Butler admired Hamilton as "the nation-builder," yet he described himself as a liberal in respect to the limits of political authority. As the tension between his nationalism and his liberalism built up in the nineteen-twenties, Butler began to talk about the soundness of Jefferson's principles. These principles which, had they prevailed at any time during the last century would have done irreparable harm, were now needed to maintain a free society at home and peace in the world. Although Butler loved Hamilton too much ever to abandon him completely, he clearly enlisted under Jefferson's standard in 1935. He condemned the decline of individual and local liberties, the use of the tax power to force social and political changes, the growth of warlike nationalism and oppressive collectivism. "All these considerations enforce the conviction that Thomas Jefferson was right; that Government must be carefully restricted in its powers and functions; that it must be held closely to them; and that every attempt on the part of Government to invade the reserved field of Liberty, no matter on what pretense, must be stoutly and stubbornly resisted." Was it argued that conditions had changed since Jefferson's day? Yes, Butler replied, but "Fundamental prin-

ciples do not change." The urgent task of the time was to restore
The Forgotten Man, and thus to redress the true liberal balance of
Jefferson and Hamilton. These two great leaders were not antago-
nistic but complementary, Butler said. He liked to think the statues
of the two rivals, as they stood on the Columbia campus, facing the
observer on the right and on the left, symbolized the idea of
American government.

The Indiana congressman, Samuel B. Pettingill, was a "Jeffersonian Democrat" who had looked upon Roosevelt as a returned
Jefferson. Gradually disillusioned, he broke with the administration
on the Court Bill. Speaking in the House a year later, Pettingill re-
called to American memory July Fourth 1826. Millions of Americans
for over a century had rejected the proofs of Jefferson's passing; a
great political party had dedicated itself to the perpetuation of his
teachings. Now, after five years of the dictatorial New Deal, the congressman solemnly announced, "the most serious of all questions
facing America and the masses of mankind everywhere is whether
Thomas Jefferson is dead." Pettingill's *Jefferson, The Forgotten Man*,
in 1938, was the most elaborate attack on the New Deal written in
Jeffersonian chapter and verse. Disclaiming any quarrel with Roosevelt's broad objectives, Pettingill said they were spoiled by non-
Jeffersonian methods. Jefferson, he wrote, "did not believe liberal
ends could be attained by illiberal means." Like Walter Lippmann,
whose *The Good Society* was a much more sophisticated statement
of the position, Pettingill thought the foundation stone of liberalism
was the "free market" economy. Just insofar as the New Deal, in its
action on the economy, substituted for the freedom of the market-
place centralized planning and control, it was Hamiltonian and a
throwback to the authoritarian mercantilist state. Assuming that the
ills of the economy arose from the business community, the New
Deal invoked the powers of the state against business. In fact,
Pettingill asserted, the root of the trouble was political, as always;
the root was government intervention of any sort, for any purpose,
in the economy. The privileges the Republicans had used in a Hamiltonian way, the New Dealers tried to use in a Jeffersonian way, not
stopping to realize that the enemy was privilege itself. The task of
liberalism, the Hoosier congressman concluded, must always be

liberation. No better guide existed than Jefferson's First Inaugural Address. The Jeffersonian, Pettingill, and the Hamiltonian, Butler, thus ended up on the same side.

A few, though not many, intellectuals joined the attack from the right on the New Deal. The historian James Truslow Adams, in the previous decade, was a typical liberal intellectual: a debunker of patriotic myths, a denouncer of Puritanism and Babbittry, a somewhat supercilious observer of the political scene. Politics made no sense, he said in 1929, because the Americans had illogically built a Hamiltonian economic machine within their Jeffersonian house of faith. "We practice Hamilton from January 1 to July 3 every year. On July 4 we hurrah like mad for Jefferson. The next day we quietly take up Hamilton again for the rest of the year as we go about our business." Adams's fantastically popular *Epic of America,* in 1931, explained how America had been brought to this soulless condition. Jefferson represented "the American dream"—the dream of the common man in constant quest of freedom and opportunity—which Adams unfolded in five great forward movements: the Revolution, Jeffersonian Democracy, Jacksonian Democracy. Lincoln Republicanism, and Wilsonian Progressivism. But the dream, betrayed by the Hamiltonian Mammon, gradually retreated into the lost world behind the city and the corporation. The question for Adams, as for other Jeffersonians of "the noble dream," was whether America could reconcile the Jeffersonian philosophy with social realities more and more distant from its fundamental postulates. Mammon had displaced God in 1931, but Adams hesitated to announce the end of the epic. He looked at the problem again in 1936. *The Living Jefferson* applied Jefferson's philosophy to the present crisis. Roosevelt had preached "sound Jeffersonian doctrine" in 1932; his administration plunged America deeper into the Hamiltonian abyss. "What we need is not a Hamilton, but a Jefferson, to persuade the masses . . . that the 'more abundant life,' if thought of only in terms of economics and state planning, will be ashes in our mouths if we cannot at the same time retain those personal liberties of action . . . which alone make life worthy."

"Beating the Living with the Bones of the Dead," Texas congressman Maury Maverick entitled a scathing review of Adams's book. Maverick unfairly accused Adams of gross ignorance of Jefferson and subservience to the Liberty League crowd. The title of the book should have been, "Jefferson Repainted: Pigments by Du Pont, Oils by Standard Oil, Canvas by Hoosac Mills, Scenery by Schecter Bros." Maverick also registered his complaint in Congress. The thin film of scholarship on *The Living Jefferson* must not be allowed to conceal the author's true purpose, he warned, which was to dig up the dead Jefferson and exhibit him as a live model reactionary. "Thomas Jefferson specifically warned future generations against beating the living with the bones of the dead.' But the Liberty Leaguers have stolen him for their hero, and have publicly paraded him before the American people in garments he never wore."

The last word on Jefferson and the New Deal was uttered by Godfrey D. Gloom, "the well-known pawpaw planter and old-fashioned Jeffersonian Democrat from Amity, Indiana," as he expired, struck down by a passing auto, on a busy Philadelphia street corner in June 1936. Gloom, the fictional creation of newsman Elmer Davis in 1920, was a figure as real as life to many readers of the *New York Times.* His grandfather, it appeared from Gloom's obituary, had always boasted to the fame of having held Jefferson's horse at his inauguration. His father had come from Virginia to Indiana, where young Gloom trained briefly in the law office of Daniel Voorhees, a peerless Jeffersonian, and then entered the bear-skinning trade. At a ripe age (he had cast his first vote for James Buchanan), Gloom developed the habit of attending national political conventions, where Davis found him in 1920 and quadrennially (except for 1928) thereafter. Surprised to discover Gloom at the Republican convention in 1936 wearing a Landon sunflower in his lapel, the reporter asked an explanation. "The modern streamlined Democrats have got no more use for Jeffersonians than they have for a Model T, to say nothing of the horse and buggy," Gloom replied. The Republicans had become the grand old party of Jefferson. But the Democratic habit was too strong; two weeks later, Gloom set aside his Jeffersonian fears and meekly endorsed Roosevelt. Then death nipped him. It was time, the "last Jeffersonian" told the crowd that gathered around to hear his dying words:

Jefferson has now been endorsed by both parties, and there seems as little prospect that the endorsement will ever be repudiated as that either

*party will ever put Jeffersonian doctrine into practice. And maybe . . .
that is just as well. For the principles of Thomas Jefferson I have un-
shaken respect; but when he translated those principles into concrete
policies he did so according to the peculiar conditions of his time, as
any man of sense would have done.*

It was impossible to return. Gloom was convinced that Jefferson,
were he alive, "would stick to his principles of standing up for the
rights of ordinary people by whatever means might seem most advantageously adapted to that end." When the self-styled Jeffersonians put a halo around the words uttered by the prophet in 1800,
then, Gloom said, "the best place for a genuine Jeffersonian is in
the tomb."

It may still be too early to say how well the New Deal, tackling
the severest crisis since the Civil War, combined "maintenance of
the symbolic code" with "fearlessness of revision"—the art of free
society, as Whitehead thought—but in the case of the Jefferson
symbol a good report may be given. Although the administration
treated Jeffersonian canons with remarkable abandon, it appealed
for justification to Jefferson's progressive spirit. "Not by ancestors,
but by practical considerations, the modern problems of liberty are
to be disentangled," wrote the prize-winning essayist of *Harpers
Magazine*'s contest in 1937 on the redefinition of "The American
Way." This Benthamite wisdom colored the New Deal far more bril-
liantly than the Jeffersonian wisdom about government. It was, however, the kind of wisdom about means which a people resolutely
committed to ancestral ideals of democracy could well afford. The
hazards of the voyage away from the old landmarks were reduced
by the fact that the compass pointed unwaveringly to freedom. "If
we think that Jefferson created a free democracy," Gilbert Seldes
remarked, "we miss the essence of democracy which is that every
moment the people must create it for themselves." Democracy was
not something Jefferson had dreamed once and for all, and which
could be had by the simple expedient of returning to his principles.
Nor was it a theory of government or a code of action valid for all
time. The old complaints on the score of "rigidity of rule" were be-
side the point. Jefferson was not doctrines but ideals. He symbolized

the faith that an informed people secure in their inalienable rights are always capable of saving themselves.

This was the end of the political tradition. After the Roosevelt Revolution, serious men stopped yearning for the agrarian utopia, politicians (and most historians too) laid aside the Jefferson-Hamilton dialogue, and almost no one any longer maintained the fiction that American government was run, or ought to be run, on the Jeffersonian model. What mattered was the faith in the power of free men constantly to rediscover their heritage and to work out their destiny in its spirit. The New Deal consummated the process by which Jefferson came to stand, above any other American, the hero of this faith, and for great clusters of civilized values as well. Paradoxically, the ultimate disintegration of the Jeffersonian philosophy of government heralded the ultimate canonization of Jefferson.

Suggestions for Additional Reading

Bibliographies

Primary and secondary Jefferson materials are abundant, but there is as yet no standard, comprehensive bibliographical guide. One of the earliest and still useful bibliographies is that compiled by Hamilton B. Tompkins, *Bibliotheca Jeffersoniana* (N.Y., 1887). The 1903 edition of *The Writings of Thomas Jefferson,* edited by A. A. Lipscomb (N.Y.), includes a useful "Contribution to a Bibliography of Thomas Jefferson." Probably the most comprehensive work is that of W. Harvey Wise and John W. Cronin, *A Bibliography of Thomas Jefferson* (Washington, 1935). William H. Peden has a significant bibliographical contribution in *Some Aspects of Jeffersonian Bibliography* (Lexington, Va., 1941). Some contemporary authors have compiled good bibliographies as a result of their writings, including notably Merrill D. Peterson's "Guide to Sources" in *The Jefferson Image in the American Mind* (N.Y., 1962) and Dumas Malone's "Select Critical Bibliography," in *Jefferson and His Time* (4 vols., Boston, 1948–   ).

Published Papers

Jefferson editors have been more active than Jefferson bibliographers. The best-known collections of Jefferson papers are Paul Leicester Ford, ed., *The Writings of Thomas Jefferson* (10 vols., N.Y., 1892–1899), and A. A. Lipscomb and A. E. Bergh, eds., *The Writings of Thomas Jefferson* (20 vols., Washington, 1903). The Ford collection is more limited but better referenced while the more extensive Lipscomb work, called the "Memorial Edition," is more difficult to use. The most notable work in progress is the projected fifty or more volume work on *The Papers of Thomas Jefferson* being edited under the direction of Julian P. Boyd (Princeton, 1950–   ). Specialized volumes of Jefferson correspondence have been published including *Official Letters of the Governor of the State of Virginia,* II, *The Letters of Thomas Jefferson,* H. R. McIlwaine, gen. ed., (Virginia State Library, 1928); Gilbert Chinard, ed., *The Letters of Lafayette and Jefferson* (Johns Hopkins, 1929); Bernard Mayo, ed.,

Jefferson Himself: The Personal Narrative of a Many-Sided American (Boston, 1942); Adrienne Koch and William Peden, eds., *The Life and Selected Writings of Thomas Jefferson* (N.Y., 1944); Edwin Morris Betts and James Adam Bear, Jr., eds., *The Family Letters of Thomas Jefferson* (Columbia, Mo., 1966); and L. J. Cappon, ed., *The Adams-Jefferson Letters* (2 vols., Chapel Hill, 1959). The Territorial Papers of Louisiana and Mississippi, American State Papers, and the Journals, Calendars, and Statutes of the State of Virginia contain valuable materials. Quite interesting and useful works are Jefferson's *Notes on the State of Virginia* available in the well-annotated edition of William H. Peden (Chapel Hill, 1955); and *Thomas Jefferson's Farm Book* (Princeton, 1953), and *Jefferson's Garden Book* (Princeton, 1944), both edited by Edwin Morris Betts.

Secondary Works

The two most outstanding earlier works on Thomas Jefferson are Henry S. Randall, *The Life of Thomas Jefferson* (3 vols., N.Y., 1865) which is the standard, older biographical account, and Henry Adams, *History of the United States During the Administrations of Jefferson and Madison* (9 vols., 1889–1891) which presents an intensive scholarly survey of the period.

There have been many excellent twentieth-century publications. The selections used in this study are recommended for further reading. Especially significant Jefferson studies that are not represented in this volume include Dumas Malone's four-volume work on *Jefferson and His Time* (Boston, 1948   ). Charles Beard's classic treatment of *The Economic Origins of Jeffersonian Democracy* (N.Y., 1915) has had considerable influence on subsequent Jefferson studies as have the popular works of Claude Bowers. Albert J. Nock's volume on *Thomas Jefferson* (N.Y., 1926) is recommended for its treatment of Jefferson as the "civilized man." Gilbert Chinard effectively analyzes the tension between Jefferson's theories and his use of presidential power in *Thomas Jefferson: The Apostle of Americanism* (Boston: Little, Brown, 1929. Reprinted by University of Michigan Press, 1957). Adrienne Koch, *The Philosophy of Thomas Jefferson* (N.Y., 1943) is a sound, thoughtful reevaluation. Marie Kimball's three volumes provide an intensive, friendly treatment of Jef-

ferson from 1743 to 1789 (N.Y., 1943, 1947, 1950). Daniel J. Boor-
stin's *The Lost World of Thomas Jefferson* re-creates the intellectual
environment of Jefferson's time. Nathan Schachner's *Thomas Jefferson: A Biography* is a recent and highly readable evaluation of
Jefferson's strengths and weaknesses (N.Y., 1951).

Recent interest in the politics of Thomas Jefferson is well ex-
emplified in Noble E. Cunningham, Jr., *Jeffersonian Republicans in
Power: Party Operations, 1801–1809* (Chapel Hill, 1967) and his *Jef-
fersonian Republicans: The Formation of a Party Organization, 1789–
1801* (Chapel Hill, 1967). Complementary studies include Joseph
Charles, *Origins of the American Party System* (N.Y., 1961) and
Leonard D. White *The Jeffersonians: A Study in Administrative His-
tory* (N.Y., 1951) as well as the studies by James MacGregor Burns,
The Deadlock of Democracy (Englewood Cliffs, N.J., 1963), William
Nisbet Chambers, *Political Parties in a New Nation: The American
Experience, 1776–1809* (Oxford, 1963), and Richard P. McCormick,
The Second American Party System (Chapel Hill, 1966) which are
represented in this volume.

Of the many useful studies of "Jefferson the Virginian," Louis B.
Wright's *First Gentlemen of Virginia* (San Marino, Cal., 1940), *Patrician and Plebian in Virginia* (N.Y., 1910), and *Give Me Liberty: The
Struggle for Self-Government in Virginia* (Philadelphia, 1958), the
latter two by Thomas J. Wertenbaker, should prove especially
informative.

There have been a number of good works on Jefferson as educa-
tor, scientist, agriculturist, and architect; and on Jefferson's religion,
Jefferson and Burr, Jefferson and Hamilton, Jefferson and the Declaration of Independence, Jefferson and States Rights, and Jefferson's
economic system, samples of which can be gleaned from the
bibliographies.

Articles

It is impossible to mention more than a few of the published articles
in such a brief bibliographical guide as this, and it would be pre-
sumptuous in any event to establish a criteria for selecting those
"better" or "most useful" to Jefferson scholars. Each has certain
merits and a usefulness of its own. One is best advised to review the
indexes to the *American Historical Review, Journal of American*

History, Journal of Southern History, Virginia Quarterly Review, Virginia Magazine of History and Biography, and *Atlantic Monthly* (among other journals) as especially fruitful sources of good Jefferson materials. Merrill Peterson's "Guide to Sources," previously mentioned, provides the best annotated compilation of Jefferson articles. A few representative articles which have been of special interest to this editor include Charles Beard, "Thomas Jefferson: A Civilized Man," *Mississippi Valley Historical Review,* XXX (September 1943); Carl Becker, "What Is Still Living in the Political Philosophy of Jefferson," *American Historical Review,* XLVIII (July 1943); Dumas Malone, "The Relevance of Mr. Jefferson," *Virginia Quarterly Review,* XXXVII (Summer 1961); Julian P. Boyd, "Thomas Jefferson's Empire of Liberty," *Virginia Quarterly Review,* XXIV (Autumn 1948); and Fletcher M. Green, "Democracy in the Old South," *Journal of Southern History,* XII (February 1946).

1 2 3 4 5 6 7 8 9 10